Voices of Liberation

Voices of Liberation

Frantz Fanon

COMPILED BY LEO ZEILIG

FOREWORD BY MIREILLE FANON-MENDÈS-FRANCE

Haymarket Books
Chicago, Illinois

© 2014 Human Sciences Research Council
First published 2014 as part of a series of titles named *Voices of Liberation*.

This edition published in 2016 by
Haymarket Books
P.O. Box 180165
Chicago, IL 60618
773-583-7884
www.haymarketbooks.org
info@haymarketbooks.org

ISBN: 978-1-60846-613-9

Extracts from *Black Skins, white masks* reproduced with permission from © Éditions du Seuil, 1952.
Excerpts from *The Wretched of the Earth* by Frantz Fanon, English translation copyright © 1963
by Présence Africaine. Used by permission of Grove/Atlantic, Inc. Any third party use of this
material, outside of this publication, is prohibited.
Extracts from Studies in a Dying Colonialism and Studies in a Dying Colonialism reproduced
with permission from Monthly Review Press.

Images supplied by Archives Frantz Fanon/IMEC and Leo Zeilig.

Copyedited by Peter Lague
Typeset by Nicole de Swardt
Cover design by Nicole de Swardt and Georgia Demertzis
Cover photo by Archives Frantz Fanon/IMEC

Trade distribution:
In the US, Consortium Book Sales and Distribution, www.cbsd.com
In Canada, Publishers Group Canada, www.pgcbooks.ca
In the UK, Turnaround Publisher Services, www.turnaround-uk.com
All other countries, Publishers Group Worldwide, www.pgw.com

This book was published with the generous support of Lannan Foundation
and Wallace Action Fund.

Library of Congress Cataloging-in-Publication data is available.

Entered into digital printing October, 2020.

Dedicated to Pierre Chaulet and David Macey

'Sans la reconnaissance de la valeur humaine de la folie,
c'est l'homme même qui disparaît'

FRANÇOIS TOSQUELLES, L'Enseignement de la Folie (1992)

'Without the recognition of the human value of madness,
it is man himself who disappears.'

(These words were the psychiatric principle that guided Fanon's work.)

CONTENTS

ACKNOWLEDGEMENTS

I read Frantz Fanon's final, greatest book *The Wretched of the Earth*, when I was living in Dakar in Senegal. I was working at the country's main university, named after historian Cheikh Anta Diop. The university, like the country, seemed to be in an advanced state of collapse. The students I taught studied hard, but knew they would struggle to find work after graduation. The promises of independence forty years before, which had briefly offered the continent the prospects of real freedom, development and an escape from poverty, had been cruelly lost. For much of the continent, the dreams of African unity and socialism had crashed on the rocks of national liberation.

Reading Fanon in my small study at the university, with the overhead fan slicing into the thick, humid air, was a revelation. Fanon described the failures of liberation and decolonisation; he described the degeneration of the leaders of the struggle for independence, a group he labelled a caste of profiteers, who took control of the new states. With astonishing, even prophetic foresight, he spoke of the national bourgeoisie, that avid and voracious class who would turn national liberation into a curse and a burden. In my slightly fevered reading of Fanon, I would find myself flipping to the first pages of the book to check the date of publication. How was it possible for someone to write with such sheering, disarming insight about postcolonial power and failure in 1961?

During those weeks I was witness to something else in Dakar. In 2000 the Socialist Party, which had held power since independence in 1960, was defeated in a peaceful, democratic election. Before the elections it was students, many of whom I taught, who had mobilised behind the movement for political change. This was a national mobilisation that pulled in school and university students with the poor and the working class calling for political liberation. With the election of Abdoulaye Wade there was going to be an end to corruption, poverty and underdevelopment. Wade was to prove a cruel and terrible disappointment, but the movement brought to me the realisation that, despite the defeat of the radical promises of independence the continent was still rocked by boisterous, extraordinary protest movements that contained the potential for transforming the world.

As I continued to read Fanon, moving on to his second book, written in 1959 during the Algerian Revolution, I found a writer who captured the empowerment – or mutation, as Fanon would write – of ordinary people involved in political struggle. Using irresistible language, Fanon spoke about how an oppressed people were recerebralised in the process of changing their conditions. The anvil of revolution could restructure consciousness, reversing an oppressed people's long-held sense of inferiority and self-doubt. Here was Fanon as a champion of revolutionary change.

I decided to investigate the circumstances of his life and write about this incredible man. In the course of my research I discovered that, although Fanon wrote for the oppressed and poor of the Third World, he understood that real liberation could only be secured if it were accompanied by political and economic transformation across the world, north and south. Fanon was an internationalist. Independence, for him, was the indispensable first stage of a global struggle for human emancipation, for a new humanism. In 1961 he cautioned his readers, those who had fought for and won this liberation, telling them that they must wage a ceaseless struggle against the national bourgeoisie, before this class could lay their hands on the spoils of the new nation.

My investigations led me to meet an extraordinary array of generous people who devoted much time to this project. Some, like Pierre and Claudine Chaulet, were Fanon's close friends, his struggle brothers and sisters. Others have written brilliantly about his life and legacy. I met Fanon's leading biographer, David Macey, in Leeds, a year before he died. We spent the day talking about Fanon. An edited extract of the interview is included in this volume. David and I exchanged cigarettes and talked about Negritude, Algeria, postcolonialism. It was a heady, moving delight to be in David's company, a man of such gentle erudition, insights and kindness. This book is dedicated to Pierre and David, both of whom died before I could finish the work.

Many other friends, comrades and colleagues have helped develop my understanding of Fanon. Ian Birchall, historian and socialist, has been a companion since the start of the research in my attempt to understand Algeria, Fanon and the French left. For me he has long been a model of an engaged, determined and brilliant researcher, writer and activist. Fanon's daughter, Mireille Fanon-Mendès-France was patient and generous with her time, agreeing to meet me in France and to write the Foreword for this collection.

Her work on her father's legacy is deeply embedded in an understanding of the continued relevance of his work. Others need to be mentioned: Andy Wynne, Kim Wale, Gillian Zeilig, Maurice Caplan, Martin Evans, Hamza Hamouchene, Philip Murphy, Lila Chouli. While I was working in Algiers I was inspired by conversations and interviews with veterans of the Algerian war against the French, particularly Miraoui Smain and Moutif Mohamed.

Finally, this collection was possible because of the incredibly professional team at HSRC Press. Jeremy Wightman and Fiona Wakelin were both passionate about Fanon. They commissioned the volume and made invaluable comments and suggestions. Jeremy has been an immensely supportive and engaged publisher who saw the relevance and necessity of this addition to the Voices of Liberation series and to debates taking place in South Africa. Charlotte Imani and Kholeka Mabeta have also been extremely helpful. Samantha Phillips has been a pleasure to work with, calming my occasional fits of enthusiasm with pointed, practical questions and deadlines.

It is my fervent hope that this volume will help a new generation of readers, as well as those already familiar with his work, to engage with Fanon's writing and life in a spirit of political engagement and criticism. Fanon would have wanted nothing else.

ACRONYMS

ALN	Armée de Libération Nationale (National Liberation Army)
AML	Amis du Manifeste et de la Liberté (Friends of the Manifesto and Liberty)
BSO	Baloch Student Federation
CNRA	National Committee of the Algerian Revolution
FLN	Front de Libération National (National Liberation Front)
GPRA	Gouvernement Provisionel de la République Algérienne (Provisional Government of the Algerian Republic)
IMF	International Monetary Fund
MNA	Mouvement National Algerien (Algerian National Movement)
MNC	Mouvement National Congolais (Congolese National Movement)
MRP	Mouvement Républicain Populaire (Popular Republican Movement)
NATO	North Atlantic Treaty Organisation
PCF	Parti Communiste Français (French Communist Party)
POUM	Partido Obrero e Unificacion Marxista (Workers Party of Marxist Unity)
PPA	Parti Populaire Algeriene (Algerian People's Party)
SFIO	Section Francaise de L'Internationale Ouvriére (the French Socialist Party)
WTO	World Trade Organisation

THE LIFE OF FRANTZ FANON

Events in the life of Frantz Fanon	Year	Related events
Fanon is born in the French West Indies, in Fort-de-France, Martinique, on **20 July**.	1925	
Fanon leaves Martinique to join the Free French fighting against the Nazi occupation of France.	1944	
Fanon returns after the war to Fort-de-France in Martinique to complete his school studies.	1945	**8 May** Europe celebrates the end of the war. On the same date in the town of Sétif in Algeria anti-colonial demonstrations break out. French army massacres thousands in the region over the following weeks.
Fanon leaves for Paris to study dentistry; transfers to Lyon where he studies medicine, later specialising in psychiatry.	1946	
Fanon's first child, Mireille Fanon, is born.	1948	
Fanon marries Marie-Josephe Dublé (known as Josie). As a trainee psychiatrist, Fanon works at the famous French psychiatric hospital in Saint Alban run by François Tosquelles. Tosquelles becomes an important influence on Fanon's work. *Black Skin, White Masks* is published.	1952	
Takes up his first appointment as a fully qualified psychiatrist in Blida, Algeria.	1953	
	1954	**March–May** The Battle of Dien Bien Phu sees the defeat of the French by Viet Minh nationalists, leading to the Geneva Accords and French withdrawal from Indochina. **1 November** The start of Algeria's bloody war and revolution against the French launched by radical Algerian nationalists (later calling themselves the Front de Libération Nationale [FLN]).
Josie gives birth to Olivier. Fanon becomes involved in supporting the Algerian Revolution against the French in his capacity as a psychiatrist and doctor.	1955	
Late in the year Fanon's position at the hospital, treating FLN fighters and supporting the war against the French, becomes impossible. Writing in his letter of resignation, 'If psychiatry is a medical technique which aspires to allow man to cease being alienated from his environment…the Arab…is permanently alienated in his own country.'	1956	French socialists come to power, led by socialist Prime Minister Guy Mollet, who escalates the war in Algeria. **August** The FLN organise the Soummam Conference in Algeria, under the leadership of Abane Ramdane. The Battle of Algiers lasts until 1957; the FLN combine 'terrorist' attacks and strikes in the Algerian capital.

Events in the life of Frantz Fanon	Year	Related events
Fanon moves with his family to Tunis, the Tunisian capital. Tunis has become an important base for FLN exiles. Fanon becomes increasingly active in the FLN, joins the team that produce the FLN's newspaper *El Moudjahid*.	1957	
	1958	**May** Charles de Gaulle returns to power following a coup attempt in Algeria.
Fanon writes *Studies in a Dying Colonialism* (published in French with the title *L'An V de la Révolution Algérienne*, translated into English as *Year Five of the Algerian Revolution*).	1959	
Fanon is made ambassador for the GPRA (Gouvernement Provisionel de la République Algérienne) in Ghana. Fanon undertakes a mission through West Africa to investigate the possibility of opening up a southern front into Algeria for the Armée de Liberation Nationale (ALN). Fanon is diagnosed with leukaemia in **December**.	1960	
Fanon writes *The Wretched of the Earth*. Meets his hero, Jean-Paul Sartre, and Simone de Beauvoir in Rome. Lectures ALN troops in Ghardimaou, Tunisia. Travels to the United States for treatment. Dies on **6 December** at the Institutes of Health in Maryland. Body returned to Tunis; buried in liberated territory in Algeria.	1961	
	1962	**5 July** Algeria gains independence from the French.

FOREWORD

Reading Frantz Fanon today
by Mireille Fanon-Mendès-France

*Mireille Fanon-Mendès-France is chairperson of the Frantz Fanon Foundation
and member of the Working Group of Experts on People of African Descent in
the United Nations Human Rights Council.*

Frantz Fanon's presence can still be felt today and his work enlightens a
large number of struggling people. Some 50 years after his death on 6 December
1961, Fanon continues to challenge the world 'disorder'. Those who oppose
poverty and exploitation can see through the false veneer of words such as
'freedom', 'justice' and 'human rights' – terms bandied about by advocates
of the neocolonial imperial order – and sense the permanent ugliness in
the world. Over these 50 years, forms of domination may have changed, as
well as the ways in which the authorities attempt to abuse the meaning of
these words. But, today, for those who experience the reality of injustice and
violence, alienation and exploitation, reading Fanon helps them understand
the new false beliefs broadcast in insidious ways by the media.

Frantz Fanon's deconstruction of the established order is especially
relevant now at a time when, in today's world order, dictated by the forces of
the global economy, many people have discovered that they are still citizens of
the Third World, that they are virtually subhuman in the eyes of their rulers,
who are more powerful and nationalistic than ever.

Fanon's work not only speaks to the dominant relationships that prevailed,
and still prevail, in what was formerly called the Third World. It equally
applies to Europe and the United States, where the dominant relationships
of those countries with the rest of the world are internally reproduced, with
a false ideology. The recent global financial and sovereign debt crises that
we have seen are indicative of the degree of subjugation and inequality that
persists in countries that claim to be democratic.

Extreme intellectual subterfuge, hyped up by massive and sophisticated
means, contributed to the social unrest and economic inequality experienced
by the poor and the victims of social exclusion. These methods are built on

fear and the authorities' insistence of the 'natural' character of the established order. Within the borders of countries one finds that certain groups are made scapegoats for the enduring unrest (e.g. migrants, immigrants, travellers, workers and Muslims), and the poor are made to oppose one another – their own countrymen. On an international level, the problem is even more visible – we are back to the old colonial gunboat diplomacy and we are seeing conflicts of extreme intensity.

Fanon tears apart the dubious arguments supporting colonialism with faultless analysis. And as the colonialism of the past wore the mask of a 'civilising' mission, today the same brutal policy is cloaked in the form of contemporary humanist concepts such as the eradication of poverty and the duty to protect people from tyrannical rulers. But the reality is otherwise: these same tyrannies have been established and are defended by those elites who claim today to protect their people.

Independence in certain countries in Africa and the Arab world is generally deemed to have been a failure and the powerful elites who govern such states must be held responsible. The major and decisive role in such states played by Western powers, either formally or informally, all the more harmful because their interventions are not bound by rule of law, in no way reduces the burden of this responsibility. So, it is not surprising today that this failure of independence and the ensuing violence and abuses we find in some regions should be invoked to justify direct military intervention. NATO's intervention in Libya, for example, showed that even the UN could be manipulated to authorise military diplomatic interventions reminiscent of the colonial era.

The same Western media that took up the cause of the poor people of Libya – forgetting how the ruling castes of their country were corrupted by General Gaddafi – turned a blind eye to the disorder caused by Western intervention in Libya (and the whole of the Sahel region, for that matter). Ironically, it was these same Western powers that created the destabilising effect, which, today, currently justifies, in their eyes, military intervention to re-stabilise the region.

These events that we hear about today centre on very much the same issues that Fanon addressed. The interaction between the colonial order and its local 'puppets' lies at the heart of the issues he writes about. Even though the main forms of colonialism no longer exist, after half a century of independence from colonial rule it is clear, however, that there is still a power system that engenders oppression, alienation poverty and inequality. Today there are groups who endure – albeit in a different context – the same suffering that their forebears endured under colonial occupation. In these postcolonial states, stillborn and without sovereignty, societies are crushed and people abandoned. As Fanon feared, their elites have failed their people and have merely replaced the old colonialist system with neocolonialism.

After the flags of independence had been hoisted, the former colonial masters' domination persisted in the corridors of power of the newly liberated states. The seizure of power by the national bourgeoisie – Fanon had clearly raised warning signals about this group, particularly in The Pitfalls of National Consciousness, a chapter of his final book, *The Wretched of Earth* – resulted in a complete confiscation of independence and a misappropriation of the gains of the anti-colonialist struggle. Fanon described with remarkable prescience, decades before it happened, how neocolonialism's corrupt and unpopular national governments would perpetuate the interests and domination of their former colonial masters:

> The national middle class which takes over power at the end of the
> colonial regime is an underdeveloped middle class. It has practically
> no economic power, and in any case it is in no way commensurate
> with the bourgeoisie of the mother country, which it hopes to replace.
> In its narcissism, the national middle class is easily convinced that it
> can advantageously replace the middle class of the mother country.
> But that same independence that literally drives it into a corner will
> give rise within its ranks to catastrophic reactions, and will oblige it
> to send out frenzied appeals for help to the former mother country
> … It is completely focussed on activities of the intermediary type. Its
> innermost vocation seems to be to keep in the running and to be part
> of the racket. The psychology of the national bourgeoisie is that of the
> businessman, not that of a captain of industry.[1]

Fanon's predictions have now become an everyday reality. To read Fanon is to open our eyes to the brutality of the contemporary world and to help us understand its origins. Reading Fanon is not a gentle exercise: it is demanding, confusing and, in the end, liberating. To read Fanon forces us to face reality in its most hideous forms, but it also provides the intellectual tools needed to deconstruct and explain it. For that reason, Fanon's work is a living body of thought. Its own dynamic allows the linking and putting into perspective of facts that seem unimportant, and integrate them into a long historical sequence. Reading Fanon allows us to understand why independence in Africa or the Arab world drifted towards authoritarianism and mismanagement on all fronts – social, economic and cultural.

This failure of independence has been caused by certain elites maintaining the general order of the former colonies, thereby preserving their own interests. And the fact that the former colonisers' influence is still present is no secret: at the strategic level, agreements provided for the installation of bases where, in major airports, for example, police-control systems are under foreign supervision, clearly reflects the real state of the sovereignty of these 'neocolonies'. Under external supervision, local elites have destroyed their countries' national identity, allowing them to regress into tribalist dictatorships. The new leaders have taken advantage of ethnic divisions within their nations, souring the relationships between emerging states or ethnic groupings – relationships that had been inherited from, and in some cases created by, colonialism. This prevented the emergence of successful independent states capable of serving their people. The same states have also allowed decisions to be made by external agents under the pretext of the right to protect and humanitarian intervention.

This process led to, for example, the division in Sudan that ended in the secession of South Sudan, opened up the way for Western intervention in Libya and Ivory Coast, and led to the endless and bloody conflict in the eastern DRC. It also allowed the establishment of NGOs that have replaced and overriden impotent states, forcing their people, particularly in rural areas, into dependency.

Independence has generally been a missed opportunity; it is still an unfinished work. It is striking, though, that Fanon's warnings were uttered at the dawn of independence, before the rot had set in. His clear analysis was surprisingly premonitory on the kinds of abuses that he predicted would occur in postcolonial states.

The neocolonial period, it turns out, is just a new form of colonisation taking place in Africa and the Arab-Muslim world. But it is also increasingly seen in the West. People everywhere from the global North and South are experiencing a worldwide neocolonial order based on the plutocracies' domination of their exploited and despised populations. This anonymous order, with a strong political and institutional foundation, has been set up for the exclusive benefit of private self-interest. Western parliamentary democracies do not generally allow for the coming to power of political leaders or groups that might give voice to popular dissent or support the views of minority groups.

For Fanon, 'Decolonization, which sets out to change the order of the world, is ... a program of complete disorder ... In decolonization, there is therefore the need [for] a complete questioning of the colonial situation. If we wish to describe it precisely, we might find it in the well-known words: "The last shall be first and the first last."'[2]

In Fanon's view, modern liberalism is deployed through propaganda and the manipulation of minds. According to him, the mass media influence public opinion, win its consent and, if needs be, introduce the rhetoric of fascism and racism, and the stigma of otherness. Out of this Fanon's reflections and actions began to take root.

Fanon's liberating criticism reveals the world's power systems for what they really are – systems of oppression and looting. Hence, the new form of imperialism we see today – which goes hand in hand with globalisation and has political support – consists in opening the markets of the least developed countries to multinational corporations. This way, the global economies permanently establish their hegemony in a global market dominated by the financial sector.

Multinational companies and international banks literally subjugated the economically advanced northern states, representing a world order that ruthlessly divides mankind between rich and poor, allowing the richest, even though they are very much a minority, to monopolise the wealth of all, condemning the rest of humanity to poverty and despair. The poorest, unlike goods and capital, which circulate freely, are shackled in poverty and denied freedom of movement.

For these dominant powers, it is essential to deal with human movement and adapt it to the needs of the global market, which means organising and controlling migration to meet both the economic and demographic requirements of the states enslaved to the multinationals. Hence, migration policies are now considered from the perspective of mobility. This process is accompanied by repressive and coercive practices, and an ideology that harks back to the darkest days of European history. It has led to state secretive surveillance justified by the authorities under the pretext of pursuing the war on terror, but which in reality has ended up criminalising the excluded and underprivileged of society, and anyone else trying to resist. In successive shifts, Western regimes have merely reintroduced colonial practices in the way they manage their societies. There is nothing new when it comes to discrimination.

Even if the colonial era has ended, its heritage casts a long shadow, and the images and forms of colonialism that Fanon referred to are perpetuated today:

> The native is declared insensible to ethics; he represents not only the absence of values, but also the negation of values. He is, let us dare to admit, the enemy of values, and in this sense he is the absolute evil. He is the corrosive element, destroying all that comes near him; he is the deforming element, disfiguring all that has to do with beauty or morality; he is the depository of maleficent powers, the unconscious and irretrievable instrument of blind forces.[3]

In many countries today racism still prevails in postcolonial society. It exists not necessarily in overt forms but in more insidious societal manifestations. Racism today can be seen in the way certain groups are excluded from the rest of society and disempowered. Racism seems to be accepted in these forms without its perpetrators necessarily being branded racist. The ideological structures of the state even encourage this racist form of exclusion by stigmatisation. This is what Fanon had observed in *Toward the African Revolution*: 'Racism is not the whole but the most visible, the most day-to-day and, not to mince matters, the crudest element of a given structure.'[4]

Paradoxically, the oppressed 'native' of Fanon's colonial world is found not only in his or her place of origin but also in what Fanon calls the 'forbidden cities', where segregation continues to occur today. He writes in *The Wretched of the Earth*:

> The colonial world is a world cut in two ... The zone where the natives live is not complementary to the zone inhabited by the settlers. The two zones are opposed, but not in the service of a higher unity ... This world divided into compartments, divided in two is inhabited by

two different species. The originality of the colonial context is that economic reality, inequality, and the immense difference of ways of life never come to mask the human realities.[5]

And is this not how the neighbourhoods of some cities were designed – to segregate groups?

From 'the black human being who did not enter into history' to a secularist struggle, essentialism is the new manifestation of old views. Cultural hierarchies aim to differentiate groups in order to divide and exploit. Skin colour, once again, is the subject of intense debate, above and beyond culture, national origin or religion. The negative characterisation of black people is equal to the removal of the supposed guilt of white people. Both are prisoners of their own alienation.

On the other hand, in light of the bloody imperial wars waged in Iraq, Afghanistan and Libya, and the colonial war in Palestine, it is clear that the warlike logic of imperialism has violently broken out once again, leading to the mutation and regression of international law, and confirming that the new world order is based on military intimidation, enslavement of the weak and overexploitation of global resources.

Fanon's views on supremacy, exploitation and alienation remain meaningful and relevant today. The revolt he advocates against an absurd and criminal social, political and economic system is the means to achieve the emancipation of all people, both the dominated and the dominant, in the humanist and universalist meaning that characterises man and his work.

For Fanon, the ultimate goal of the political struggle is human liberation sustained without any forms of disalienation, dogmatic prejudice or rigidity. He remains, despite attempts by some to discredit him, an incontestable thinker who stood firmly by his views. Fanon cannot reduced to one single dimension of the struggle. He was an anti-racist in the name of universalism and an anti-colonialist in the name of justice and freedom. His independence of thought and clear views gained him the admiration and respect of freedom fighters such as Che Guevara, Amílcar Cabral, Agostinho Neto, Nelson Mandela, Mehdi Ben Barka and many other liberation-movement leaders. Even today, he continues to inspire new generations of activists and intellectuals in both the global South and North.

In Fanon's work, there is no desire for revenge or to stigmatise white people, as some proponents of imperialism and supporters of the existing hierarchy of civilisation would like to portray him today. His critics, certain capitalist intellectuals, would present him as a theoretician of blind and excessive violence, precisely because his work is the radical antidote to the lies and deceit that they incarnate.

The violent resistance that he advocated, which he saw as the means of securing the freedom of those who are denied their rights, exploited and reduced to slavery, is a self-defence mechanism for the oppressed who suffer the violent consequences of domination, dispossession and contempt. In this sense, his thinking is still today an antidote to relinquishing one's human rights. It is the expression of pure anger and legitimate indignation behind the ceaseless struggle for the freedom, justice and dignity of all women and men.

More than fifty years after his death, Fanon's call for people to resist oppression and continue the struggle for justice and freedom meets the aspirations of men and women, in all their diversity, all over the world.

NOTES

For a more detailed essay on Fanon's work by his daughter, please see *Frantz Fanon. Recueil de textes introduit* by Mireille Fanon-Mendès-France, (Geneva : Editions du CETIM, 2013) www.cetim.ch

1   F. Fanon, *The Wretched of the Earth* (New York: Grove Press Edition, 1963), pp. 149–150.

2   Ibid., pp. 36–37.

3   Ibid., p. 41.

4   F. Fanon, *Toward the African Revolution* (New York: Grove Press Edition, 1967), p. 32.

5   Fanon, *The Wretched of the Earth*, p. 40.

His
life

Why revisit Fanon?

DELEGATES ATTENDING THE ALL African People's Conference in December 1958 in independent Ghana came from across the African continent. Most spoke of the continuing struggle against colonialism. In the Congo, labelled an empire of silence, the Mouvement National Congolais (MNC) faced repression by Belgium, a colonial power that refused to entertain any notion of genuine independence. In South Africa the apartheid regime was confident that it could keep the increasing demands for change north of its borders at bay. Meanwhile, in France, in a referendum on 13 September, President Charles de Gaulle had offered all French African colonies limited sovereignty under the French authority in a so-called Franco-African community. Only Guinea, under Ahmed Sékou Touré, had insisted on immediate independence, famously commenting: 'We prefer poverty in freedom to riches in slavery.'[1] In certain colonies, where there was a large white 'settler' presence, the struggle against colonial rule was deeper and more protracted. In other colonies, the colonial metropolis had begun to accept the inevitability of decolonisation.

Ghana had already gained its independence the previous year – the first sub-Saharan country run by a black government and led by a black prime minister, Kwame Nkrumah. He spoke openly of breaking the chains of colonialism and imperialism on the continent as part of a pan-African vision of continental unity. After generations of slavery, colonialism and racism, Ghana seemed to declare to the world what a victorious and united liberation movement could achieve.

Ghana had become both the de facto sub-Saharan headquarters for liberation movements on the continent still reaching towards independence for their countries, and a laboratory for nationhood and independence. Although already a collection of vivid and painful contradictions, Ghana was the model for many countries under colonial rule. Independent since 1957, after years as a British colony, Ghana was a paradoxical place. The former colonists of the Gold Coast, Ghana's colonial name, had stayed on to assist the new government. Even the Ghanaian army was run by British officers who were on lease to the Ghanaians until its own officers had been trained. At the same time, the Nkrumah was an outspoken advocate for pan-Africanism. For a generation of young militants, he was the figure to emulate. Fanon learned much in Ghana.

Many people spoke well that day at the All Africa People's conference. On 8 December 1958, Frantz Fanon, using the name Dr Omar Fanon, spoke about the struggle against the French in Algeria. This slight, Caribbean-born doctor and revolutionary had only been a self-declared militant and partisan of the Algerian struggle for a few years. When he mounted the podium to speak, his eyes fixed on his text, most delegates had no idea who he was. His eyes shone with the usual urgency and intensity as he spoke: 'If Africa is to be free we cannot beg, we must tear away by force what belongs to us ... all forms of struggle must be adopted, not excluding violence.'[2]

The audience was transfixed. One South African, reporting on the conference, observed:

> Dr Fanoh Omar [sic] of Algeria is certainly the highlight of the session.
> He does not mince words. What FLN man can afford the luxury
> anyway? Algerians have no other recourse but fight back he says, and
> the FLN means to go through with it. In staccato French he carries his
> audience to the horrible scene of French atrocities on Algerians. He
> gets the loudest and longest ovation of all speakers.[3]

For Fanon, it was not enough to celebrate the achievements of decolonisation: it was also necessary to educate, to strain at the limits of national freedom and to provoke and generate debate. The All African People's Conference was the place to learn about the liberation movements on the continent and, where necessary, to educate these movements about the violent struggle against the French in the north.

Since his death in 1961, Frantz Fanon has been appropriated for almost every cause. Five years after his death he emerged as the preferred theorist of the emergent Black Power movement in the United States, influencing Bobby Seale and Huey P. Newton in the Black Panther Party. In 1967 Dan Watts, the editor of the radical Black Power newspaper, *Liberator*, described the extent of Fanon's influence on the revolt of black America as follows:

> You're going along thinking all the brothers in these riots are old winos. Nothing could be further from the truth. These cats are ready to die for something. And they know why. They all read. Read a lot. Not one of them hasn't read the Bible ... Fanon ... You'd better get this book. Every brother on a rooftop can quote Fanon.[4]

In the 1960s and 1970s, Fanon was the quintessential Third Worldist. His ideas were taken up by movements that looked to the guerrilla struggle launched from the countryside. In newly decolonised countries, Fanon's last book (*The Wretched of the Earth*) became a manual for Maoists predicting an imminent revolutionary wave. The proletariat could not be trusted – these movements, following Fanon, would be based on other political forces. In the 1990s Fanon was taken up with renewed vigour by the academic community. Cultural critics and postmodernists focused exclusively on his work on identity, and presented a largely decontextualised Fanon, shorn of history. Here was Fanon with his revolutionary urgency (and heart) ripped out.

Fanon became the privileged thinker of the 'post-colony', and Anglo-American academics made careers researching Fanon's body of thought. As Fanon's biographer, David Macey, explained:

> In itself there's nothing wrong with that – better to study Fanon ... But I think it is necessary to put Fanon back in his context – stop abstracting from it and start exploring what are the implications today of ... Fanon ... in a more positive sense ... we won't do that by discussing Fanon in seminars in Yale University ... it's got to go beyond that. And I think that's the problem with post-colonial studies ... it doesn't actually link up with what virtually anybody goes through everyday.[5]

Yet most of Fanon's life and writing was dedicated to revolutionary change. Soon after he moved to Algeria in 1953, he devoted himself the to Front de Libération Nationale (FLN). He wrote about the ensuing revolutionary movement in Algeria and how people were transformed by their involvement in the struggle for liberation. Relationships between men and women, and families and their children, which had seemed frozen into the fabric of society and traditions, came apart in a process that Fanon described as 'radical mutation', as the battle against the French rippled across Algerian society. But Fanon did much more than celebrate these changes – he also sought to explain how they could be deepened. He saw how national liberation could become a curse, unless it was extended beyond the immediate goal of independence from former colonial powers and linked to regional and international processes of popular transformation. For this to happen, Fanon argued that the right type of organisation had to be built and he warned against the danger of an absence of ideology.

Why is it important to return to Fanon, analyse his work and read his books? Once again, the world is being rocked by rebellion and revolution. North Africa has become the fulcrum of revolutionary change. Resisting austerity in Europe has led to mass protests in Portugal, Spain and Greece. Governments in Turkey and Brazil have been shaken by protests. In South Africa, one academic writes of the 'rebellion of the poor' as an explanation for the record levels of strikes and protests over the last decade.[6] Fanon's work is a useful and necessary place to return to, so we can place current challenges to the status quo in context and shed light on these political movements. In addition, Fanon's vision of human emancipation through popular and revolutionary struggle continues to tantalise contemporary activists, even if his work is marked by serious pitfalls and contradictions.[7]

Understanding Fanon (and his time) can still be useful for those seeking to understand (and undertake) social change. Fanon's questions and concerns are also ours: what are the limitations of revolutionary movements? What political forces usurp revolutionary struggles after national liberation? What is the role of leadership in political movements? How are nationalist movements and national consciousness inherently restrictive to political and social transformation?

Despite the scope of Fanon's work, this short biographical essay will limit itself to a general introduction of the main contours of Fanon's life and work.

This introduction should help contextualise the selection of Fanon's writings that follow.[8]

Inside Martinique: Racism, war and France

Fanon was born in 1925 to a middle-class family in Martinique, an island in the Caribbean. His childhood was comfortable, and relatively unremarkable. But life in Martinique permanently marked his identity. The island was, and still is, a place of profound racism, in its own composition and its relationship to metropolitan France. The island's communities were, in Fanon's youth, divided into a small class of white planters and businessmen, the békés (the descendants of European settlers), the mulattos and the blacks. In a society obsessively demarcated by colour, these categories signified a family's place in the world. On the island, pigmentation – specifically how close your skin was to white – to a large extent determined your trajectory in life and your own sense of self-worth. Fanon's family had some white ancestry, and were ambitious and mobile. His mother was a proud shop owner, his father a civil servant in the customs service. Fanon attended school at the Lycée Schoelcher in the capital, Fort-de-France, and gained a reputation for being an avid reader and keen footballer who was also confident and bright. The family considered themselves French, and no one felt this more keenly than their brightest son.

The year 1946 was a turning point in the island's history because in that year, together with Guadeloupe, Martinique joined La Réunion and Guyane to be known collectively as a *Département d'Outre-mer* (oversea territory) of the French Republic. This marked the official assimilation of Martinique and Guadeloupe into France. The departmentalisation was presented as a humane alternative to colonisation, as other French colonies had begun to speak of decolonisation and to revolt against their European master. Today these islands are holiday destinations for tourists. Guidebooks describe lush, green mountains, turquoise oceans and whitewashed colonial style houses. The islands are presented as exotic destinations and romantic hideaways for discerning and intelligent travellers.

Martinique was 'founded' in 1635 for the French by trader Pierre Belain d'Esnambuc. Local Carib resistance to the invasion was crushed by superior European arms. Martinique, Guadeloupe and Guyane were part of France's transatlantic empire in the 17th century. The colonial system that developed was vicious, using indentured labourers, frequently press-ganged from France's Atlantic coast. They produced primary products – cotton, tobacco and coffee – on plantations run by the French bourgeoisie. Apart from a brief period at the end of the 18th century under British occupation, Martinique remained solidly in French hands. The island was an inherently unequal economy and society, producing goods for the global market in conditions of modern agricultural production. While smallholders principally grew tobacco, sugar cultivation required labour intensity that the independent producers could not provide. Labour for this new crop came from West Africa. In 1664 Martinique had an estimated 2 900 white inhabitants, with a black population of 3 138. By 1750 the total population had grown to 56 000, the overwhelming majority of them slaves. Slave merchants from Nantes, Bordeaux, La Rochelle and Le Havre commissioned and paid for the 2 800 ships that were involved in the transatlantic slave trade. These ships exported products from France, which were exchanged for men and women captured on the western seaboard of Africa, who were then transported as slaves to French colonies in the 'West Indies'. This slave-trade triangle was completed when ships returned to France transporting sugar from the Caribbean. Thousands of the captured men and women did not survive the ocean crossing; as many as 15 per cent of the human cargo perished on the voyage.[9]

Slavery was established by France's *Code Noir* decree, in force from 1685. This was a brutal document with barbaric provisions. For example, for a slave to strike a free man or master was punishable by death; a runaway slave could have an eye removed and would be branded; a second bid to escape would result in the slicing of their hamstrings. The slave was a commodity and had no rights. Marking the birth of capitalism, the islands were used solely for the exploitation of export crops for a growing capitalist market.

Slave revolts were a regular occurrence, but nothing was on the scale of the revolution that broke out in the French Caribbean colony of San Domingo in 1791. Inspired by the revolutionary events in France, this slave revolt was led by Toussaint L'Ouverture, a freed black slave. In 1794 the French revolutionary convention in Paris, the Nationale Révolutionnaire, abolished slavery. In 1804, after 10 years of revolutionary struggle, Haiti declared itself independent – the first independent country in Latin America and the world's first black republic. By 1801, however, Napoleon had restored slavery across the rest of the French colonies in the French Caribbean, but the memory of the slave revolt was never completely obliterated from Caribbean or world history. [10]

These events did not have a direct effect on Martinique, which was under British control during the revolutionary years, reverting to French control soon afterwards. After 1848 and the definitive abolition of slavery, the plantation economy continued. While colonial plantations were compensated any losses that resulted from the abolition of slavery, most free slaves were obliged to work for a wage on the same plantations where they had been slaves. But, even without slavery, life on Martinique was miserable. Sugar could only be produced by creating seasonal unemployment, which led to debt and credit. As David Macey puts it, 'unofficial debt bondage replaced institutionalised slavery'.[11] Abolition created other illusions. Slaves now became, officially at least, French citizens and had the formal right to vote. Life on the island, however, was dominated by the békés, the white class who could trace their ancestors to the plantation owners and original settlers.

The béké was at the apex of a taxonomy of colour on the island that was so complex that one 18th-century planter with mathematical pretensions identified 128 mixed blood types.[12] The categories included bodily attributes, all defined in relation to their degree of whiteness, such as eye colour and nature of hair (wavy, straight or curly). Fanon wrote eloquently about the terrible preoccupation with colour in the Antilles in his first book, *Peau Noire, Masques Blancs*:

> Let me point out once more that every Antillean expects all the
> others to perceive him in terms of the essence of the white man …
> It is in white terms that one perceives one's fellows. People will say
> of someone, for instance, that he is 'very black'; there is nothing
> surprising, within a family, in hearing a mother remark that 'X is the
> blackest of my children' – it means that X is the least white.[13]

The attention to colour and pigmentation of the non-white community was vital to the island Fanon knew.

The Second World War fundamentally reshaped politics on the island. In 1944 Fanon fled Martinique, disobeying his mother's orders not to join the Free French.[14] Fanon served in Morocco, Algeria and finally in France. To Fanon's

analysis, while also enabling the reader to be touched and moved. In his first book, he cites novelists and poets on a similar quest, such as Richard Wright and Chester Himes, who describe with force the experiences of racism and blackness. But these writers were also part of a generation that was politically committed – a commitment with which Fanon identified as well.

Black Skin, White Masks

Fanon was no stranger to racism in France. He started to write *Peau Noire, Masques Blancs* (*Black Skin, White Masks*), while still a student of medicine. The book is an attempt to describe the lived experience of a black person. It was published in 1952. It is, to some extent, autobiographical, as well as a call for mutual recognition and an end to racism. Drawing on Sartre's work on anti-Semitism, Fanon explains that being black is made in confrontation with others and created by the racist's gaze. Race and racism, Fanon argues in the book, is a relationship of intersubjectivity that orbits around a superiority and inferiority complex, with whiteness at the centre of a supposed superiority.[21]

Fanon further argues in the book that he is cast into his blackness by racism, and literally becomes the insults and stereotypes of the racist. When a black person is confronted with racism, they are immediately broken apart: 'I was responsible for my body, responsible for my race, responsible for my ancestors … He is all the clichés of anti-black racism: "the negro is stupid, the negro is bad, the negro is wicked, the negro is ugly.[22]"'
But, as Fanon is confined to his blackness by the racist gaze and insult, so the white person is trapped by his whiteness. There is a tension in the book between Fanon's need to declare: '*Je suis mon propre fondement*' ('I am my own foundation'), to assert himself individually, and the realisation that such a foundation can only be established collectively.

Following Hegel, *Black Skin, White Masks* makes an appeal for humanism that Fanon maintains throughout his work. According to him, this universality and humanism can, however, only be acquired with the recognition by others – the acknowledgement of the humanity of black (and later colonised) peoples. Yet this recognition is not a benevolent gesture, bestowed on black people, but one that must be seized and reached for in struggle and collective action. Recognition and humanity cannot be granted.

Fanon drew on Hegel's master–slave dialectic to understand the nature of oppression, violence and resistance. Following Hegel, Fanon emphasised the centrality of the risk of life in the struggle for reciprocal recognition. Because the slave accepts servitude for fear of death and is unwilling to die for freedom, the master is tyrannical and violent without limit. The slave's oppression intensifies until he discovers that his oppressor can be killed, and this discovery shakes his social and psychological world.

Fanon explains how this discovery for the slave bursts the omnipotence of the oppressor, who becomes demystified. The slave is then psychologically ejected from the self, and his self-confidence is restored. The fear of physical death is replaced with a desire for social and historical life, even if the result is physical death. The slave realises that there are many kinds of death, and in choosing physical life, he sacrifices social life. When he decides that it is social life and freedom that are more important, this ushers in revolutionary struggles and transformation.[23] As Fanon writes at the end of *Black Skin, White Masks*:

> … the Negro knows nothing of the cost of freedom, for he has not
> fought for it. The former slave, who can find in his memory no trace
> of the struggle for liberty … sits unmoved before the young white man
> singing and dancing on the tightrope of existence … The former slave
> needs a challenge to his humanity, he wants a conflict, a riot.[24]

In the conclusion of the book Fanon asserts, contrary to the ideas of Negritude, that there is no 'black' task, history or politics separate or distinct from the project of human emancipation and development. In a hymn to a radical humanism that never leaves him Fanon writes:

> There is no Negro mission; there is no white burden. I find myself
> suddenly in a world … in which I am summoned into battle … There is
> no white world; there is no white ethic, anymore than there is a white
> intelligence. There are in every part of the world men who search.[25]

At this stage, in *Black Skin, White Masks*, Fanon was still not clear what a struggle for 'recognition' would entail, or how such recognition could be practically sought, even if the language he used remains compelling today: 'Yes to life. Yes to love. Yes to generosity ... No to scorn of man. No to degradation of man. No to exploitation of man. No to the butchery of what is most human in man: freedom.'[26] Algeria helped to actualise Fanon's philosophy.

In *Black Skin, White Masks*, Fanon developed a style that was distinct and powerful. His prose is full of poetry and rhythm, and demands to be read aloud. He was not satisfied with academic language, but craved to reach his readers emotionally, a desire that never left him. As he puts it: 'The situation that I have examined ... is not a classic one. Scientific objectivity was barred to me, for the alienated, the neurotic, was my brother, my sister, my father.'[27] In Fanon's writing in general, but particularly in his first book, he is telling a story about race relations as a prose-poet. He does not give the reader an analysis of categories that are distanced and sociological. Rather, the book aims to invoke in the reader an experience of what race and racism really mean and how they are felt. This is a phenomenological approach that attempted to penetrate how people experience the world. Fanon had learnt his style, politics and philosophy from the phenomenology of Merleau-Ponty and Sartre. He provided an account of the structures of experience through which racism is lived.[28] Nothing like Fanon's book had been published before.

Fanon submitted the manuscript of *Black Skin, White Masks* as a dissertation for his final medical degree, but, not unfairly, it was rejected. When the book was published, it gave Fanon little exposure to Parisian literary circles: there were few readers and fewer reviews. But the book was a marker for Fanon, identifying him as a serious thinker, a young black intellectual whose language and arguments demanded a response.

After graduating Fanon took up his first major post at Saint Alban, the renowned psychiatric hospital in France, then headed by François Tosquelles. Tosquelles became an important influence on Fanon. He was a proponent of institutional psychiatry, which involved revolutionising the psychiatric hospital by introducing group therapy and social activities long before they became fashionable, in an attempt to create a 'neo-society' that would help the patient eventually readjust to society. Tosquelles was a militant anti-Stalinist who had been a senior member of the far-left *Partido Obrero e Unificacion Marxista* (POUM) (Workers Party of Marxist Unity) in the Spanish Civil War. He was a central intellectual figure in Fanon's life, and his only mentor.

Learning radical psychiatry: Saint Alban

In 1952, at Saint Alban, Fanon was plunged into a world of radical politics and psychiatry. Tosquelles was a psychiatrist with revolutionary ideas about transforming the hospital and psychiatric medicine by incorporating neurology, biology and phenomenology. He had been thrust into the continent's first armed struggle (and revolution) against fascism in Spain in the 1930s, which exposed the counter-revolutionary role of the Soviet-led Communist Party. It was these betrayals that contributed to the eventual defeat of the republican government. Tosquelles's life was indelibly marked by these experiences.[29]

The psychiatric hospital dominated the small town of Saint Alban, in the remote Lozère department of southern France. Still hard to reach today, in the 1950s it took many hours to access on poor roads from Lyon. The large hospital was built on a hill, with land that the patients farmed. Newer buildings were built around an old castle where the patients carried out therapeutic activities, and lived and slept in dormitories. Fanon would have felt the extreme separation of the hospital from the world.[30]

At Saint Alban, Tosquelles insisted on breaking down the rigid medical hierarchy between patient and doctor, and doctor and auxiliary staff. Similar to the scrapping of ranks in the POUM militias, democratic decision-making was introduced under his influence at the hospital. Elected delegates from the hospital community made decisions on the library, film group and newspaper. A therapeutic environment was created to include intensive group work; antipsychotic drugs and electroconvulsive therapy were used when necessary. Jean Oury, a French psychiatrist, described the atmosphere and activism of the hospital during and immediately after the Second World War as follows:

> What we had at Saint-Alban for example (and this is going back some time!) was a fervent inter-disciplinary research: phenomenologists, psychologists, neurologists, surrealist poets, immunologists from the Pasteur Institute, and then all the activities and projects renewed in the wake of the French Liberation with groups such as the *Travail et Culture* or TEC (Work and Culture) which later gave rise to the *Theatre Nationale Populaire* or TNP (National Popular Theatre). It was a magnificent effort which had no dealings with Stalinism ... from 1944–45, for example, there were the 'caravans' for the children of

factory workers: they would have the chance to go away on holiday, to go on excursions into the mountains, etc.[31]

One of the principal activities of the staff and patients was the hospital newspaper *Trait d'Union*. The paper was written, printed and circulated by the patients, carrying news about activities and social events, as well as techniques and therapeutic practice. The content of the paper was discussed at weekly editorial meetings, bringing patients and staff together. Articles were debated not only during group activities, but also in the pages of the paper. Tosquelles often wrote the lead articles in *Trait d'Union*, but more junior psychiatrists, including Fanon, also made contributions. During his short stay at the hospital, he wrote a number of editorials. In the 26 December 1952 issue Fanon wrote the front page editorial about lassitude, literally a state of weariness or listlessness, and the crisis of middle age:

> One must not confuse weariness and rest. Weariness is the refusal to
> continue, unaccountable weight in the legs, an unusual emptiness
> in the head and especially an anxiety, which troubles the chest ... If
> at 40 years old, and it must be said that it is especially at 40 that this
> happens, is born in me a desire to no longer do anything ... I notice on
> waking on a beautiful morning that I have the desire for nothing, how
> are we to understand this? ... In a sense to be forty is to say to hell with
> the world, damn others, damn life, damn me ... to hell with those who
> want to be kind with me, to hell with all those who I don't like.

In a later issue a patient took umbrage with Fanon's discussion on lassitude, (which extended over a number of front-page editorials), responding in a letter to the paper with some anger:

> We have done everything we could to please our doctors and nurses,
> only for us to be described as layabouts by Doctor Fanon. I would
> also like to say that my health is not improving, that I am not feeling
> very strong, take the 'ratatouille' that we eat which made me sick. The
> nurses will tell you about it ... I hope that the doctors will take note.[32]

Fanon was influenced by Tosquelles' psychiatric practice at Saint Alban. He was inspired by his mentor's commitment to democratic and egalitarian principles, where there was no whiff of racism or segregation, and where patients could criticise their doctors openly and in print. Fanon was an active member of the clubs and social events, and would later attempt to institute similar programmes in the hospitals in Algeria and Tunisia where he assumed responsibility for social activities. Tosquelles, in common with many others, was impressed by Fanon's gift for polemic and his refusal to be bound by the so-called virtue of patience. Fanon learnt from Tosquelles the vital role that patients must play in their own treatment – the self-activity of these weakened brothers and sisters of humanity. Written on a plaque outside the hospital today are Tosquelles's words: 'Without the recognition of the human value of madness, it is man himself who disappears.' These words were the psychiatric principle that guided Fanon's work.

In 1952 Fanon made a brief return to Martinique on a working holiday. He had not been back since leaving for Paris in 1946. His contact with the island during his absence had been through newspapers, letters and stories from his brothers and sisters. For a student, and then a poorly paid trainee doctor, the passage back to Martinique was a luxury he could barely afford. The trip home was a mixed blessing. He saw his family and worked as a GP from a friend's house. But if he had entertained a hope that he could return to live and work on the island, he decided after a short time that Martinique would suffocate him. After less than two months he returned to Lyon. He never returned again to his home.

Algeria: Resistance and repression

At the end of 1953 Fanon took up a job in Blida-Joinville, a town a short distance from Algiers. Algeria was then a territory of France, firmly under the boot of French authority, as it had been since 1848. Invaded by France in 1830, Algeria was not fully integrated for another 18 years, as the French struggled to pacify native resistance. When 'integration' finally took place, the Arab-Berber population (or *indigènes*) were not accorded French citizenship and remained subjects with few rights. Fanon, writing to his brother to tell him of the move, explained, 'I'm going to Algeria. You understand: the French have enough psychiatrists to take care of their madmen. I'd rather go to a country where they need me.'[33]

The decision to go to Algeria was not because Fanon had a vision of the future success of *Les Damnés de la Terre* (*The Wretched of the Earth*). Fanon may have been militant and angry, but he was also an ambitious doctor who had little chance of finding a post in France. His decision was therefore pragmatic and he no doubt would have stayed in France had there been opportunities for him.

Algeria was eventually legally constituted as an administrative department of France. The process of this incorporation was brutal. It cast pre-colonial Algerian society into backwardness, so that trade, education and human development were systematically underdeveloped by French colonialism. Algerian historian Mostefa Lacheraf, in an important historical account, explains these developments powerfully:

> Algeria was no barbarian country inhabited by illiterate people with anarchic or sterile institutions. Its human and economic values attained a high level ... Patriarchal, agricultural and civic life-styles co-existed ... throughout there was a marked sense of energy and industry: in maritime and artisanal techniques, in para-industrial methods, in city organisation, in the commerce with Africa and across the Mediterranean, in a system of intellectual values which was strongly impregnated with legal traditions, formal logic, more or less rationalist theology, with Arabic and Maghrebine folk traditions ... a widely diffused culture, generalised through its written and oral expression ... Algeria in the earlier 19th century displayed far fewer deficiencies, far more chance of progress in relation to the civilisation of the period and the general movement of free peoples than it did by the end of the century, stripped of its millions of hectares of forest, robbed of its mines, of its liberty, of its institutions and thus of the essential prop and motor of any collective progress.[34]

Schooling, which had been relatively widespread when the French arrived in 1830, was almost completely wiped out. By 1950 UNESCO reported 90 per cent illiteracy among the local population.[35] Under the impact of the French invasion, millions of Algerians lost their lives as a result of direct killing, displacement and the collapse of food security, as communities were forced off the land and fertile agricultural regions were taken over for the cultivation of vines for the export of wine to Europe. Algeria's population fell to approximately 3.5 million in 1852, from 6 million in 1830.

But the French did not have an easy time. Quelling resistance took them many years (and arguably never fully succeeded), and there were only a few years between 1830 and 1871 when there was no fighting. Though new social forces were beginning to emerge from the dramatic mutation of Algerian society under French occupation, these were inherently contradictory, involving neither the total eradication of the past, nor a clear project for the future.[36]

Although Algeria's modern war of independence and national liberation are popularly seen as starting in 1954, the 1930s and 1940s were dominated by a number of different constitutional nationalist parities. One of the most important figures of the period was Messali Hadj, whose Parti Populaire Algérien (PPA) (Algerian People's Party) was formed in 1937. The PPA regarded junior civil servants and the working class (especially the largely coastal working class in the docks) as its main constituency in the, and agricultural workers as its main constituency in the rural areas. Throughout the Second World War, there was a wave of working-class militancy that escalated until 1945. In many ways, these strikes and demonstration, infused with a combination of nationalist ideas and bread-and-butter demands, were the first phase of a regional explosion of labour activism that was about to erupt. The extent of radicalisation can barely be exaggerated. Writers Roger Murray and Tom Wengraf, writing about this period, describe it as follows:

> By early 1945 a revolutionary situation existed in Algeria: the political agitation generated by the Friends of the Manifesto and Liberty (Amis du Manifeste et de la Liberté AML) [an organisation bringing together a variety of nationalist parties] was escaping its control. An acute economic crisis, detonated by the notably bad harvest of the previous year, had developed out of the departure of large numbers of troops at a time when the effects of long-term inflation were making themselves felt ... Large-scale demonstrations of unemployed and starving men took place in many parts of the country; fights with the police were frequent and anti-French feeling was at a peak ... the progressive *elus* [conservative nationalists] grew increasingly apprehensive as the social situation became more volatile and inflammatory. In May Algeria was shaken by an uprising whose dimensions and violence were unparalleled since 1871.[37]

Massive demonstrations took place in Oran, Algiers and other cities mobilised by the Confédération Générale du Travail (General Confederation of Labour). Across Algeria for two days after armistice celebrations the same account explains how 'the whole area was out of military and administrative control'.[38]

The French, however, were determined to gain the upper hand. On 8 May 1945 – as Europe was celebrating victory against the Nazis – there was a French crackdown in the town of Sétif, 250 km from the capital, Algiers. After a series of pro-independence demonstrations in Sétif, between 20 000 and 30 000 Algerians were massacred by the French authorities in the surrounding areas in the east of the country over a number of weeks.[39] As one war ended, another started. The massacre hardened anger inside the Algerian nationalist movement, which had been dominated by several organisations, including the Mouvement pour le Triomphe des Libertés Démocratiques and Ferhat Abbas's Union Démocratique du Manifeste Algérien.

France never admitted there was a war in Algeria. Since Algeria was part of France, it could not launch or fight a war on its own territory. At that time – and for years afterwards – the government in France used linguistic devices to hide the conflict.[40] So there were 'events' and 'terrorist action' but not war. Only in 1999 did the French government accept that a war had taken place. However, like the Vichy period of collaboration with the Nazis, Algeria remains un passé qui ne passe pas ('a past which does not pass').[41]

The Front de Libération Nationale, activism and psychiatry

In 1954 the FLN was born. The timing of the FLN insurrection on 1 November 1954 was carefully chosen. Earlier that year the French had suffered a humiliating defeat in Vietnam at Dien Bien Phu, which signalled the end of the French colonial presences in South East Asia. The FLN were determined to strike hard on the back of this defeat. The strategy pursued by the old nationalist organisation in Algeria had reached an impasse, the FLN claimed. The insurrection was initially led by a small group of Algerians, who subsequently became lionised as the forefathers of Algeria's independence.[42] Although the FLN was initially a small minority of Algerian nationalists committed to violent and armed confrontation with France, by 1955 there was a fuller mobilisation of nationalist forces around the strategy that the FLN had started to develop. Abane Ramdane, radical nationalist, was the principal force behind these initiatives.[43]

From early in its life, the FLN was a ruthless organisation. It fought a low-intensity war on the streets of both France and Algeria against the supporters of Messali Hadj's party, renamed the Mouvement National Algérien (MNA).[44] Much of this fighting was to ensure access to Algerian workers in France who paid 'taxes' to nationalist organisations. The FLN was dependent on this solidarity to fund the war, but the MNA had deeper roots in many Algerian communities. The FLN sought to maintain hegemony over its own forces and to pacify potential competitors.[45]

Despite attempts to present itself as a monolithic organisation, the FLN was divided by serious political differences. The Soummam Conference, held in August 1956 in occupied Algeria, radically asserted the importance of an internal leadership over an exiled one and of political supremacy over military action. Organised by Ramdane, the Soummam declaration, established a militant agenda for the Algerian Revolution, but it was firmly subordinated to a political strategy. The fight, Ramdane argued, would be taken to the cities and towns. This story is told in the film by Gillo Pontecorvo, *The Battle of Algiers*, set in 1956–57. The Battle of Algiers occurred at a time when the FLN was at its peak as an urban organisation and influenced by Ramdane. The combination of strike action and a bombing campaign against French settlers in the capital was finally defeated by the French in 1957. Ramdane and other militants were forced into exile. The Soumman Conference had argued that a social republic would follow independence.

In 1956 Soummam reinstated the FLN's commitment to an Islamic republic. However, this commitment to Islam must not be confused with the radical Islamism much spoken about today. That period addressed very distinct concerns and it was then possible to envisage a progressive project of social reforms and nationalist liberation under the banner of Islam. An independent Algeria, in Soummam's vision, would be a broad and multi-ethnic state, shorn of the religious exclusivity that has wrongly come to characterise the appellation 'Islamic'. The fact that Algeria did not develop as originally envisaged it was not because of the Islamic pronouncements in the FLN's Soummam statement. The conference stated this commitment clearly: 'The birth of an Algerian state in the form of a democratic and social Republic … is not a restoration of the monarchy or a dead theocracy.'[46]

Soummam also placed the Armée de Libération Nationale (ALN)

(the National Liberation Army) on a firm footing. The ALN became an army that recruited broadly from students, workers and intellectuals. As a people's Army, inspired if not modelled on General Giáp's North Vietnamese counterpart, it relied on popular support. *Moussebilines* and *fidayines* were essentially soldiers without uniform. The *moussebilines* were recruited and operated locally, and were involved in acts of sabotage, frequently acting as 'guides' to the ALN. The *fidayines* were local fighters who took part in attacks on police stations and the military police.

Africa had seen mass revolts and armed resistance before Algeria. The struggle of the Mau Mau against European settlers in Kenya was a vital staging post for decolonisation on the continent (and was admired by Fanon). But the Algerian Revolution was on an entirely grander scale, posing an existential threat not only to French colonialism in North Africa, but to the entire French Empire. It was the first time that an armed struggle of this size had taken place in Africa. Soummam had firmly placed the radical wing in control of the nationalist struggle.

Fanon threw himself into the frenzy. If he had arrived in Algeria as a radical in 1953 with vague notions of political action, he left Algeria three years later a revolutionary, determined to dedicate his life to the Algerian cause. Soon after November 1954 Fanon, with colleagues, helped to turn Blida-Joinville's hospital into a place where wounded and traumatised FLN fighters could be treated (and hidden). Fanon, however, acting out of his own radical humanism ended up also treating war-damaged French policemen in need of nerve specialists, so they could continue to torture 'terrorist' suspects. For a man widely and inaccurately regarded as the apostle of violence, he treated both tortured and torturer, with equal concern and in most cases kept the identities and confidences of both a secret.

If Fanon had no plans to move to Algeria, he was quickly made aware that he had joined an oppressive branch of French colonial medicine. Doctors were not the agents of an objective science. Frequently, local doctors were important members of the property-owning class. They cheated and patronised their Algerian patients, seeing their work with Algerians as little more than a veterinary service, as a farmer treats his livestock. Four years after he had arrived in Algeria, Fanon wrote powerfully about the role of many of the doctors in colonial Algeria.

When Algeria was first invaded and occupied by the French expeditionary army, the force included a large contingent of doctors. There was no clear distinction between medical and military work they marched together into Algeria's interior. Africa was conquered, according to the saying, with the Bible and gun but it could not have proceeded without the doctor's syringe. Doctors performed experiments and carried out research that became the intellectual justification for defining the Algerians as a peculiar and separate race, inferior to the European conqueror.

Medicine may have been midwife to the violent French colonialism in the 20th century, but not all doctors and psychiatrists in Algeria saw themselves as handmaidens to this civilising mission. In some respects, the Algerian school pioneered by Antoine Porot prided itself on serious reforms, though it was deeply committed to the colonial project. Porot argued that in order to better execute their duty to their Algerian patients, doctors should speak Arabic and understand their traditions and customs. Knowledge of Arabic and Muslim customs would help deepen the colonial project and treat mental pathologies. But despite Porot's so-called enlightenment, he still regarded Algerians as children. For example, in an article published in 1918, Porot decried 'the Muslim native's remarkable propensity for the passive life, his habitual insouciance about the future, and his childlike credulity and stubbornness'.[47]

The hierarchies that the colonial state used to divide up Algerians operated on many levels. Fanon, now a well-paid doctor in a large French hospital in Algeria, was part of the colonial medical establishment. However, as a black doctor, he was at the same time alienated by the establishment. Being black cast him to the margins of the colonial system in Algeria; he was not automatically regarded as an insider to the Algerian cause. He did not speak Arabic and did not know Algeria. Nonetheless, Fanon attempted to breathe Tosquelles's reforming zeal into the hospital in Blida. In contrast to the regimented discipline of the hospital's old staffers, with their fixed working hours and visits, Fanon worked irregular hours, sometimes starting early in the morning, and made both regular and impromptu visits to the ward. He cut an impressive figure, meticulously turned out in tailored white coats and shirts that he would sometimes change twice a day.

As a result of Fanon's more liberal care of his patients, there is some legend and myth surrounding his sojourn at Blida. Some reports have him moving around the hospital, releasing patients from chains and straitjackets, and playing the part of Jack Nicholson's character Randle Patrick McMurphy in the film *One Flew over the Cuckoo's Nest*. His close friend and fellow doctor Pierre Chaulet seems to repeat the myth when he recalled:

> At Blida, Fanon not only removed the chains from some of the sick, but he abolished the use of straitjackets, and most importantly he organised social and leisure activities (the Moorish café, football games, Algerian music concerts, Muslim religious festivals and a printer for a hospital newspaper).[48]

The historical record gives us a more ambivalent account of Fanon as the hospital's liberator, casting off chains and freeing patients from their straitjackets. Colleagues at Blida have explained that chains were not used at the hospital and that although Fanon was a psychiatrist with radical notions of democratisation and institutional psychiatry, he also had a pragmatic willingness, even an enthusiasm, to employ the full panoply of psychiatric methods: strong antipsychotic drugs, electric-shock treatment and narco-therapy. Removing straitjackets was an important part of Fanon's treatment, but – in his view – traumatised and alienated patients might also need medical restraints and aggressive drug therapy.

Nonetheless, ever flexible in his approach, Fanon realised that the methods of institutional psychiatry had to be adapted. Techniques he had learnt at Saint Alban were culturally bound with limited benefit beyond European patients. His Algerian patients had good reasons to reject them. Consequently, Fanon started to work with a local Algerian musician to develop a musical therapy as a new way to reach his Algerian patients. But a more fundamental truth emerged.

As great, even heroic, as Fanon's efforts were to break down the barriers between doctor and patient, he only succeeded in reproducing these hierarchies. Built into his position was an inherent contradiction. Introducing an interpreter to facilitate discussions produced the opposite of the intended result: it reinforced distance and hardened hostility towards the reforms. He learnt that parties and celebrations were largely meaningless – what was the point of a party separated from family or religious occasions?[49] The solution was further adaptation. Fanon tore apart the old practices of institutional psychiatry. An Algerian café was created, decorated with local art, an imam was invited to take Friday prayers and traditional storytellers came to entertain the patients. But in the immediate pre-war period these practices were risky. When Algerian patients were given tools to plough and cultivate the hospital allotment, European staff were aghast. Peasant tools had been used in Sétif in 1945 to kill European settlers. Macey records the service manager of the hospital complaining that his Martiniquan head doctor was 'madder than the madmen'.[50]

Conditions eventually became impossible at the hospital as the war and Fanon's involvement in it escalated. Towards the end of 1956, Fanon decided he could no longer stay in Algeria – for the safety of his wife and son but also because he could not practise his profession. He resigned, stating in letter to Algeria's resident minister (governor): 'If psychiatry is a medical technique which aspires to allow man to cease being alienated from his environment, I owe it to myself to assert that the Arab, who is permanently alienated in his own country, lives in a state of absolute depersonalisation.'[51]

His last days at the hospital were tense. Fanon had now identified himself openly with the enemy. He left for France, his wife, Josie, and young son following shortly afterwards.

Exile in Tunisia – through France

Fanon was still not entirely clear where he would go. He knew that his family was not going to stay in France, the country he had now rejected and, although he was committed to the Algerian struggle, he did not leave immediately for Tunisia, where the FLN had set up a regional headquarters. In France he spent a prolonged period with the French Trotskyist, Jean Ayme. A close friend of Fanon's and follow psychiatrist Alice Cherki records that Fanon seemed in no particular rush to leave:

> He continued to sleep three hours per night and to devour books.
> Amongst the documents that Ayme gave him to read, he was fascinated to discover the transcripts of the first four congresses of the Communist International ... Fanon spent entire nights in their company.[52]

Ayme also observed that although Fanon was incredibly smart, with an impressive knowledge of philosophy and psychiatry, he did not have much political training. He had not been an activist and did not have a thorough knowledge of revolutionary history. Fanon was undergoing a rapid education.

Eventually Fanon's family left for Tunisia in early 1957. Tunisia had become independent the previous year and was rapidly becoming the principal base for the FLN's exiled leadership, with a large community of Algerians who had been forced out of their country taking refuge there. Fanon lived in Tunis for the rest of his life. Together with other exiles, he helped write and edit the organisation's newspaper *El Moudjahid*. Pierre and Claudine Chaulet, who were close friends and fellow militants of the FLN in Algeria, had also been forced to move to Tunis after Pierre's release from prison in mid-1957. They were among the few Algerians of French origin who had committed themselves to the liberation war. The couple had introduced Fanon to the FLN in Algiers. This is their vivid description of Fanon during his years in Tunis:

> Brilliant talker, charmer, adored using words from the medical and psychiatric lexicon to express a core meaning (such as 'muscular vigilance'), he seemed to have read everything, sometimes in a spin of words, taking lyrical flight, attentive to the reactions of his listeners, pushing sometimes reason to the point of paradox to provoke discussion and at the same time a disciplined militant, modest and accepting criticism of certain improper expressions or exaggerations.[53]

Fanon continued to work as a psychiatrist, publishing papers on his experiments and attempting to reform the hospital regime in the two psychiatric units where he worked. He also wrote regularly for *El Moudjahid* and devoted himself to the work of the FLN. Fanon was not a natural journalist. He did not type and, instead, he would dictate his articles to secretaries, rarely carrying out interviews or original research. But he had an extraordinary gift for polemical and passionate prose that expressed the spirit of the revolution.

The newspaper was a strange beast. Produced fortnightly, it was made up of reports and appeals but with little actual reporting. It was sold widely in France and was smuggled into Algeria. This is how Pierre Chaulet recalls the collective spirit that prevailed at the paper:

> Freedom of discussion was total within the editorial board. Each person took turns to speak on the proposed themes ... The reciprocal

influence of one on another makes it difficult to discern a single influence: we shared the same analysis and we had the same objectives within the editorial board. Fanon was one of us, not more, and what we wrote was the result of a collective reflection.[54]

Year Five of the Algerian Revolution

Fanon wrote *L'An V de la Révolution Algérienne* (*Year Five of the Algerian Revolution*, currently published in English under the title *Studies in a Dying Colonialism*) in 1959. The book was an attempt to garner support for the FLN and engage with the French left. It was a publication of pro-Algerian and FLN propaganda that celebrated the popular involvement of the Algerian people in the war of liberation. The French left had equivocated and failed to support the FLN and the war. The PCF was the largest extra-parliamentary force on the left and, though individual members supported the war, the party's pronouncements were scandalous. The PCF argued that the revolution would take place not in Algeria, but in France, and that Algerian nationalists must follow the political lead of the French proletariat, as Algeria was not ready for independence. The greatest threat, the PCF stated, was that an independent Algeria could fall into the clutches of American imperialism. In this respect, the PCF did not raise objections to the anti-American justification for the war offered by Charles de Gaulle, who after he returned to power in 1958 continued the war (even though he eventually conceded defeat).[55] However, there were influential anti-Stalinists, including *les porteurs de valises* (literally the carriers of suitcases), who smuggled money out of France for the FLN, who refused to take the side of the French republic and supported the FLN. Though the achievements of these militants should not be exaggerated, these were courageous and inspiring acts of solidarity. In Algeria, the communist party did play a significant role fighting the French, though Fanon did not seem to have been aware of the extent of this involvement.[56]

In contrast to the general negative sentiment that the left in France and those fighting for Algerian independence had towards the PCF, when the Section Française de L'Internationale Onvrière (French Socialist Party) (SFIO) came to power in 1956, there was jubilation among progressive forces in France and Algeria. This sentiment was based on the prospect that the new socialist prime minister, Guy Mollet, would end the war against Algeria and lead negotiation towards Algeria's independence. Instead, however, Mollet capitulated to pressure from the white settlers in Algeria and escalated the war, forcing ever more French conscripts into the bloodbath. He also appointed Robert Lacoste to the post of resident minister of Algeria. Those in Algeria who had resisted the FLN – sometimes because of genuine doubts about the front's politics and strategy – now felt they had no alternative to joining and supporting the front. The FLN was, more or less, the pre-eminent organisation of national liberation. Fanon's long-standing colleague and collaborator in his psychiatric work, Charles Geromini, described how any political choice was taken away after Mollet's betrayal:

> There was no longer any choice other than between Lacoste and
> the Front. A third force could have had meaning only if it had been
> supported by the French left. Since the French left were playing the
> game of Algerian fascism, any attempt to organise liberal action in
> Algiers was doomed to failure.[57]

Across the spectrum, the forces on the left were without a socialist alternative. On the radical left, this had been closed off by the PCF, while the parliamentary and socialist left had now been discredited by their terrible and tragic confrontation with the FLN.

The title of Fanon's book, *L'An V de la Révolution Algérienne*, is a reference to the French Revolution. It is also an indication that Fanon, like leading members of the FLN, saw 1954 as signalling a new epoch of liberation and that everything previous could be ignored or, in the case of Messali's MNA, erased. But Fanon's arguments in the book about the Algerian Revolution were more nuanced than those of the FLN. The popular mobilisation of the Algerian people for the war after 1954 marked the start of a new Algeria. The revolution, which lasted until Algeria eventually attained independence in 1962, had seen an extraordinary flowering of human capacity that overturned old attitudes, habits and the deeply embedded sense of colonial and racial inferiority. Algerians were beginning to stand up for themselves, and to resist and be proud of themselves.

L'An V de la Révolution Algérienne starts with a sense of disbelief that 'five years of struggle have bought no political change',[58] despite the fact that this bitter war, which was still going on, had been fought for a cause almost universally supported. Fanon speaks in an autobiographical tone when he refers to the devastating betrayal and feelings of outrage of those who had fought alongside the French in the Second World War, only now to see the French army occupy Algeria and attempt to crush its people into subservience.

But Fanon holds back his greatest condemnation for the hypocrisy of French so-called supporters of the war for independence, lampooning their position: 'In a war of liberation, the colonised people must win, but they must do so ... without barbarity.'[59] When a European nation, he continues, indulges in torture and barbarity, it is a blight on their civilisation and history. Yet, when the colonised respond, it is the fulfilment of their underdeveloped nature. So an 'underdeveloped nation is obliged to practise fair play, even while its adversary ventures, with a clear conscience, into unlimited ... terror.'[60] Fanon goes on to underline this double standard, pointing out that the colonised are therefore imprisoned again when they fight back because they are merely confirming their primitive essence. They will only be given European support if they fight and resist as we dictate.[61]

Fanon presents an argument for revolutionary terror, which he bases on a pragmatic assessment of the violence of the oppressed:

> Because we want a democratic ... Algeria, because we believe one
> cannot rise and liberate oneself in one area and sink in another, we
> condemn, with pain in our hearts, those brothers who have flung
> themselves into revolutionary action with ... brutality that centuries of
> oppression give rise to and feed.[62]

Fanon goes on to argue that violence emerges because of the horrors of colonisation and French occupation, and that the expression of this initial violence, of revolutionary action, contains elements of brutality, pride, freedom from humiliation and a desire to cast off servility.

The French democrat, Fanon tells us, wants liberation without the dreadful cries of the oppressed. He is prepared to celebrate the struggle for independence, but 'with a minimum of errors'. This, Fanon argues, is an abstraction that exists only in the salons and cafés of the Parisian intelligentsia. The democrat is neither honest about the role of his enlightened European nation, nor realistic about the struggles of the colonised. Instead, he is caught in a racist trap, blind to the way colonisation and violence are inextricably linked. Torture is not an aberration of settler colonialism but an intrinsic and natural outgrowth.

But full support for the war is important for the people of the colonising nation. Fanon argues that a colonising nation (and the people in that nation) cannot free itself while holding down another nation or people. The colonial state is caught in a racist world, as the colonised are caught in a web of repression and violence. Real transcendence will come when the humanity and transformation of the oppressed are recognised, and the European working class throws off racist myths. This change in consciousness is only possible by breaking with one's past – a break that can only be made through struggle.

With little effort, we can see an important vein of continuity linking Fanon's first book with his 1959 volume. Fanon held fast to the belief that psychiatry could play a role healing those who carried out some of the worst violence for the French. Writing about the hordes of torturers, he expresses his hope in the book:

> Those men belong nowhere. Now that the French colonial empire is being shaken by its last spasms, the French would do well to identify them ... Jackals do not take to feeding on milk overnight. The taste of blood and of crime is deeply embedded in the very being of these creatures who, it should be said, must be retrieved by psychiatry. [63]

Forever the psychiatrist, Fanon articulates an almost naive hope that these 'jackals' can indeed be retrieved.

Struggle – the *real struggle* – was the key to Fanon in 1959, as it was for black people seeking recognition in 1952. This involved the popular participation of ordinary Algerians in the revolution. The book is part declaration of this popular ownership of revolutionary struggle and of the liberating wind sweeping through Algerian society. It is also a lyrical and poetic celebration of how people are, in Fanon's medical lexicon, re-cerebralised by revolutions often in their most private and intimate relationships. Describing the transformation taking place between men and women, Fanon writes:

> The couple is no longer shut in upon itself. It no longer finds its end in itself. It is no longer the result of the natural instinct of perpetuation of the species, nor the institutionalised means of satisfying one's sexuality ... The Algerian couple, in becoming a link in the revolutionary organisation, is transformed into a unit of existence.[64]

Contrary to the accusations made against him, Fanon was not exaggerating or being sentimental about revolutions.[65] Algeria during this period was undergoing profound changes. The years 1956 to 1960 showed all the signs of radical transformation. The struggle that had been launched in 1954 by a small group of men had become a mass movement that pulled in urban and rural areas, men and women, Muslim and Jew, as well as the armed struggles and city demonstrations, riots and strikes.

Political discussions became widespread. The radio – previously an object treated with suspicion as an alien technology – was commandeered (or subverted) by the population as an alternative source of information. Fanon wrote about the democratisation of the radio during the revolution. The FLN radio station, The Voice of Fighting Algeria, had started broadcasting from Cairo in 1956. Moutif Mohamed grew up in Algiers during the revolution and years later recalled listening to the FLN radio station:

> We listened to the radio, *The Voice of Fighting Algeria*, to understand
> what was happening, but there was lots of static and my father would
> say, 'Be quiet, let me listen to what's going on.' Then he would say, 'You
> see my son, we are fighting the French. We have an army.' At the time
> we lived right next to the road and he was anxious that we would be
> heard listening to the radio. He would tell us, 'Be careful, we don't know
> who is behind the door, the military might be passing.' If the French had
> found the radio they would have burnt it. They burnt radios.'[66]

In *L'An V de la Révolution Algérienne*, Fanon captures the sense of expectation and hope as old servile relationships collapsed. Cultural habits and traditions changed as women became active in the war. The French could be resisted, and their power broken. These changes were not limited to narrow groups of Algerian fighters, but tens of thousands of ordinary Algerians who had begun to contemplate independence and freedom for the first time. These were the years of Algeria's revolution.

As the revolution progressed through the 1950s and early 1960s, it pulled in widening layers of society who were transformed and radicalised by the struggle against the French. For example, men and women, as we have seen, were forced to re-examine their relationships, as women became involved in political activity. In 1974 the Algerian government estimated that about 11 000

Algerian women fought for the liberation of Algeria (about 3 per cent of them fought in combat). This is almost certainly a serious underestimate.[67]

L'An V de la Révolution Algérienne describes (and celebrates) the nature of Algeria's popular revolution. As Fanon scholar Nigel Gibson explains:

> L'An V really speaks of this experience of revolution. It is interesting that many criticized Fanon as a 'romantic' or 'utopian' but ... the revolution, as revolutions do, turned things upside down, upset the old social relations. That these changes did not remain, that they were turned back (re-revolved?) does not mean that they didn't happen. I think Fanon also understood the fragility of new social relations, not only from outside but also from inside the revolution, and that is a reason why he remains relevant today.[68]

Fanon's involvement in the FLN grew and he assumed more responsibilities, writing and now speaking on behalf of the FLN in press conferences and attending international conferences.

The Wretched of the Earth

Fanon was diagnosed with leukaemia at the end of 1960 and knew immediately that he was dying, and that he had, at best, only a year or two to live. His life bunched up. A man not used to holding himself back, he now strained to almost inhuman lengths to write and influence a movement in which he had begun to have serious misgivings and fears. In 1960 he had been made ambassador of the Gouvernement Provisionel de la République Algérienne (Provisional Government of the Algerian Republic) to Ghana, where he met leaders of the nationalist movements from the continent. Initially, he refused treatment in the USA, which he reputedly labelled a country of racists and lynch mobs, and instead travelled to Moscow. The leukaemia death sentence drove Fanon on and he became possessed with the need to assist the FLN and the ALN, its armed wing. In 1961, months before his death, he completed his final work, The Wretched of the Earth. The book shows Fanon as a revolutionary thinker in continual development. It is extremely rich and complex (and even includes a discussion on pottery and sculpture), but I will limit my discussion to the book's main arguments.

Even though Fanon was intimately involved in the FLN and the national liberation movement, he was gaining, almost unique in his generation, critical insight into the limitations of the very national freedom and independence they were fighting for. *The Wretched of the Earth* can be read as a warning to Algeria – and to the rest of the decolonised and decolonising world – about how the national bourgeoisie decay into

> ... a sort of little greedy caste, avid and voracious, with the mind of a huckster, only too glad to accept the dividends that the former colonial power hands out to it. This get-rich-quick middle class shows itself incapable of great ideas or of inventiveness. It remembers what it has read in European textbooks and imperceptibly it becomes not even the replica of Europe, but its caricature.[69]

But Fanon also attempted to address how this degeneration could be avoided.

The Wretched of the Earth grasped the predicament that independence presented to the movements and leadership of national liberation. Postcolonial power was caught between an enfeebled national bourgeoisie and the global limitations imposed on any newly developing nation in the modern world. In this context, it was inevitable that the new national bourgeoisies would act to suppress those in their own people whose demands could not be met within the existing economic and political system. The pseudo-bourgeoisie – described in a variety of terms in the book, often as a 'profiteering caste' – is not a real bourgeoisie. They own nothing, Fanon tells us, and they will bring nothing. They have no national programme of development, seeking simply to become the favoured middlemen for metropolitan capital.

Fanon was able to describe, with extraordinary power, how national freedom often became its opposite, the curse of independence. How could he recognise, with such shearing accuracy, developments that had hardly started to emerge? There are several indications as to why. Fanon's close friend and leader of the FLN, Abane Ramdane, associated with the radical wing, had been assassinated in 1958. This led to Fanon's serious questioning of the organisation to which he had devoted his life. After the murder, it was clear that some elements of the FLN would deal with internal opponents who they disagreed with. Fanon was a critical student of what was happening within the FLN.

He also saw, and attempted to analyse, the parties of national independence in Ghana and Senegal. The contrast between the rhetoric of national freedom and the reality of independence was great in Ghana. The radical rhetoric of the country's first leader of independent Ghana, Kwame Nkrumah, contrasted with the continuity of colonial power after its independence in 1957. Fanon's personal disappointment can also be felt in the pages of his classic. Césaire, for a short time his schoolteacher and hero, turned his back on independence and accepted continued incorporation into France under a deal set out by De Gaulle in 1958. But that was not all. The great poet of Negritude and new president of Senegal, Léopold Senghor, betrayed the Algerian Revolution – voting in the French Assembly for an extension of emergency powers to prosecute the war in Algeria. Senghor also accepted De Gaulle's compromise of a French community of African states. African freedom and independence were being revealed as a false prophet.

But there were two events, one contemporary and the other historical, that pulled back the curtains on newly independent African nations for Fanon, to reveal the dangers they faced. The first was the Congo crisis, which Fanon saw unfold before him. A nationalist party was elected to power in 1960 in democratic and transparent elections, and to the jubilations of the Congolese. But days after the official ceremony of independence, the country ruptured. Two mineral-rich provinces, Katanga and Kasai, broke away, backed and armed by Belgium, the former colonial power. Seven months after his election, in January 1961, the leader of the nationalist MNC and the elected prime minister, Patrice Lumumba – whom Fanon had met in Ghana and the Congo – was murdered by the Belgians, and their Congolese puppets in the break away province.[70] Real economic and political independence would not be countenanced by the parting colonial powers. The conclusion that Fanon drew was that Africa must craft its own tools and wage a relentless battle against imperial invasion and the pseudo-bourgeoisie who usurp the powerful forces of national liberation.

The second event that exposed the dangers of independence for Fanon was a deep historical understanding of events in Central and South America that he came across in his reading. As a voracious reader, Fanon studied history and philosophy with a gusto that left his contemporaries astonished. As his friend Chaulet reminisced, he 'seemed to have read everything'. Latin America had experienced independence generations before Africa. Independence, he noted, had been keenly fought for, but hopelessly compromised. He concurred with Césaire that in Haiti – the country that had won independence from France after a slave revolution in the 1790s – the colonial problem had first been posed in its great contradictions, as the country fought for, won and then saw the impotence of this freedom in a world dominated by several imperialist states.[71] Fanon writes despairingly in *The Wretched of the Earth*: 'The African bourgeoisie of certain under-developed countries have learnt nothing from books. If they had looked closer at the Latin American countries they doubtless would have recognised the dangers which threatened them.'[72] Fanon was a figure of the black Atlantic, his life, experiences and thinking criss-crossed the Atlantic, picking up and developing insights from the Caribbean and the Americas, which then enriched and expanded his analysis of decolonisation in Africa.

The Wretched of the Earth sounded the emergency alarm. He saw how the FLN was developing in a similar way to these other nationalist formations. The book was an attempt to pull back the FLN – as much as he could in a single volume – and prevent the development of the caste of profiteers. Fanon has been criticised for his sweeping generalisations in the book, but on preventing the growth of a national bourgeoisie, he is quite specific about what needs to be done.[73]

The peasantry or workers?

Like many thinkers of his time, Fanon was influenced by Maoist interpretations of socialism, which emphasised the central role of the peasantry in revolutionary struggle while holding a deep suspicion towards the proletariat. He articulates this view in *The Wretched of the Earth*:

> ... the proletariat is the nucleus of the colonised population which has been most pampered by the colonial regime. The embryonic proletariat of the towns is in a comparatively privileged position. In capitalist countries, the working class has nothing to lose; it is they who in the long run have everything to gain. In the colonial countries the working class has everything to lose; in reality it represents that fraction of the colonised nation which is necessary and irreplaceable if the colonial

machine is to run smoothly: it includes tram conductors, taxi-drivers, miners, dockers, interpreters, nurses and so on ...[74]

Fanon accepted the widespread argument that the organised African working class had been effectively bought off with the profits of imperialist exploitation, and that revolutionary action against the new African ruling classes would only come from the poorest African rural masses and the lumpenproletariat of unemployed and semi-employed in urban areas.

It was to the peasantry, therefore, that Fanon turned for his revolutionary agents. As he put it:

[I]t is clear that in the colonial countries the peasants alone are revolutionary, for they have nothing to lose and everything to gain. The starving peasant, outside the class system is the first among the exploited to discover that only violence pays. For him there is no compromise, no possible coming to terms; colonisation and decolonisation are simply a question of relative strength.[75]

There is a real sense in *The Wretched of the Earth* that the role Marx gave to the working class could be taken over by the peasantry. This displays Fanon's failure to understand what Marx meant by the pivotal role of the working class and its relationship to the oppressed.

As we have seen, Fanon's relationship with Marxism was strained. Fanon seems to have been relatively unschooled in Marxism, though by no means unaware of Marx's major writings. Gibson explains it like this:

I don't think he is that 'versed' in Marx. I don't think he was a Marxist; he was not claiming it and didn't feel he needed to. I think the *18th Brumaire* struck him and the *Communist Manifesto*, in that the bourgeoisie he discovers on the ground, so to speak, are not the ones that Marx writes of. But his intellectual appetite meant he read Marx.[76]

Macey goes further, arguing that, 'Fanon showed little interest in Marxist theory and whilst he had obviously absorbed its general principles there are few signs that he ever studied it in any depth.'[77]

The actual history of decolonisation in Africa reveals a boisterous working class, often leading the struggle for national liberation. This group was able to paralyse the colonial machine by their position at the heart of the system's profit-making in factories, mines and docks.[78] This power of the working class can be seen in many parts of late colonial sub-Saharan Africa, and even more so in North Africa and the Middle East. For example, there was a widening and radicalising wave of working-class militancy after 1945 in Egypt, Syria and Iraq. In addition, arguably it was the working-class demonstrations in the cities and towns across Algeria in December 1960 that forced the French to accept that they would have to leave. This wave of working-class dissent was a movement that was not controlled or organised by the FLN, and has been labelled the Algeria's Dien Bien Phu moment in the revolution.[79]

But there were also important weaknesses in these urban-based struggles – which Fanon's own analysis of the petty-bourgeois intelligentsia points to. There was an absence of working-class leadership within these strikes and protests, which could have made an argument for an urban, worker-led movement of a national and socialist revolution in a single and ongoing process of revolutionary change linked to the countryside. There were, of course, many reasons why these politics could not emerge, not least the role of the Stalinised communist parties, which sought either to limit these revolts to nationhood, or argue, in the case of Algeria, for the need to follow the lead of the European working class. There were also serious weaknesses in working-class politics. Faced with these problems often the leadership of national and decolonising movements fell into other hands – quite distinct from the working class and poor (and Fanon's peasantry). A nationalist intelligentsia assumed control of diverse movements for national liberation. This intelligentsia had often been educated in the West, with a strong sense of the humiliation at their perceived national backwardness. In Egypt in 1952, it was a class of nationalist Free Officers who led the revolution in deposing King Farouk's regime. Fanon knew prominent members of this class, both personally and from afar, including Senghor, Lumumba, Césaire and Nkrumah.

In addition, many labour movements on the continent *were* able to resist their total incorporation into the nationalist project and maintain their own autonomy from hegemonic nationalist parties, but their biggest problem was their inability to generate intellectual or ideological alternatives to the focus on national economic development dominant among both Stalinists and nationalists. As a consequence, trade unions sometimes adopted syndicalist or economistic approaches, rejecting nationalist or new state ideologies and arguing that their role was non-political. This unfortunately seemed to confirm the accusation, present in *The Wretched of the Earth*, that organised workers represented, in an African context, a labour aristocracy whose selfish defence of their privileges was at the expense of other, particularly rural, sections of society.[80]

The idea of combining national democratic and social transformation into a permanent regional and global revolution was lost with the degeneration of the Russian Revolution after 1917. Yet Fanon tantalises us with insights into the role of the national bourgeoisie in a colonised and Third-World setting. He also recognised the need in his last book to enrich the revolution with social transformation and that the project for a new humanism could only be achieved on a global scale.

On violence

It is in the chapter dedicated to violence in *The Wretched of the Earth* that Fanon has suffered his greatest misreading and denunciations. Building on his previous work, Fanon writes clearly that 'at the level of individuals, violence is a cleansing force. It frees the native from his inferiority complex and from his despair and inaction; it makes him fearless and restores his self-respect.'[81] Shorn of their context, statements such as this seem to extol violence, but this was not Fanon's intention. Fanon was writing about the necessity of resistance that involves violence, when one is up against overwhelming odds. The experience of colonialism, Fanon explains, has been of unremitting violence and its overthrow will require force. The violence of the oppressed, he argues, is a necessary and inevitable part of decolonisation. Liberation without it is impossible – a cruel dream shimmering beautifully in the distance, always out of reach.

But there is a further element to his argument. The violence of the oppressed has the therapeutic effect of ridding the colonised of their deeply held feelings of inferiority. The colonisers can be hurt, their violence countered and broken. The result, when the colonisers are defeated – as it is with all popular upheavals – is a sense of strength and pride the oppressed have in their own value and self-worth – a collective struggle, involving violence, maybe, but an inherently personal transformation from inferiority to self-assertion and self-recognition. Therefore, any real struggle of the oppressed will require counter-violence. Non-violence, Fanon writes, is an invention of the colonial intelligentsia, whereas

> violence alone, violence committed by the people, violence organised
> and educated by its leaders, makes it possible for the masses to
> understand social truths and gives the key to them. Without that
> struggle, without that knowledge of the practice of action, there's
> nothing but a fancy-dress parade and the blare of trumpets. There's
> nothing save a minimum of re-adaptation, a few reforms at the top,
> a flag waving: and down there at the bottom an undivided mass, still
> living in the Middle Ages, endlessly marking time.[82]

Fanon was not the apostle of violence, but its subtle and pragmatic analyst.

Endgame

After a momentary respite in his illness, knowing that he had only a very short time to live, Fanon insisted on lecturing ALN troops in Ghardimaou on the Tunisian/Algerian border, on draft versions of the famous chapter *Mésaventures de la conscience nationale* (Pitfalls of national consciousness). But he was also inspired to speak to them on what he had learnt from Sartre's *Critique de la Raison Dialectique*, which he had recently and enthusiastically read. As important as their cause was, Fanon told the troops, it had to be extended and deepened into the social and economic life of the new nation. Independence was no panacea for the colonised, and unless the transformation that they (the ALN troops he was lecturing) were committed to was enriched and spread not only inside Algerian society, but also regionally and globally, then the national liberation that they sought was in danger of becoming its opposite – a curse or a prison that would solve few of the problems that Algerians had given their lives for.[83]

Returning to Tunis, Fanon dictated the last chapters of his book, in a period of intense activity and tragedy captured by Pierre Chaulet:

> *The Wretched of the Earth* is to be read like an urgent message,
> delivered in a raw state, uncorrected – we did not dare question certain
> passages in front a man who was reading his text to the close friends
> that we were, while pacing up and down his room in Tunis, sick and

aware that he was condemned, desiring with all his force, in a superb language, to say what he had to say.[84]

As night spread quickly across the sky, Fanon's life did not wane but rather became focused more sharply. There is a limit, however, to what one book (and one extraordinary life force) as brilliant and problematic as Fanon's could do.

Finally accepting that treatment in the USA might prolong his life, he left for Washington in early October 1961. Eight weeks later, he died at the National Institutes of Health in Maryland. Fanon fought death until the end. When he was finally hospitalised, he was joined by his wife and young son. The disease silenced him. The startling and brilliant loudhailer of colonial liberation, revolution and radical humanism was dead. Fanon's last request was that his body be buried in liberated Algeria. Before he had left for the USA, he lamented to his brothers and sisters in the FLN: 'You are lucky, you will see the independence of Algeria, but I will not.'[85]

NOTES

1 Sékou Touré, 'Nous préférons la pauvreté dans la liberté à l'opulence dans l'esclavage', http://www.fondationsekoutoure.org, accessed August 2013.

2 'All African People's Conference' in an unnamed newspaper report (December, 1958), Institute of Commonwealth Studies, London.

3 'All African People's Conference' in an unnamed newspaper report.

4 P. N. Singh, 'The Black Panthers and the "Undeveloped Countries" of the Left' in Charles E. Jones (ed.), Black Panther Party Reconsidered (Baltimore: Black Classic Press, 1998), p. 76.

5 David Macey, interview, Leeds 14 October 2010. Sadly Macey died in October 2011. I am indebted to his impressive work on Fanon but particularly the patience and generosity he showed me in 2010.

6 See P. Alexander, 'South Africa after Marikana', International Socialism 137 (2013).

7 There has been no shortage of excellent biographies, memoirs and serious studies. Among the long list several that stand out include: D. Macey, Frantz Fanon: A Biography (New York: Picador, 2001); N. Gibson, Fanon: The Postcolonial Imagination (London: Polity Press, 2003); N. Gibson (ed.), Rethinking Fanon: The Continuing Dialogue (New York: Humanity Books, 1999); A. Cherki, Frantz Fanon: A Portrait (Paris: Seuil, 2000); I. Gendzier, Frantz Fanon (Paris: Seuil, 1976).

8 This introduction is part of ongoing work into Frantz Fanon; see also L. Zeilig, 'Frantz Fanon, Une Vie Révolutionnaire', Contretemps 2:10 (2011) and 'Pitfalls and Radical Mutations: Frantz Fanon's Revolutionary Life', International Socialism, 134 (2012). The essay includes interviews with those who knew Fanon, or were involved in the same struggles. Many ideas in the article have benefited immensely from suggestions and conversations with Ian Birchall, Alex Callinicos and David Macey, and from Pierre Chaulet's severe but justified criticism of an earlier version of the work. Sadly, Chaulet died on 5 October 2012.

9 Cited in Macey, *Frantz Fanon: A Biography*, p. 43

10 C. L. R. James, *The Black Jacobins: Toussaint L'Ouverture and the San Domingo Revolution* (London: Vintage, 1989).

11 Macey, *Frantz Fanon: A Biography*, p. 43.

12 Macey, *Frantz Fanon: A Biography*, p. 46.

13 F. Fanon, *Peau Noire, Masques Blancs* (Paris: Seuil, 1952), p. 163.

14 The Free French was constituted by French officers, led by De Gaulle, who were determined to fight against the Nazi occupation and the capitulation of the French elite.

15 Macey, interview.

16 Cited in Macey, *Frantz Fanon: A Biography*, pp. 103–104.

17 A. Césaire, *Cahier d'un Retour au Pays Natal* (Paris: Presence Africaine, 1983), pp. 57–58.

18 Fanon, *Peau Noire, Masques Blancs*.

19 I. Birchall, 'Socialism or Identity Politics: A Reply to Linda A Bell', *Sartre Studies International* 4:2 (1998), p. 70.

20 A complex philosophical tradition, phenomenology asserts one's presence in the world and the centrality of multiple lived experiences.

21 D. Macey, '"I am My Own Foundation": Frantz Fanon as a Source of Continued Political Embarrassment', *Theory, Culture and Society* 27:7–8 (2011), p. 41.

22 Fanon, *Peau Noire, Masques Blancs*, pp. 116–117.

23 See H. Bulhan, *Frantz Fanon and the Psychology of Oppression* (London: Plenum Press, 1985).

24 Fanon, *Peau Noire, Masques Blancs*, p. 221.

25 Fanon, *Peau Noire, Masques Blancs*, p. 220.

26 Fanon, *Peau Noire, Masques Blancs*, p. 222.

27 Fanon, *Peau Noire, Masques Blancs*, p. 216.

28 I am grateful to Kim Wale for this insight.

29 See D. Reggio, 'Jean Oury – iatros philosophos', http://www.gold.ac.uk/history/news-events/inallcases/, accessed September 2012

30 Today the hospital is called *Centre Hospitalier François-Tosquelles*. Though the cradle of institutional psychiatry, today the hospital is a shell of its former self: patients are locked up for hours and heavily drugged, the early experiments of the hospital only a faint memory to the staff.

31 David Reggio, 'An Interview with Dr Jean Oury', http://www.gold.ac.uk/media/interview1-jean-oury.pdf, accessed June 2013.

32 Fanon, 'Lassitude' *Trait d'Union*, n. 128 (1952); Lettre, Amayen Roger, n. 129 (1953), Saint Alban library, accessed August 2012.

33 Cited in Macey, *Frantz Fanon: A Biography*, p. 203.

34 Cited in R. Murray and T. Wengraf, 'The Algerian Revolution – 1', *New Left Review* 1:22 (1963), pp. 22–23.

35 F. Jeanson, *La Révolution Algérienne* (Paris: Feltrinelli, 1962), p. 29.

36 Murray and Wengraf, 'The Algerian Revolution', pp. 15–30.

37 Often referred to as the Kabyle insurrection, the uprising involved approximately 250 different groups and almost a third of the Algerian population; see for an account M. Ferro, *Colonisation: A Global History* pp. 53–54 (London: Routledge, 1994); Murray and Wengraf, 'The Algerian Revolution', pp. 53–54.

38 Murray and Wengraf, 'The Algerian Revolution', pp. 53–54.

39 J. L. Planche, *Sétif 1945: Histoire d'un Massacre Annoncé* (Paris: Perrin, 2006).

40 The war lasting until 1962 cost an estimated 1 million Algerian lives.

41 Macey, '"I am my own foundation"', p. 37.

42 The nine historical leaders of the FLN were Krim Belkacem, Mostefa Ben Boulaid, Larbi Ben M'hidi, Rabah Bitat, Mohamed Boudiaf, Mourad Didouche, Hocine Ait Ahmed, Ahmed Ben Bella and Mohamed Khider.

43 I am grateful to Pierre Chaulet for these insights; interview, Algiers, 28 September 2011.

44 The 'war' within in a war is brilliantly captured in Rachid Bouchareb's film *Outside the Law* (2010).

45 See M. Harbi and B. Stora, *La Guerre d'Algérie* (Paris: Robert Laffont, 2004).

46 Panaf Editors, *Frantz Fanon* (London: Panaf, 1975), p. 182.

47 Cited in N. Lazarus *The Postcolonial Unconscious* (Cambridge: Cambridge University Press, 2011), p. 171.

48 P. and C. Chaulet, interview, Paris, 14 November 2010.

49 Macey, *Frantz Fanon: A Biography*, p. 232.

50 Macey, *Frantz Fanon: A Biography*, p. 233.

51 F. Fanon, *Pour la Revolution Africaine* (Paris: Francois Maspero, 1964), p. 60.

52 Cherki, *Frantz Fanon*, p. 135.

53 P. and C. Chaulet, interview.

54 P. and C. Chaulet, interview.

55 The PCF did have a point. The USA was determined to break the power of European imperialisms, in order to extend its own global hegemony; the Suez Crisis illustrated this point. It was also the reason why the Soviet Union was reluctant to give the FLN full support. See A. Drew, *Visions of Liberation: Communism and Nationalism in Algeria* (Manchester: Manchester University Press, forthcoming 2014).

56 S. Pattieu, *Les Camarades des Frères: Trotskistes et Libertaires dans la Guerre d'Algérie* (Paris: Editions Syllepse, 2002).

57 C. Geromini, 'Appendix 1' in F. Fanon, *L'An V de la Révolution Algérienne* (Paris: La Découverte, 2001), p. 174.

58 F. Fanon, *L'an V*, p. 5.

59 Fanon, *L'an V*, p. 6.

60 Fanon, *L'an V*, p. 6.

61 This argument neatly reflects the hypocritical support of European and American politicians and commentators on the recent revolutions in Egypt, Libya and Tunisia. The 'masses' on the streets of North Africa can be celebrated as long as they are 'non-violent' and 'peace-loving'.

62 Fanon, *L'an V*, p. 7.

63 Fanon, *L'an V*, p. 152

64 Fanon, *L'an V* p. 114.

65 Macey, *Frantz Fanon: A Biography*, p. 402.

66 M. Mohamed, interview, Algiers, 4 October 2011.

67 M. Turshen, 'Algerian Women in the Liberation Struggle and the Civil War: From Active Participants to Passive Victims?', *Social Research* 69:3 (2002).

68 N. Gibson, interview, London, 3 November 2010.

69 F. Fanon, *Les Damnés de la Terre* (Paris: François Maspero, 1961), p.131.

70 See L. Zeilig, *Voices of Liberation: Patrice Lumumba* (Cape Town: HSRC Press, 2013).

71 See C. Høgsbjerg, 'CLR James and the Black Jacobins', *International Socialism*, www.isj.org.uk/index.php4?id=639&issue=126, accessed July 2013.

72 Fanon, *Les Damnés*, p. 130.

73 D. Caute, *Frantz Fanon* (New York: The Viking Press, 1970), pp. 73–74.

74 Fanon, *Les Damnés*, pp. 146–147.

75 Fanon, *Les Damnés*, pp. 91–92.

76 Gibson, interview.

77 Macey, *Frantz Fanon: A Biography*, p. 479.

78 See L. Zeilig (ed.), *Class Struggle and Resistance in Africa* (Chicago: Haymarket, 2009).

79 H. Elsenhans, 'Les Manifestations de Décembre 1960 et la Reconnaisance de la Révolution Algérienne' in *11 Décembre 1960. Le Diên Biên Phu Politique de la Guerre d'Algérie* (Paris: Petite collection – Histoire, 2010), pp. 29–62.

80 But it is hard to escape the sense that Fanon's approach reflected Abane's failure to turn the Algerian Revolution to the cities and urban areas, rather than a serious consideration of the role of the working class in the developing world.

81 Fanon, *Les Damnés*, p. 70.

82 Fanon, *Les Damnés*, p. 110.

83 R. Bernasconi, 'Fanon's *The Wretched of the Earth* as the Fulfilment of Sartre's *Critique of Dialectical Reason*', *Sartre Studies International* 16:2 (2010).

84 P. and C. Chaulet, interview.

85 P. and C. Chaulet, interview.

His
Voice

Fanon during a press conference at the Congress of Black African Writers, 1959

BLACK SKIN, WHITE MASKS
From Chapter 7: The Negro and Recognition

I wonder sometimes whether school inspectors and government functionaries are aware of the role they play in the colonies. For twenty years they poured every effort into programmes that would make the Negro a white man. In the end, they dropped him and told him, 'You have an indisputable complex of dependence on the white man.'

The Negro and Hegel

Self-consciousness exists in itself and for itself, in that and by the fact that it exists for another self-consciousness; that is to say, it is only by being acknowledged or recognised.

    – *Hegel*, The Phenomenology of Mind.[1]

Man is human only to the extent to which he tries to impose his existence on another man in order to be recognised by him. As long as he has not been effectively recognised by the other, that other will remain the theme of his actions. It is on that other being, on recognition by that other being, that his own human worth and reality depend. It is that other being in whom the meaning of his life is condensed.

There is not an open conflict between white and black. One day the White Master, *without conflict*, recognised the Negro slave.

But the former slave wants to *make himself recognised.*

At the foundation of Hegelian dialectic there is an absolute reciprocity which must be emphasised. It is in the degree to which I go beyond by own immediate being that I apprehend the existence of the other as a natural and more than natural reality. If I close the circuit, if I prevent the accomplishment of movement in two directions, I keep the other within myself. Ultimately, I deprive him even of this being-for-itself.

The only means of breaking this vicious circle that throws me back on myself is to restore to the other, through mediation and recognition, his human reality, which is different from natural reality. The other has to perform the same operation. 'Action from one side only would be useless, because what is to happen can only be brought about by means of both. ...'; '*they recognise themselves as mutually recognising each other.*'[2]

In its immediacy consciousness of self is simple being-for-itself. In order to win the certainty of oneself, the incorporation of the concept of recognition is essential. Similarly, the other is waiting for recognition by us, in order to burgeon into the universal consciousness of self. Each consciousness of self is in quest of absoluteness. It wants to be recognised as a primal value without reference to life, as a transformation of subjective certainty (*Gewissheit*) into objective truth (*Wahrheit*).

When it encounters resistance from the other, self-consciousness undergoes the experience of *desire* – the first milestone on the road that leads to the dignity of the spirit. Self-consciousness accepts the risk of its life, and consequently it threatens the other in his physical being. 'It is solely by risking life that freedom is obtained; only thus is it tried and proved that the essential nature of self-consciousness is not *bare existence*, is not the merely immediate form in which it at first makes its appearance, is not its mere absorption in the expanse of life.'[3]

Thus human reality in-itself-for-itself can be achieved only through conflict and through the risk that conflict implies. This risk means that I go beyond life toward a supreme good that is the transformation of subjective certainty of my own worth into a universally valid objective truth.

As soon as I *desire* I am asking to be considered. I am not merely here-and-now, sealed into thingness. I am for somewhere else and for something else. I demand that notice be taken of my negating activity insofar as I pursue something other than life, insofar as I do battle for the creation of a human world – that is, of a world of reciprocal recognitions.

He who is reluctant to recognise me opposes me. In a savage struggle I am willing to accept convulsions of death, invincible dissolution, but also the possibility of the impossible.[4]

The other, however, can recognise me without struggle: 'The individual, who has not staked his life, may, no doubt, be recognised as a *person*, but he has not attained the truth of this recognition as an independent self-consciousness.'[5]

Historically, the Negro steeped in the inessentiality of servitude was set free by his master. He did not fight for his freedom.

Out of slavery the Negro burst into the lists where his masters stood. Like those servants who are allowed once every year to dance in the drawing room, the Negro is looking for a prop. The Negro has not become a master. When there are no longer slaves, there are no longer masters.

The Negro is a slave who has been allowed to assume the attitude of a master.

The white man is a master who has allowed his slaves to eat at his table.

One day a good white master who had influence said to his friends, 'Let's be nice to the niggers. ...'

The other masters argued, for after all it was not an easy thing, but then they decided to promote the machine-animal-men to the supreme rank of *men*.

Slavery shall no longer exist on French soil.

The upheaval reached the Negroes from without. The black man was acted upon. Values that had not been created by his actions, values that had not been born of the systolic tide of his blood, danced in a hued whirl round him. The upheaval did not make a difference in the Negro. He went from one way of life to another, but not from one life to another. Just as when one tells a much improved patient that in a few days he will be discharged from the hospital, he thereupon suffers a relapse, so the announcement of the liberation of the black slaves produced psychoses and sudden deaths.

It is not an announcement that one hears twice in a lifetime. The black man contented himself with thanking the white man, and the most forceful proof

49

of the fact is the impressive number of statues erected all over France and the colonies to show white France stroking the kinky hair of this nice Negro whose chains had just been broken.

'Say thank you to the nice man,' the mother tells her little boy ... but we know that often the little boy is dying to scream some other, more resounding expression. ...

The white man, in the capacity of master,[6] said to the Negro, 'From now on you are free.'

But the Negro knows nothing of the cost of freedom, for he has not fought for it. From time to time he has fought for Liberty and Justice, but these were always white liberty and white justice; that is, values secreted by his masters. The former slave, who can find in his memory no trace of the struggle for liberty or of that anguish of liberty of which Kierkegaard speaks, sits unmoved before the young white man singing and dancing on the tightrope of existence.

When it does happen that the Negro looks fiercely at the white man, the white man tells him: "Brother, there is no difference between us." And yet the Negro knows that there is a difference. He *wants* it. He wants the white man to turn on him and shout: "Damn nigger." Then he would have that unique chance-to "show them. ..."

But most often there is nothing-nothing but indifference, or a paternalistic curiosity.

The former slave needs a challenge to his humanity, he wants a conflict, a riot. But it is too late: The French Negro is doomed to bite himself and just to bite. I say "the French Negro," for the American Negro is cast in a different play. In the United States, the Negro battles and is battled. There are laws that, little by little, are invalidated under the Constitution. There are other laws that forbid certain forms of discrimination. And we can be sure that nothing is going to be given free.

There is war, there are defeats, truces, victories.

In the same way, the slave here is in no way identifiable with the slave who loses himself in the object and finds in his work the source of his liberation.

The Negro wants to be like the master.

Therefore he is less independent than the Hegelian slave.

In Hegel the slave turns away from the master and turns toward the object.

Here the slave turns toward the master and abandons the object.

50

"The twelve million black voices"[7] howled against the curtain of the sky. Torn from end to end, marked with the gashes of teeth biting into the belly of interdiction, the curtain fell like a burst balloon.

On the field of battle, its four corners marked by the scores of Negroes hanged by their testicles, a monument is slowly being built that promises to be majestic.

And, at the top of this monument, I can already see a white man and a black man *hand in hand*.

For the French Negro the situation is unbearable. Unable ever to be sure whether the white man considers him consciousness in-itself-for-itself, he must forever absorb himself in uncovering resistance, opposition, challenge.

This is what emerges from some of the passages of the book that Mounier has devoted to Africa.[8] The young Negroes whom he knew there sought to maintain their alterity. Alterity of rupture, of conflict, of battle.

The self takes its place by opposing itself, Fichte said. Yes and no.

I said in my introduction that man is a yes. I will never stop reiterating that.

Yes to life. *Yes* to love. *Yes* to generosity.

But man is also a *no*. *No* to scorn of man. *No* to degradation of man. *No* to exploitation of man. *No* to the butchery of what is most human in man: freedom.

Man's behavior is not only reactional. And there is always resentment in a reaction. Nietzsche had already pointed that out in *The Will to Power*.

To educate man to be actional, preserving in all his relations his respect for the basic values that constitute a human world, is the prime task of him who, having taken thought, prepares to act.

NOTES

1 G.W.F. Hegel, *The Phenomenology of Mind*, trans by J.B. Baillie, 2nd rev. ed. (London: Allen & Unwin, 1949), pp. 230–231.

2 Hegel, *The Phenomenology of Mind*, pp. 230–231.

3 Hegel, *The Phenomenology of Mind*, p. 233.

4 When I began this book, I wanted to devote one section to a study of the death wish among Negroes. I believed it necessary because people are forever saying Negroes never commit suicide.

  M. Achille did not hesitate to maintain this in a lecture, and Richard Wright, in one of his stories, has a white character say, 'If I were a Negro I'd kill myself … ' in the sense that only a Negro could submit to such treatment without feeling drawn to suicide.

Since then, M. Deshaies has taken the question of suicide as the subject for his thesis. He demonstrated that the studies by Jaensch, who contrasted the disintegrated-personality 'type' (brown eyes and skin), are predominantly specious.

According to Durkheim, Jews never committed suicide. Now it is the Negroes. Very well: 'The Detroit municipal hospital found that 16.6% of its suicide cases were Negroes, although the proportion of Negroes in the total population is only 7.6%. In Cincinnati, the number of Negro suicides is more than double that of whites; this may result in part from the amazing sexual disparity among Negro suicides: 358 women against 76 men.' (Gabriel Deshaies, *Psychologie du suicide*, note 23).

5 Hegel, *The Phenomenology of Mind*, p. 233.

6 I hope I have shown that here the master differs basically from the master described by Hegel. For Hegel there is reciprocity; here the master laughs at the consciousness of the slave. What he wants from the slave is not recognition but work. In the same way, the slave here is no way identifiable with the slave who loses himself in the object and finds in his work the source of his liberation.

The Negro wants to be like the master.

Therefore he is less independent than the Hegelian slave.

In Hegel the slave turns away from the master and turns toward the object.

Here the slave turns toward the master and abandons the object.

7. In English in the original. (Translator's note)

8. Emmanuel Mounier, *L'éveil de l'Afrique noire* (Paris, Éditions du Sevil. 1948).

From Chapter 8: By Way of Conclusion

The social revolution ... cannot draw its poetry from the past, but only from the future. It cannot begin with itself before it has stripped itself of all its superstitions concerning the past. Earlier revolutions relied on memories out of world history in order to drug themselves against their own content. In order to find their own content, the revolutions of the nineteenth century have to let the dead bury the dead. Before, the expression exceeded the content; now, the content exceeds the expression.

- *Karl Marx*, The Eighteenth Brumaire.

I can already see the faces of all those who will ask me to be precise on this or that point, to denounce this or that mode of conduct.

It is obvious – and I will never weary of repeating this – that the quest for disalienation by a doctor of medicine born in Guadeloupe can be understood only by recognising motivations basically different from those of the Negro labourer building the port facilities in Abidjan. In the first case, the alienation is of an almost intellectual character. Insofar as he conceives of European culture as a means of stripping himself of his race, he becomes alienated. In the second case, it is a question of a victim of a system based on the exploitation of a given race by another, on the contempt in which a given branch of humanity is held by a form of civilisation that pretends to superiority.

I do not carry innocence to the point of believing that appeals to reason or to respect for human dignity can alter reality. For the Negro who works on a sugar plantation in Le Robert, there is only one solution: to fight. He will embark on this struggle, and he will pursue it, not as the result of a Marxist or idealistic analysis but quite simply because he cannot conceive of life otherwise than in the form of a battle against exploitation, misery, and hunger.

It would never occur to me to ask these Negroes to change their conception of history. I am convinced, however, that without even knowing it they share my views, accustomed as they are to speaking and thinking in terms of the present. The few working-class people whom I had the chance to know in Paris never took it on themselves to pose the problem of the discovery of a Negro past. They knew they were black, but, they told me, that made no difference in anything. In which they were absolutely right.

In this connection, I should like to say something that I have found in many other writers: Intellectual alienation is a creation of middle-class society. What I call middle-class society is any society that becomes rigidified in predetermined forms, forbidding all evolution, all gains, all progress, all discovery. I call middle class a closed society in which life has no taste, in which the air is tainted, in which ideas and men are corrupt. And I think that a man who takes a stand against this death is in a sense a revolutionary.

The discovery of the existence of a Negro civilisation in the fifteenth century confers no patent of humanity on me. Like it or not, the past can in no way guide me in the present moment.

The situation that I have examined, it is clear by now, is not a classic one. Scientific objectivity was barred to me, for the alienated, the neurotic, was my brother, my sister, my father. I have ceaselessly striven to show the Negro that in a sense he makes himself abnormal; to show the white man that he is at once the perpetrator and the victim of a delusion.

There are times when the black man is locked into his body. Now, 'for a being who has acquired consciousness of himself and of his body, who has attained to the dialectic of subject and object, the body is no longer a cause of the structure of consciousness, it has become an object of consciousness.'[1]

The Negro, however sincere, is the slave of the past. None the less I am a man, and in this sense the Peloponnesian War is as much mine as the invention of the compass. Face to face with the white man, the Negro has a past to legitimate, a vengeance to exact; face to face with the Negro, the contemporary white man feels the need to recall the times of cannibalism. A few years ago, the Lyon branch of the Union of Students From Overseas France asked me to reply to an article that made jazz music literally an irruption of cannibalism into the modern world. Knowing exactly what I was doing, I rejected the premises on which the request was based, and I suggested to the defender of European purity that he cure himself of a spasm that had nothing cultural in it. Some men want to fill this world with their presence. A German philosopher described this mechanism as *the pathology of freedom*. In the circumstances, I did not have to take up a position on behalf of Negro music against white music, but rather to help my brother to rid himself of an attitude in which there was nothing healthful.

The problem considered here is one of time. Those Negroes and white men will be disalienated who refuse to let themselves be sealed away in the materialised Tower of the Past. For many other Negroes, in other ways, disalienation will come into being through their refusal to accept the present as definitive.

I am a man, and what I have to recapture is the whole past of the world. I am not responsible solely for the revolt in Santo Domingo.

Every time a man has contributed to the victory of the dignity of the spirit, every time a man has said no to an attempt to subjugate his fellows, I have felt solidarity with his act.

In no way should I derive my basic purpose from the past of the peoples of colour.

In no way should I dedicate myself to the revival of an unjustly unrecognised Negro civilisation. I will not make myself the man of any past. I do not want to exalt the past at the expense of my present and of my future.

It is not because the Indo-Chinese has discovered a culture of its own that he is in revolt. It is because 'quite simply' it was, in more than one way, becoming impossible for him to breathe. When one remembers the stories with which, in 1938, old regular sergeants described the land of piastres and rickshaws, of cut-rate boys and women, one understands only too well the rage with which the men of the Viet-Minh go into battle.

An acquaintance with whom I served during the Second World War recently returned from Indo-China. He has enlightened me on many things. For instance, the serenity with which young Vietnamese of sixteen or seventeen faced firing squads. 'On one occasion,' he told me, 'we had to shoot from a kneeling position: The soldiers' hands were shaking in the presence of those young "fanatics".' Summing up, he added: 'The war that you and I were in was only a game compared to what is going on out there.'

Seen from Europe, these things are beyond understanding. There are those who talk of a so-called Asiatic attitude toward death. But these basement philosophers cannot convince anyone. This Asiatic serenity, not so long ago, was a quality to be seen in the 'bandits' of Vercors and the 'terrorists' of the Resistance.

The Vietnamese who die before the firing squads are not hoping that their sacrifice will bring about the reappearance of the past. It is for the sake of the present and of the future that they are willing to die.

If the question of practical solidarity with a given past ever arose for me, it did so only to the extent to which I was committed to myself and to my neighbour to fight for all my life and with all my strength so that never again would a people on the earth be subjugated. It was not the black world that laid down my course of conduct. My black skin is not the wrapping of specific values. It is a long time since the starry sky that took away Kant's breath revealed the last of its secrets to us. And the moral law is not certain of itself.

As a man, I undertake to face the possibility of annihilation in order that two or three truths may cast their eternal brilliance over the world.

Sartre has shown that, in the line of an unauthentic position, the past 'takes' in quantity, and, when solidly constructed, *informs* the individual. He is the past in a changed value. But, too, I can recapture my past, validate it, or condemn it through my successive choices.

The black man wants to be like the white man. For the black man there is only one destiny. And it is white. Long ago the black man admitted the unarguable superiority of the white man, and all his efforts are aimed at achieving a white existence.

Have I no other purpose on earth, then, but to avenge the Negro of the seventeenth century?

In this world, which is already trying to disappear, do I have to pose the problem of black truth?

Do I have to be limited to the justification of a facial conformation?

I as a man of colour do not have the right to seek to know in what respect my race is superior or inferior to another race.

I as a man of colour do not have the right to hope that in the white man there will be a crystallisation of guilt toward the past of my race.

I as a man of colour do not have the right to seek ways of stamping down the pride of my former master.

I have neither the right nor the duty to claim reparation for the domestication of my ancestors.

There is no Negro mission; there is no white burden.

I find myself suddenly in a world in which things do evil; a world in which I am summoned into battle; a world in which it is always a question of annihilation or triumph.

I find myself – I, a man – in a world where words wrap themselves in silence; in a world where the other endlessly hardens himself.

No, I do not have the right to go and cry out my hatred at the white man. I do not have the duty to murmur my gratitude to the white man.

My life is caught in the lasso of existence. My freedom turns me back on myself. No, I do not have the right to be a Negro.

I do not have the duty to be this or that …

If the white man challenges my humanity, I will impose my whole weight as a man on his life and show him that I am not that 'sho' good eatin'' that he persists in imagining.

I find myself suddenly in the world and I recognise that I have one right alone: That of demanding human behaviour from the other.

One duty alone: That of not renouncing my freedom through my choices.

I have no wish to be the victim of the *Fraud* of a black world.

My life should not be devoted to drawing up the balance sheet of Negro values.

There is no white world, there is no white ethic, any more than there is a white intelligence.

There are in every part of the world men who search.

I am not a prisoner of history. I should not seek there for the meaning of my destiny.

I should constantly remind myself that the real *leap* consists in introducing invention into existence.

In the world through which I travel, I am endlessly creating myself.

I am a part of Being to the degree that I go beyond it.

And, through a private problem, we see the outline of the problem of Action. Placed in this world, in a situation, 'embarked,' as Pascal would have it, am I going to gather weapons?

Am I going to ask the contemporary white man to answer for the slave-ships of the seventeenth century?

Am I going to try by every possible means to cause Guilt to be borne in minds?

Moral anguish in the face of the massiveness of the Past? I am a Negro, and tons of chains, storms of blows, rivers of expectoration flow down my shoulders.

But I do not have the right to allow myself to bog down. I do not have the right to allow the slightest fragment to remain in my existence. I do not have the right to allow myself to be mired in what the past has determined.

I am not the slave of the Slavery that dehumanised my ancestors.

To many coloured intellectuals European culture has a quality of exteriority. What is more, in human relationships, the Negro may feel himself a stranger to the Western world. Not wanting to live the part of a poor relative, of an adopted son, of a bastard child, shall he feverishly seek to discover a Negro civilisation?

Let us be clearly understood. I am convinced that it would be of the greatest interest to be able to have contact with a Negro literature or architecture of the third century before Christ. I should be very happy to know that a correspondence had flourished between some Negro philosopher and Plato. But I can absolutely not see how this fact would change anything in the lives of the eight-year-old children who labour in the cane fields of Martinique or Guadeloupe.

No attempt must be made to encase man, for it his destiny to be set free.

The body of history does not determine a single one of my actions.

I am my own foundation.

And it is by going beyond the historical, instrumental hypothesis that I will initiate the cycle of my freedom.

The disaster of the man of colour lies in the fact that he was enslaved.

The disaster and inhumanity of the white man lie in the fact that somewhere he has killed man.

And even today they subsist, to organise this dehumanisation rationally. But I as a man of colour, to the extent that it becomes possible for me to exist absolutely, do not have the right to lock myself into a world of retroactive reparations.

I, the man of colour, want only this:

That the tool never possess the man. That the enslavement of man by man cease forever. That is, of one by another. That it be possible for me to discover and to love man, wherever he may be.

The Negro is not. Any more than the white man.

Both must turn their backs on the inhuman voices which were those of their respective ancestors in order that authentic communication be possible. Before it can adopt a positive voice, freedom requires an effort at disalienation. At the beginning of his life a man is always clotted, he is drowned in contingency. The tragedy of the man is that he was once a child.

It is through the effort to recapture the self and to scrutinise the self, it is through the lasting tension of their freedom that man will be able to create the ideal conditions of existence for a human world.

Superiority? Inferiority?

Why not the quite simple attempt to touch the other, to feel the other, to explain the other to myself?

Was my freedom not given to me then in order to build the world of the *You*?

At the conclusion of this study, I want the world to recognise, with me, the open door of every consciousness.

My final prayer:

O my body, make of me always a man who questions!

NOTE
1 M. Merleau-Ponty, *La Phénoménologie de la Perception* (Paris: Gallimard, 1945), p. 277.

STUDIES IN A DYING COLONIALISM
Chapter 1: Algeria Unveiled

The way people clothe themselves, together with the traditions of dress and finery that custom implies, constitutes the most distinctive form of a society's uniqueness, that is to say the one that is the most immediately perceptible. Within the general pattern of a given costume, there are of course always modifications of detail, innovations which in highly developed societies are the mark of fashion. But the effect as a whole remains homogeneous, and great areas of civilisation, immense cultural regions, can be grouped together on the basis of original, specific techniques of men's and women's dress.

It is by their apparel that types of society first became known, whether through written accounts and photographic records or motion pictures. Thus, there are civilisations without neckties, civilisations with loin-cloths, and others without hats. The fact of belonging to a given cultural group is usually revealed by clothing traditions. In the Arab world, for example, the veil worn by women is at once noticed by the tourist. One may remain for a long time unaware of the fact that a Moslem does not eat pork or that he denies himself daily sexual relations during the month of Ramadan, but the veil worn by the women appears with such consistency that it generally suffices to characterise Arab society.

In the Arab Maghreb, the veil belongs to the clothing traditions of the Tunisian, Algerian, Moroccan and Libyan national societies. For the tourist and the foreigner, the veil demarcates both Algerian society and its feminine component.[1] In the case of the Algerian man, on the other hand, regional modifications can be noted: the *fez* in urban centres, turbans and *djellabas*[2] in the countryside. The masculine garb allows a certain margin of choice, a modicum of heterogeneity. The woman seen in her white veil unifies the perception that one has of Algerian feminine society. Obviously what we have here is a uniform which tolerates no modification, no variant.[3]

The *haïk*[4] very clearly demarcates the Algerian colonised society. It is of course possible to remain hesitant before a little girl, but all uncertainty vanishes at the time of puberty. With the veil, things become well-defined and ordered. The Algerian woman, in the eyes of the observer, is unmistakably 'she who hides behind a veil.'

We shall see that this veil, one of the elements of the traditional Algerian garb, was to become the bone of contention in a grandiose battle, on account of which the occupation forces were to mobilise their most powerful and most varied resources, and in the course of which the colonised were to display a surprising force of inertia. Taken as a whole, colonial society, with its values, its areas of strength, and its philosophy, reacts to the veil in a rather homogeneous way. The decisive battle was launched before 1954, more precisely during the early 1930s. The officials of the French administration in Algeria, committed to destroying the people's originality, and under instructions to bring about the disintegration, at whatever cost, of forms of existence likely to evoke a national reality directly or indirectly, were to concentrate their efforts on the wearing of the veil, which was looked upon at this juncture as a symbol of the status of the Algerian woman. Such a position is not the consequence of a chance intuition. It is on the basis of the analyses of sociologists and ethnologists that the specialists in so-called native affairs and the heads of the Arab Bureaus coordinated their work. At an initial stage, there was a pure and simple adoption of the well-known formula, 'Let's win over the women and the rest will follow.' This definition of policy merely gave a scientific coloration to the 'discoveries' of the sociologist.

Beneath a patrilineal pattern of Algerian society, the specialists described a structure of matrilineal essence. Arab society has often been presented by Westerners as a formal society in which outside appearances are paramount. The Algerian woman, an intermediary between obscure forces and the group, appeared in this perspective to assume a primordial importance. Behind the visible, manifest patriarchy, the more significant existence of a basic matriarchy was affirmed. The role of the Algerian mother, that of the grandmother, the aunt and the 'old woman,' were inventoried and defined.

This enabled the colonial administration to define a precise political doctrine: 'If we want to destroy the structure of Algerian society, its capacity for resistance, we must first of all conquer the women; we must go and find them behind the veil where they hide themselves and in the houses where the men keep them out of sight.' It is the situation of woman that was accordingly taken as the theme of action. The dominant administration solemnly undertook to defend this woman pictured as humiliated, sequestered, cloistered ... It described the immense possibilities of woman, unfortunately transformed by the Algerian man into an inert, demonetised, indeed dehumanised object. The behaviour of the Algerian was very firmly denounced and described as medieval and barbaric. With infinite science, a blanket indictment against the 'sadistic and vampirish' Algerian attitude toward women was prepared and drawn up. Around the family life of the Algerian, the occupier piled up a whole mass of judgments, appraisals, reasons, accumulated anecdotes and edifying examples, thus attempting to confine the Algerian within a circle of guilt.

Mutual aid societies and societies to promote solidarity with Algerian women sprang up in great number. Lamentations were organised. 'We want to make the Algerian ashamed of the fate that he metes out to women.' This was a period of effervescence, of putting into application a whole technique of infiltration, in the course of which droves of social workers and women directing charitable works descended on the Arab quarters.

The indigent and famished women were the first to be besieged. Every kilo of semolina distributed was accompanied by a dose of indignation against the veil and the cloister. The indignation was followed up by practical advice. Algerian women were invited to play 'a functional, capital role' in the transformation of their lot. They were pressed to say no to a centuries-old subjection. The immense role they were called upon to play was described to them. The colonial administration invested great sums in this combat. After it had been posited that the woman constituted the pivot of Algerian society, all efforts were made to obtain control over her. The Algerian, it was assured, would not stir, would resist the task of cultural destruction undertaken by the occupier, would oppose assimilation, so long as his woman had not reversed the stream. In the colonialist programme, it was the woman who was given the historic mission of shaking up the Algerian man. Converting the woman, winning her over to the foreign values, wrenching her free from her status, was at the same time achieving a real power over the man and attaining a practical, effective means of destructuring Algerian culture.

Still today, in 1959, the dream of a total domestication of Algerian society by means of 'unveiled women aiding and sheltering the occupier' continues to haunt the colonial authorities.[5]

The Algerian men, for their part, are a target of criticism for their European comrades, or more officially for their bosses. There is not a European worker who does not sooner or later, in the give and take of relations on the job site, the shop or the office, ask the Algerian the ritual questions: 'Does your wife wear the veil? Why don't you take your wife to the movies, to the fights, to the café?'

European bosses do not limit themselves to the disingenuous query or the glancing invitation. They use 'Indian cunning' to corner the Algerian and push him to painful decisions. In connection with a holiday – Christmas or New Year, or simply a social occasion with the firm – the boss will invite *the Algerian employee and his wife.* The invitation is not a collective one. Every Algerian is called in to the director's office and invited by name to come with 'your little family.' 'The firm being one big family, it would be unseemly for some to come without their wives, you understand? ...' Before this formal summons, the Algerian sometimes experiences moments of difficulty. If he comes with his wife, it means admitting defeat, it means 'prostituting his wife,' exhibiting her, abandoning a mode of resistance. On the other hand, going alone means refusing to give satisfaction to the boss; it means running the risk of being out of a job. The study of a case chosen at random – a description of the traps set by the European in order to bring the Algerian to expose himself, to declare: 'My wife wears a veil, she shall not go out,' or else to betray: 'Since you want to see her, here she is,' – would bring out the sadistic and perverse character of these contacts and relationships and would show in microcosm the tragedy of the colonial situation on the psychological level, the way the two systems directly confront each other, the epic of the colonised society, with its specific ways of existing, in the face of the colonialist hydra.

With the Algerian intellectual, the aggressiveness appears in its full intensity. The *fellah*, 'the passive slave of a rigidly structured group,' is looked upon with a certain indulgence by the conqueror.[6] The lawyer and the doctor, on the other hand, are severely frowned upon. These intellectuals, who keep their wives in a state of semi-slavery, are literally pointed to with an accusing finger. Colonial society blazes up vehemently against this inferior status of the Algerian woman. Its members worry and show concern for those unfortunate women, doomed 'to produce brats,' kept behind walls, banned.

Before the Algerian intellectual, racialist arguments spring forth with special readiness. For all that he is a doctor, people will say, he still remains an Arab. 'You can't get away from nature.' Illustrations of this kind of race prejudice can be multiplied indefinitely. Clearly, the intellectual is reproached for limiting the extension of learned Western habits, for not playing his role as an active agent of upheaval of the colonised society, for not giving his wife the benefit of the privileges of a more worthy and meaningful life ... In the large population centres it is altogether commonplace to hear a European confess acidly that he has never seen the wife of an Algerian he has known for twenty years. At a more diffuse, but highly revealing, level of apprehension, we find the bitter observation that 'we work in vain' ... that 'Islam holds its prey.'

The method of presenting the Algerian as a prey fought over with equal ferocity by Islam and France with its Western culture reveals the whole approach of the occupier, his philosophy and his policy. This expression indicates that the occupier, smarting from his failures presents in a simplified and pejorative way the system of values by means of which the colonised person resists his innumerable offensives. What is in fact the assertion of a distinct identity, concern with keeping intact a few shreds of national existence, is attributed to religious, magical, fanatical behaviour.

This rejection of the conqueror assumes original forms, according to circumstances or to the type of colonial situation. On the whole, these forms of behaviour have been fairly well studied in the course of the past twenty years; it cannot be said, however, that the conclusions that have been reached are wholly valid. Specialists in basic education for underdeveloped countries or technicians for the advancement of retarded societies would do well to understand the sterile and harmful character of any endeavour which illuminates preferentially a given element of the colonised society. Even within the framework of a newly independent nation, one cannot attack this or that segment of the cultural whole without endangering the work undertaken (leaving aside the questions of the native's psychological balance). More precisely, the phenomena of counter-acculturation must be understood as the organic impossibility of a culture to modify any one of its customs without at the same time re-evaluating its deepest values, its most stable models. To speak of counter-acculturation in a colonial situation is an absurdity. The phenomena of resistance observed in the colonised must be related to an attitude of counter-assimilation, of maintenance of a cultural, hence national, originality.

The occupying forces, in applying their maximum psychological attention to the veil worn by Algerian women, were obviously bound to achieve some results. Here and there it thus happened that a woman was 'saved,' and symbolically unveiled.

These test-women, with bare faces and free bodies, henceforth circulated like sound currency in the European society of Algeria. These women were surrounded by an atmosphere of newness. The Europeans, over-excited and wholly given over to their victory, carried away in a kind of trance, would speak of the psychological phenomena of conversion. And in fact, in the European society, the agents of this conversion were held in esteem. They were envied. The benevolent attention of the administration was drawn to them.

After each success, the authorities were strengthened in their conviction that the Algerian woman would support Western penetration into the native society. Every rejected veil disclosed to the eyes of the colonialists horizons until then forbidden, and revealed to them, piece by piece, the flesh of Algeria laid bare. The occupier's aggressiveness, and hence his hopes, multiplied ten-fold each time a new face was uncovered. Every new Algerian woman unveiled announced to the occupier an Algerian society whose systems of defence were in the process of dislocation, open and breached. Every veil that fell, every body that became liberated from the traditional embrace of the haïk, every face that offered itself to the bold and impatient glance of the occupier, was a negative expression of the fact that Algeria was beginning to deny herself and was accepting the rape of the coloniser. Algerian society with every abandoned veil seemed to express its willingness to attend the master's school and to decide to change its habits under the occupier's direction and patronage.

We have seen how colonial society, the colonial administration, perceives the veil, and we have sketched the dynamics of the efforts undertaken to fight it as an institution and the resistances developed by the colonised society. At the level of the individual, of the private European, it may be interesting to follow the multiple reactions provoked by the existence of the veil, which reveal the original way in which the Algerian woman manages to be present or absent.

For a European not directly involved in this work of conversion, what reactions are there to be recorded?

The dominant attitude appears to us to be a romantic exoticism, strongly tinged with sensuality.

And, to begin with, the veil hides a beauty.

A revealing reflection – among others – of this state of mind was communicated to us by a European visiting Algeria who, in the exercise of his profession (he was a lawyer), had had the opportunity of seeing a few Algerian women without the veil. These men, he said, speaking of the Algerians, are guilty of concealing so many strange beauties. It was his conclusion that a people with a cache of such prizes, of such perfections of nature, owes it to itself to show them, to exhibit them. If worst came to worst, he added, it ought to be possible to force them to do so.

A strand of hair, a bit of forehead, a segment of an 'overwhelmingly beautiful' face glimpsed in a streetcar or on a train, may suffice to keep alive and strengthen the European's persistence in his irrational conviction that the Algerian woman is the queen of all women.

But there is also in the European the crystallisation of an aggressiveness, the strain of a kind of violence before the Algerian woman. Unveiling this woman is revealing her beauty; it is baring her secret, breaking her resistance, making her available for adventure. Hiding the face is also disguising a secret; it is also creating a world of mystery, of the hidden. In a confused way, the European experiences his relation with the Algerian woman at a highly complex level. There is in it the will to bring this woman within his reach, to make her a possible object of possession.

This woman who sees without being seen frustrates the coloniser. There is no reciprocity. She does not yield herself, does not give herself, does not offer herself. The Algerian has an attitude toward the Algerian woman which is on the whole clear. He does not see her. There is even a permanent intention not to perceive the feminine profile, not to pay attention to women. In the case of the Algerian, therefore, there is not, in the street or on a road, that behaviour characterising a sexual encounter that is described in terms of the glance, of the physical bearing, the muscular tension, the signs of disturbance to which the phenomenology of encounters has accustomed us.

The European faced with an Algerian woman wants to see. He reacts in an aggressive way before this limitation of his perception. Frustration and aggressiveness, here too, evolve apace. Aggressiveness comes to light, in the first place, in structurally ambivalent attitudes and in the dream material that can be revealed in the European, whether he is normal or suffers from neuropathological disturbances.[7]

In a medical consultation, for example, at the end of the morning, it is common to hear European doctors express their disappointment. The women who remove their veils before them are commonplace, vulgar; there is really nothing to make such a mystery of. One wonders what they are hiding.

European women settle the conflict in a much less roundabout way. They bluntly affirm that no one hides what is beautiful and discern in this strange custom an 'altogether feminine' intention of disguising imperfections. And they proceed to compare the strategy of the European woman, which is intended to correct, to embellish, to bring out (beauty treatments, hairdos, fashion) with that of the Algerian woman, who prefers to veil, to conceal, to cultivate the man's doubt and desire. On another level, it is claimed that the intention is to mislead the customer, and that the wrapping in which the 'merchandise' is presented does not really alter its nature, nor its value.

The content of the dreams of Europeans brings out other special themes. Jean-Paul Sartre, in his *Réflections Sur la Question Juive*, has shown that on the level of the unconscious, the Jewish woman almost always has an aura of rape about her.

The history of the French conquest in Algeria, including the overrunning of villages by the troops, the confiscation of property and the raping of women, the pillaging of a country, has contributed to the birth and the crystallisation of the same dynamic image. At the level of the psychological strata of the occupier, the evocation of this freedom given to the sadism of the conqueror, to his eroticism, creates faults, fertile gaps through which both dreamlike forms of behaviour and, on certain occasions, criminal acts can emerge.

Thus the rape of the Algerian woman in the dream of a European is always preceded by a rending of the veil. We here witness a double deflowering. Likewise, the woman's conduct is never one of consent or acceptance, but of abject humility.

Whenever, in dreams having an erotic content, a European meets an Algerian woman, the specific features of his relations with the colonised society manifest themselves. These dreams evolve neither on the same erotic plane, nor at the same tempo, as those that involve a European woman.

With an Algerian woman, there is no progressive conquest, no mutual revelation. Straight off, with the maximum of violence, there is possession, rape, near-murder. The act assumes a para-neurotic brutality and sadism, even in a normal European. This brutality and this sadism are in fact emphasised by the frightened attitude of the Algerian woman. In the dream, the woman-victim screams, struggles like a doe, and as she weakens and faints, is penetrated, martyrised, ripped apart.

Attention must likewise be drawn to a characteristic of this dream that appears important to us. The European never dreams of an Algerian woman taken in isolation. On the rare occasions when the encounter has become a binding relationship that can be regarded as a couple, it has quickly been transformed by the desperate flight of the woman who, inevitably, leads the male 'among women'. The European always dreams of a group of women, of a field of women, suggestive of the gynaeceum, the harem — exotic themes deeply rooted in the unconscious.

The European's aggressiveness will express itself likewise in contemplation of the Algerian woman's morality. Her timidity and her reserve are transformed in accordance with the commonplace laws of conflictual psychology into their opposite, and the Algerian woman becomes hypocritical, perverse, and even a veritable nymphomaniac.

We have seen that on the level of individuals the colonial strategy of destructuring Algerian society very quickly came to assign a prominent place to the Algerian woman. The colonialist's relentlessness, his methods of struggle were bound to give rise to reactionary forms of behaviour on the part of the colonised. In the face of the violence of the occupier, the colonised found himself defining a principled position with respect to a formerly inert element of the native cultural configuration. It was the colonialist's frenzy to unveil the Algerian woman, it was his gamble on winning the battle of the veil at whatever cost, that were to provoke the native's bristling resistance. The deliberately aggressive intentions of the colonialist with respect to the *haïk* gave a new life to this dead element of the Algerian cultural stock — dead because stabilised, without any progressive change in form or colour. We here recognise one of the laws of the psychology of colonisation. In an initial phase, it is the action, the plans of the occupier that determine the centres of resistance around which a people's will to survive becomes organised.

It is the white man who creates the Negro. But it is the Negro who creates negritude. To the colonialist offensive against the veil, the colonised opposes the cult of the veil. What was an undifferentiated element in a homogeneous whole acquires a taboo character, and the attitude of a given Algerian woman with respect to the veil will be constantly related to her overall attitude with respect to the foreign occupation. The colonised, in the face of the emphasis given by the colonialist to this or that aspect of his traditions, reacts very violently. The attention devoted to modifying this aspect, the emotion the conqueror puts into his pedagogical work, his prayers, his threats, weave a whole universe of resistances around this particular element of the culture. Holding out against the occupier on this precise element means inflicting upon him a spectacular setback; it means more particularly maintaining 'co-existence' as a form of conflict and latent warfare. It means keeping up the atmosphere of an armed truce.

Upon the outbreak of the struggle for liberation, the attitude of the Algerian woman, or of native society in general, with regard to the veil was to undergo important modifications. These innovations are of particular interest in view of the fact that they were at no time included in the programme of the struggle. The doctrine of the Revolution, the strategy of combat, never postulated the necessity for a revision of forms of behaviour with respect to the veil. We are able to affirm even now that when Algeria has gained her independence such questions will not be raised, for in the practice of the Revolution the people have understood that problems are resolved in the very movement that raises them.

Until 1955, the combat was waged exclusively by the men. The revolutionary characteristics of this combat, the necessity for absolute secrecy, obliged the militant to keep his woman in absolute ignorance. As the enemy gradually adapted himself to the forms of combat, new difficulties appeared which required original solutions. The decision to involve women as active elements of the Algerian Revolution was not reached lightly. In a sense, it was the very conception of the combat that had to be modified. The violence of the occupier, his ferocity, his delirious attachment to the national territory, induced the leaders no longer to exclude certain forms of combat. Progressively, the urgency of a total war made itself felt. But involving the women was not solely a response to the desire to mobilise the entire nation. The women's entry into the war had to be harmonised with respect for the revolutionary nature of the war. In other words, the women had to show as much spirit of sacrifice as the men. It was therefore necessary to have the same confidence in them as was required from seasoned militants who had served several prison sentences. A moral evaluation and a strength of character that were altogether exceptional would therefore be required of the women. There was no lack of hesitations.

The revolutionary wheels had assumed such proportions; the mechanism was running at a given rate. The machine would have to be complicated; in other words its network would have to be extended without affecting its efficiency. The women could not be conceived of as a replacement product, but as an element capable of adequately meeting the new tasks.

In the mountains, women helped the *guerrilla* during halts or when convalescing after a wound or a case of typhoid contracted in the *djebel*.[8] But deciding to incorporate women as essential elements, to have the Revolution depend on their presence and their action in this or that sector, was obviously a wholly revolutionary step. To have the Revolution rest at any point on their activity was an important choice.

Such a decision was made difficult for several reasons. During the whole period of unchallenged domination, we have seen that Algerian society, and particularly the women, had a tendency to flee from the occupier. The tenacity of the occupier in his endeavour to unveil the women, to make of them an ally in the work of cultural destruction, had the effect of strengthening the traditional patterns of behaviour. These patterns, which were essentially positive in the strategy of resistance to the corrosive action of the coloniser, naturally had negative effects. The woman, especially the city woman, suffered a loss of ease and of assurance. Having been accustomed to confinement, her body did not have the normal mobility before a limitless horizon on avenues, of unfolded sidewalks, of houses, of people dodged or bumped into. This relatively cloistered life, with its known, categorised, regulated comings and goings, made any immediate revolution seem a dubious proposition. The political leaders were perfectly familiar with these problems, and their hesitations expressed their consciousness of their responsibilities. They were entitled to doubt the success of this measure. Would not such a decision have catastrophic consequences for the progress of the Revolution?

To this doubt there was added an equally important element. The leaders hesitated to involve the women, being perfectly aware of the ferocity of the coloniser. The leaders of the Revolution had no illusions as to the enemy's criminal capacities. Nearly all of them had passed through their jails or had had sessions with survivors from the camps or the cells of the French judicial police. Not one of them failed to realise that any Algerian woman arrested would be tortured to death. It is relatively easy to commit oneself to this path and to accept among different eventualities that of dying under torture. The matter is a little more difficult when it involves designating someone who manifestly runs the risk of certain death. But the decision as to whether or not the women were to participate in the Revolution had to be made; the inner oppositions became massive, and each decision gave rise to the same hesitations, produced the same despair.

In the face of the extraordinary success of this new form of popular combat, observers have compared the action of the Algerian women to that of certain women resistance fighters or even secret agents of the specialised services. It must be constantly borne in mind that the committed Algerian woman learns both her role as 'a woman alone in the street' and her revolutionary mission instinctively. The Algerian woman is not a secret agent. It is without apprenticeship, without briefing, without fuss, that she goes out into the street with three grenades in her handbag or the activity report of an area in her bodice. She does not have the sensation of playing a role she has read about ever so many times in novels, or seen in motion pictures. There is not that coefficient of play, of imitation, almost always present in this form of action when we are dealing with a Western woman.

What we have here is not the bringing to light of a character known and frequented a thousand times in imagination or in stories. It is an authentic birth in a pure state, without preliminary instruction. There is no character to imitate. On the contrary, there is an intense dramatisation, a continuity between the woman and the revolutionary. The Algerian woman rises directly to the level of tragedy.[9]

The growth in number of the FLN cells, the range of new tasks – finance, intelligence, counter-intelligence, political training – the necessity to provide for one active cell three or four replacement cells to be held in reserve, ready to become active at the slightest alert concerning the front cell, obliged the leaders to seek other avenues for the carrying out of strictly individual assignments. After a final series of meetings among leaders, and especially in view of the urgency of the daily problems that the Revolution faced, the decision to concretely involve women in the national struggle was reached.

The revolutionary character of this decision must once again be emphasised. At the beginning, it was married women who were contacted. But rather soon these restrictions were abandoned. The married women whose husbands were militants were the first to be chosen. Later, widows or divorced women were designated. In any case, there were never any unmarried girls – first of all, because a girl of even twenty or twenty-three hardly ever has occasion to leave the family domicile unaccompanied. But the woman's duties as mother or spouse, the desire to limit to the minimum the possible consequences of her arrest and her death, and also the more and more numerous volunteering of unmarried girls, led the political leaders to make another leap, to remove all restrictions, to accept indiscriminately the support of all Algerian women.

Meanwhile the woman who might be acting as a liaison agent, as a bearer of tracts, as she walked some hundred or two hundred metres ahead of the man under whose orders she was working, still wore a veil; but after a certain period the pattern of activity that the struggle involved shifted in the direction of the European city. The protective mantle of the Kasbah, the almost organic curtain of safety that the Arab town weaves round the native, withdrew, and the Algerian woman, exposed, was sent forth into the conqueror's city. Very quickly she adopted an absolutely unbelievable offensive tactic. When colonised people undertake an action against the oppressor, and when this opposition is exercised in the form of exacerbated and continued violence as in Algeria, they must overcome a considerable number of taboos. The European city is not the prolongation of the native city. The colonisers have not settled in the midst of the natives. They have surrounded the native city; they have laid siege to it. Every exit from the Kasbah of Algiers opens on enemy territory. And so it is in Constantine, in Oran, in Blida, in Bone.

The native cities are deliberately caught in the conqueror's vise. To get an idea of the rigour with which the immobilising of the native city, of the autochthonous population, is organised, one must have in one's hand the plans according to which a colonial city has been laid out, and compare them with the comments of the general staff of the occupation forces.

Apart from the charwomen employed in the conquerors' homes, those whom the coloniser indiscriminately calls the 'Fatmas', the Algerian women, especially the young Algerian women, rarely venture into the European city. Their movements are almost entirely limited to the Arab city. And even in the Arab city their movements are reduced to the minimum. The rare occasions on which the Algerian woman abandons the city are almost always in connection with some event, either of an exceptional nature (the death of a relative residing in a nearby locality), or, more often, traditional family visits for religious feasts, or a pilgrimage. In such cases, the European city is crossed in a car, usually early in the morning. The Algerian woman, the young Algerian woman – except for a very few students (who, besides, never have the same ease as their European counterparts) – must overcome a multiplicity of inner resistances, of subjectively organised fears, of emotions. She must at the same time confront the essentially hostile world of the occupier and the mobilised, vigilant, and efficient police forces. Each time she ventures into the European city, the Algerian woman must achieve a victory over herself, over her childish fears. She must consider the image of the occupier lodged somewhere in her mind and in her body, remodel it, initiate the essential work of eroding it, make it inessential, remove something of the shame that is attached to it, devalidate it.

Initially subjective, the breaches made in colonialism are the result of a victory of the colonised over their old fear and over the atmosphere of despair distilled day after day by a colonialism that has incrusted itself with the *prospect of enduring forever.*

The young Algerian woman, whenever she is called upon, establishes a link. Algiers is no longer the Arab city, but the autonomous area of Algiers, the nervous system of the enemy apparatus. Oran, Constantine, develop their dimensions. In launching the struggle, the Algerian is loosening the vise that was tightening around the native cities. From one area of Algiers to another, from the Ruisseau to Hussein-Dey, from El-Biar to the rue Michelet, the Revolution creates new links. More and more, it is the Algerian woman, the Algerian girl, who will be assuming these tasks.

Among the tasks entrusted to the Algerian woman is the bearing of messages, of complicated verbal orders learned by heart, sometimes despite complete absence of schooling. But she is also called upon to stand watch, for an hour and often more, before a house where district leaders are conferring.

During those interminable minutes when she must avoid standing still, so as not to attract attention, and avoid venturing too far since she is responsible for the safety of the brothers within, incidents that are at once funny and pathetic are not infrequent. An unveiled Algerian girl who 'walks the street' is very often noticed by young men who behave like young men all over the world, but who use a special approach as the result of the idea people habitually have of one who has discarded the veil. She is treated to unpleasant, obscene, humiliating remarks. When such things happen, she must grit her teeth, walk away a few steps, elude the passers-by who draw attention to her, who give other passers-by the desire either to follow their example, or to come to her defence. Or it may be that the Algerian woman is carrying in her bag or in a small suitcase twenty, thirty, forty million francs, money belonging to the Revolution, money which is to be used to take care of the needs of the families of prisoners, or to buy medicine and supplies for the guerrillas.

This revolutionary activity has been carried on by the Algerian woman with exemplary constancy, self-mastery, and success. Despite the inherent, subjective difficulties and notwithstanding the sometimes violent incomprehension of a part of the family, the Algerian woman assumes all the tasks entrusted to her.

But things were gradually to become more complicated. Thus the unit leaders who go into the town and who avail themselves of the women-scouts, of the girls whose function it is to lead the way, are no longer new to political activity, are no longer unknown to the police. Authentic military chiefs have now begun to pass through the cities. These are known, and are being looked for. There is not a police superintendent who does not have their pictures on his desk.

These soldiers on the move, these fighters, always carry their weapons – automatic pistols, revolvers, grenades, sometimes all three. The political leader must overcome much resistance in order to induce these men, who under no circumstance would allow themselves to be taken prisoner, to entrust their weapons to the girl who is to walk ahead of them, it being up to them, if things go badly, to recover the arms immediately. The group accordingly makes its way into the European city. A hundred metres ahead, a girl may be carrying a suitcase and behind her are two or three ordinary-looking men. This girl who is the group's lighthouse and barometer gives warning in case of danger. The file makes its way by fits and starts; police cars and patrols cruise back and forth.

There are times, as these soldiers have admitted after completing such a mission, when the urge to recover their weapons is almost irresistible because of the fear of being caught short and not having time to defend themselves. With this phase, the Algerian woman penetrates a little further into the flesh of the Revolution.

But it was from 1956 on that her activity assumed really gigantic dimensions. Having to react in rapid succession to the massacre of Algerian civilians in the mountains and in the cities, the revolutionary leadership found that if it wanted to prevent the people from being gripped by terror it had no choice but to adopt forms of terror which until then it had rejected. This phenomenon has not been sufficiently analysed; not enough attention has been given to the reasons that lead a revolutionary movement to choose the weapon that is called terrorism.

During the French Resistance, terrorism was aimed at soldiers, at Germans of the Occupation, or at strategic enemy installations. The technique of terrorism is the same. It consists of individual or collective attempts by means of bombs or by the derailing of trains. In Algeria, where European settlers are numerous and where the territorial militias lost no time in enrolling the postman, the nurse and the grocer in the repressive system, the men who directed the struggle faced an absolutely new situation.

The decision to kill a civilian in the street is not an easy one, and no one comes to it lightly. No one takes the step of placing a bomb in a public place without a battle of conscience.

The Algerian leaders who, in view of the intensity of the repression and the frenzied character of the oppression, thought they could answer the blows received without any serious problems of conscience, discovered that the most horrible crimes do not constitute a sufficient excuse for certain decisions.

The leaders in a number of cases cancelled plans or even in the last moment called off the *fidaï*[10] assigned to place a given bomb. To explain these hesitations there was, to be sure, the memory of civilians killed or frightfully wounded. There was the political consideration not to do certain things that could compromise the cause of freedom. There was also the fear that the Europeans working with the Front might be hit in these attempts. There was thus a threefold concern: not to pile up possibly innocent victims, not to give a false picture of the Revolution, and finally the anxiety to have the French democrats on their side, as well as the democrats of all the countries of the world and the Europeans of Algeria who were attracted by the Algerian national ideal.

Now the massacres of Algerians, the raids in the countryside, strengthened the assurance of the European civilians, seemed to consolidate the colonial status and injected hope into the colonialists. The Europeans who, as a result of certain military actions on the part of the Algerian National Army in favour of the struggle of the Algerian people, had soft-pedalled their race prejudice and their insolence, recovered their old arrogance, their traditional contempt.

I remember a woman clerk in Birtouta who, on the day of the interception of the plane transporting the five members of the National Liberation Front, waved their photographs in front of her shop, shrieking: 'They've been caught! They're going to get their what-you-call'ems cut off!'

Every blow dealt the Revolution, every massacre perpetrated by the adversary, intensified the ferocity of the colonialists and hemmed in the Algerian civilian on all sides.

Trains loaded with French soldiers, the French Navy on manoeuvres and bombarding Algiers and Philippeville, the jet planes, the militiamen who descended on the *douars*[11] and decimated uncounted Algerians, all this contributed to giving the people the impression that they were not defended, that they were not protected, that nothing had changed, and that the Europeans could do what they wanted. This was the period when one heard Europeans announcing in the streets: 'Let's each one of us take ten of them and bump them off and you'll see the problem solved in no time.' And the Algerian people, especially in the cities, witnessed this boastfulness which added insult to injury and noted the impunity of these criminals who did not even take the trouble to hide. Any Algerian man or woman in a given city could in fact name the torturers and murderers of the region.

A time came when some of the people allowed doubt to enter their minds, and they began to wonder whether it was really possible, quantitatively and qualitatively, to resist the occupant's offensives. Was freedom worth the consequences of penetrating into that enormous circuit of terrorism and counter-terrorism? Did this disproportion not express the impossibility of escaping oppression?

Another part of the people, however, grew impatient and conceived the idea of putting an end to the advantage the enemy derived by pursuing the path of terror. The decision to strike the adversary individually and by name could no longer be eluded. All the prisoners 'shot and killed while trying to escape,' and the cries of the tortured, demanded that new forms of combat be adopted.

Members of the police and the meeting places of the colonialists (cafés in Algiers, Oran, Constantine) were the first to be singled out. From this point on the Algerian woman became wholly and deliberately immersed in the revolutionary action. It was she who would carry in her bag the grenades and the revolvers that a *fidaï* would take from her at the last moment, before the bar, or as a designated criminal passed. During this period Algerians caught in the European city were pitilessly challenged, arrested, searched.

This is why we must watch the parallel progress of this man and this woman, of this couple that brings death to the enemy, life to the Revolution. The one supporting the other, but apparently strangers to each other. The one radically transformed into a European woman, poised and unconstrained, whom no one would suspect, completely at home in the environment, and the other, a stranger, tense, moving toward his destiny.

The Algerian *fidaï*, unlike the unbalanced anarchists made famous in literature, does not take dope. The *fidaï* does not need to be unaware of danger, to befog his consciousness, or to forget. The 'terrorist', from the moment he undertakes an assignment, allows death to enter into his soul. He has a rendezvous with death. The *fidaï*, on the other hand, has a rendezvous with the life of the Revolution, and with his own life. The *fidaï* is not one of the sacrificed. To be sure, he does not shrink before the possibility of losing his life or the independence of his country, but at no moment does he choose death.

If it has been decided to kill a given police superintendent responsible for tortures or a given colonialist leader, it is because these men constitute an obstacle to the progress of the Revolution. Froger, for example, symbolised a colonialist tradition and a method inaugurated at Sétif and at Guelman in 1954.[12]

Moreover, Froger's apparent power crystallised the colonisation and gave new life to the hopes of those who were beginning to have doubts as to the real solidity of the system. It was around people like Froger that the robbers and murderers of the Algerian people would meet and encourage one another. This was something the *fidaï* knew, and that the woman who accompanied him, his woman-arsenal, likewise knew.

Carrying revolvers, grenades, hundreds of false identity cards or bombs, the unveiled Algerian woman moves like a fish in the Western waters. The soldiers, the French patrols, smile to her as she passes, compliments on her looks are heard here and there, but no one suspects that her suitcases contain the automatic pistol which will presently mow down four or five members of one of the patrols.

We must come back to that young girl, unveiled only yesterday, who walks with sure steps down the streets of the European city teeming with policemen, parachutists, militiamen. She no longer slinks along the walls as she tended to do before the Revolution. Constantly called upon to efface herself before a member of the dominant society, the Algerian woman avoided the middle of the sidewalk which in all countries in the world belongs rightfully to those who command.

The shoulders of the unveiled Algerian woman are thrust back with easy freedom. She walks with a graceful, measured stride, neither too fast nor too slow. Her legs are bare, not confined by the veil, given back to themselves, and her hips are free.

The body of the young Algerian woman, in traditional society, is revealed to her by its coming to maturity and by the veil. The veil covers the body and disciplines it, tempers it, at the very time when it experiences its phase of greatest effervescence. The veil protects, reassures, isolates. One must have heard the confessions of Algerian women or have analysed the dream content of certain recently unveiled women to appreciate the importance of the veil for the body of the woman. Without the veil she has an impression of her body being cut up into bits, put adrift; the limbs seem to lengthen indefinitely. When the Algerian woman has to cross a street for a long time she commits errors of judgment as to the exact distance to be negotiated. The unveiled body seems to escape, to dissolve. She has an impression of being improperly dressed, even of being naked. She experiences a sense of incompleteness with great intensity. She has the anxious feeling that something is unfinished, and along with this a frightful sensation of disintegrating. The absence of the veil distorts the Algerian woman's corporal pattern. She quickly has to invent new dimensions for her body, new means of muscular control. She has to create for herself an attitude of unveiled-woman-outside. She must overcome all timidity, all awkwardness (for she must pass for a European), and at the same time be careful not to overdo it, not to attract notice to herself. The Algerian woman who walks stark naked into the European city relearns her body, re-establishes it in a totally revolutionary fashion. This new dialectic of the body and of the world is primary in the case of one revolutionary woman.[13]

But the Algerian woman is not only in conflict with her body. She is a link, sometimes an essential one, in the revolutionary machine. She carries weapons, knows important points of refuge. And it is in terms of the concrete dangers that she faces that we must gauge the insurmountable victories that she has had to win in order to be able to say to her chief, on her return: 'Mission accomplished ... R.A.S.'[14]

Another difficulty to which attention deserves to be called appeared during the first months of feminine activity. In the course of her comings and goings, it would happen that the unveiled Algerian woman was seen by a relative or a friend of the family. The father was sooner or later informed. He would naturally hesitate to believe such allegations. Then more reports would reach him. Different persons would claim to have seen 'Zohra or Fatima unveiled, walking like a ... My Lord, protect us! ...' The father would then decide to demand explanations. He would hardly have begun to speak when he would stop. From the young girl's look of firmness the father would have understood that her commitment was of long standing. The old fear of dishonour was swept away by a new fear, fresh and cold – that of death in battle or of torture of the girl. Behind the girl, the whole family – even the Algerian father, the authority for all things, the founder of every value – following in her footsteps, becomes committed to the new Algeria.

Removed and reassumed again and again, the veil has been manipulated, transformed into a technique of camouflage, into a means of struggle. The virtually taboo character assumed by the veil in the colonial situation disappeared almost entirely in the course of the liberating struggle. Even Algerian women not actively integrated into the struggle formed the habit of abandoning the veil. It is true that under certain conditions, especially from 1957 on, the veil reappeared. The missions in fact became increasingly difficult. The adversary now knew, since certain militant women had spoken under torture, that a number of women very Europeanised in appearance were playing a fundamental role in the battle. Moreover, certain European women of Algeria were arrested, to the consternation of the adversary who discovered that his own system was breaking down. The discovery by the French authorities of the participation of Europeans in the liberation struggle marks a turning point in the Algerian Revolution. From that day, the French patrols challenged every person. Europeans and Algerians were equally suspect. All historic limits crumbled and disappeared. Any person carrying a package could be required to open it and show its contents. Anyone was entitled to question anyone as to the nature of a parcel carried in Algiers, Phillipeville, or Batna. Under those conditions it became urgent to conceal the package from the eyes of the occupier and again to cover oneself with the protective *haïk*.

Here again, a new technique had to be learned: how to carry a rather heavy object dangerous to handle under the veil and still give the impression of having one's hands free, that there was nothing under this *haïk*, except a poor woman or an insignificant young girl. It was not enough to be veiled. One had to look so much like a 'fatma' that the soldier would be convinced that this woman was quite harmless.

Very difficult. Three metres ahead of you the police challenge a veiled woman who does not look particularly suspect. From the anguished expression of the unit leader you have guessed that she is carrying a bomb, or a sack of grenades, bound to her body by a whole system of strings and straps. For the hands must be free, exhibited bare, humbly and abjectly presented to the soldiers so that they will look no further. Showing empty and apparently mobile and free hands is the sign that disarms the enemy soldier.

The Algerian woman's body, which in an initial phase was pared down, now swelled. Whereas in the previous period the body had to be made slim and disciplined to make it attractive and seductive, it now had to be squashed, made shapeless and even ridiculous. This, as we have seen, is the phase during which she undertook to carry bombs, grenades, machine-gun clips.

The enemy, however, was alerted, and in the streets one witnessed what became a commonplace spectacle of Algerian women glued to the wall, on whose bodies the famous magnetic detectors, the 'frying pans', would be passed. Every veiled woman, every Algerian woman became suspect. There was no discrimination. This was the period during which men, women, children, the whole Algerian people, experienced at one and the same time their national vocation and the recasting of the new Algerian society.

Ignorant or feigning to be ignorant of these new forms of conduct, French colonialism, on the occasion of May 13th, re-enacted its old campaign of Westernising the Algerian woman. Servants under the threat of being fired, poor women dragged from their homes, prostitutes, were brought to the public square and *symbolically* unveiled to the cries of '*Vive l'Algérie française!*'

Before this new offensive old reactions reappeared. Spontaneously and without being told, the Algerian women who had long since dropped the veil once again donned the *haïk*, thus affirming that it was not true that woman liberated herself at the invitation of France and of General de Gaulle.

Behind these psychological reactions, beneath this immediate and almost unanimous response, we again see the overall attitude of rejection of the values of the occupier, even if these values objectively be worth choosing. It is because they fail to grasp this intellectual reality, this characteristic failure (the famous sensitivity of the colonised), that the colonisers rage at always 'doing them good in spite of themselves.' Colonialism wants everything to come from it. But the dominant psychological feature of the colonised is to withdraw before any invitation of the conqueror's. In organising the famous cavalcade of May 13th, colonialism has obliged Algerian society to go back to methods of struggle already outmoded. In a certain sense, the different ceremonies have caused a turning back, a regression.

Colonialism must accept the fact that things happen without its control, without its direction. We are reminded of the words spoken in an international assembly by an African political figure. Responding to the standard excuse of the immaturity of colonial peoples and their incapacity to administer themselves, this man demanded for the underdeveloped peoples 'the right to govern themselves badly.' The doctrinal assertions of colonialism in its attempt to justify the maintenance of its domination almost always push the colonised to the position of making uncompromising, rigid, static counter-proposals.

After the 13th of May, the veil was resumed, but stripped once and for all of its exclusively traditional dimension.

There is thus a historic dynamism of the veil that is very concretely perceptible in the development of colonisation in Algeria. In the beginning, the veil was a mechanism of resistance, but its value for the social groups remained very strong. The veil was worn because tradition demanded a rigid separation of the sexes, but also because the occupier *was bent on unveiling Algeria*. In a second phase, the mutation occurred in connection with the Revolution and under special circumstances. The veil was abandoned in the course of revolutionary action. What had been used to block the psychological or political offences of the occupier became a means, an instrument. The veil helped the Algerian woman to meet the new problems created by the struggle.

6 *fellah* – a peasant. (Translator's note)

7 Attention must be called to a frequent attitude, on the part of European women in particular, with regard to a special category of evolved natives. Certain unveiled Algerian women turn themselves into perfect Westerners with amazing rapidity and unsuspected ease. European women feel a certain uneasiness in the presence of these women. Frustrated in the presence of the veil, they experience a similar impression before the bared face, before that unabashed body which has lost all awkwardness, all timidity, and become downright offensive. Not only is the satisfaction of supervising the evolution and correcting the mistakes of the unveiled woman withdrawn from the European woman, but she feels herself challenged on the level of feminine charm, of elegance, and even sees a competitor in this novice metamorphosed into a professional, a neophyte transformed into a propagandist. The European woman has no choice but to make common cause with the Algerian man who had fiercely flung the unveiled woman into the camp of evil and of depravation. 'Really!' the European women will exclaim, 'these unveiled women are quite amoral and shameless.' Integration, in order to be successful, seems indeed to have to be simply a continued, accepted paternalism.

8 *djebel* – mountain. (Translator's note)

9 We are mentioning here only realities known to the enemy. We therefore say nothing about the new forms of action adopted by women in the Revolution. Since 1958, in fact, the tortures inflicted on women militants have enabled the occupier to have an idea of the strategy used by women. Today new adaptations have developed. It will therefore be understood if we are silent as to these.

10 *fidaï* – a death volunteer, in the Islamic tradition. (Translator's note)

11 *douar* – a village. (Translator's note)

12 Froger, one of the colonialist leaders. Executed by a *fidaï* in late 1956.

13 The woman, who before the Revolution never left the house without being accompanied by her mother or her husband, is now entrusted with special missions such as going from Oran to Constantine or Algiers. For several days, all by herself, carrying directives of capital importance for the Revolution, she takes the train, spends the night with an unknown family, among militants. Here too she must harmonise her movements, for the enemy is on the lookout for any false step. But the important thing here is that the husband makes no difficulty about letting his wife leave on an assignment. He will make it, in fact, a point of pride to say to the liaison agent when the latter returns, 'You see, everything has gone well in your absence.' The Algerian's age-old jealousy, his 'congenital' suspiciousness, have melted on contact with the Revolution. It must be pointed out also that militants who are being sought by the police take refuge with other militants not yet identified by the occupier. In such cases the woman, left alone all day with the fugitive, is the one who gets him his food, the newspapers, the mail, showing no trace of suspicion or fear. Involved in the struggle, the husband or the father learns to look upon the relations between the sexes in a new light. The militant man discovers the militant woman, and jointly they create new dimensions for Algerian society.

14 R.A.S. – *Rien à signaler* – a military abbreviation for 'Nothing to report'.

We here go on to a description of attitudes. There is, however, an important piece of work to be done on the woman's role in the Revolution: the woman in the city, in the *djebel*, in the enemy administrations; the prostitute and the information she obtains; the woman in prison, under torture, facing death, before the courts. All these chapter headings, after the material has been sifted, will reveal an incalculable number of facts essential for the history of the national struggle.

Chapter 3: The Algerian Family
Part 1

We have seen the transformation of the Algerian woman taking place through her revolutionary commitment and her instrumentalisation of the veil. It will readily be understood that this radical change could not occur without having profound repercussions on the other components of Algerian family life.

The struggle for national liberation and the more and more total character of the repression have inflicted grave traumatisms upon the family group: a father taken into custody in the street in the company of his children, stripped along with them, tortured before their eyes; the sharply experienced brotherhood of men with bare, bruised, bloody shoulders; a husband arrested, dragged away, imprisoned. The women are then left to find ways of keeping the children from starving to death. We shall come back to this special and very important aspect of the Algerian conflict. We would like here to trace the evolution of the Algerian family, its transformation, the great modifications it has undergone because of and in the course of the war for liberation.

The most important point of this modification, it seems to us, is that the family, from being homogeneous and virtually monolithic, has broken up into separate elements. Each member of this family has gained in individuality what it has lost in its belonging to a world of more or less confused values. Individual persons have found themselves facing new choices, new decisions. The customary and highly structured patterns of behaviour that were the crystallisation of traditional ideas suddenly proved ineffective and were abandoned. Tradition, in fact, is not solely a combination of automatic gestures and archaic beliefs. At the most elementary level, there are values, and the need for justification. The father questioned by the child explains, comments, legitimises.

It is important to show that the colonised father at the time of the fight for liberation gave his children the impression of being undecided, of avoiding the taking of sides, even of adopting an evasive and irresponsible attitude. Such an experience, which is traumatic for a child when its points of reference are confined to the family circle, now loses its harmfulness. This experience, in fact, was occurring on a national scale and was part and parcel of the great upheaval incidental to the creation of a new world which was felt throughout the territory.

Before 1954, the existence of nationalist parties had already introduced changes into the native private life. The nationalist parties, the parliamentary political action, the spreading of slogans advocating splitting off from France, had already given rise to certain contradictions within the family. These developments invited the inert resistance of the colonised society to turn into action. For the tense immobility of the dominant society, the nationalist parties tried to substitute awareness, movement, creation. The people, as a whole, agreed with these parties, but they had a sharp memory of the legendary ferocity of the French military and police. Witnesses of the colonial invasion, still alive 30 or 40 years ago, had often related to them episodes of the conquest. In many regions of Algeria the accounts of massacres and the burning of villages were still vividly remembered. The conqueror had settled in such numbers, he had created so many centres of colonisation, that a certain passivity encouraged by the colonial domination made itself evident and gradually took on a tinge of despair.

Before 1954, the son who adopted a nationalist position never did so, really, against his father's wishes, but his activity as a militant in any case never in any respect modified his filial behaviour within the framework of the Algerian family. The relations based on the absolute respect due to the father and on the principle that the truth is first of all the unchallengeable property of the elders were not encroached upon. Modesty, shame, the fear of looking at the father, of speaking aloud in his presence, remained intact, even in the case of the nationalist militant. The absence of actual revolutionary action kept the personality in its customary channels.

For a long time, political action in a colonised country is a legal action that is carried on within the parliamentary framework. After a certain period, when official and peaceful channels are exhausted, the militant hardens his position. The political party passes over to direct action, and the problems that the son faces are problems of life or death for the country. In a parallel way, his attitude toward his father and the other members of the family frees itself of everything that proves unnecessary and detrimental to the revolutionary situation. The person is born, assumes his autonomy, and becomes the creator of his own values. The old stultifying attachment to the father melts in the sun of the Revolution. In Algeria, after Sétif and the different combats waged by the nationalist parties during the postwar period, positions sharpened and the people's political maturity markedly progressed.

On November 1, 1954, the Revolution reopened all the problems: those of colonialism, but also those of the colonised society. *The colonised society perceived that in order to succeed in the gigantic undertaking into which it had flung itself, in order to defeat colonialism and in order to build the Algerian nation, it would have to make a vast effort of self-preparation, strain all its joints, renew its blood and its soul.* In the course of the multiple episodes of the war, the people came to realise that if they wished to bring a new world to birth they would have to create a new Algerian society from top to bottom. In order to fulfil his aspirations, the Algerian must adapt himself at an exceptional pace to this new situation. The truth, for once, eluded its traditional trustees and placed itself within reach of any seeker. The group, which formerly looked to the father to determine its values, now had to seek these each for himself, as circumstances dictated.

Every Algerian faced with the new system of values introduced by the Revolution is compelled to define himself, to take a position, to choose.

The Son and the Father

At the time when the people were called upon to adopt radical forms of struggle, the Algerian family was still highly structured. But on the level of national consciousness, the father lagged far behind the son. A new world had come into being long before, which the parents knew nothing about, and which was developing with exceptional rapidity. In a confused way, it is true, the father had caught in passing a few snatches of phrases, a few sharp-edged meanings, but never came to the decision to fight the occupant, weapons in hand. Yet there was not an Algerian who had not faced the challenge of the oppression and wondered what was to be done. Every Algerian, at least at one time in his life, in the course of a meeting, or simply a discussion, had wished for the defeat of colonialism. At the market, in a café, on a pilgrimage, in the course of the traditional holidays, there always came a moment when the Algerian plotted against the occupier. But these exchanges were like the desperate lamentations of all the humiliated of all the countries in the world. The deep hold taken by colonial society, its frenzy to transform itself into a necessity, the wretchedness on which it was built, gave to life that familiar tinge of resignation that specialists in underdeveloped countries describe under the heading of *fatalism*.

marry. Considered a minor indefinitely, the woman owes it to herself to find a husband as soon as possible, and the father is haunted by the fear of dying and abandoning his daughter without support and therefore unable to survive.

All these restrictions were to be knocked over and challenged by the national liberation struggle. The unveiled Algerian woman, who assumed an increasingly important place in revolutionary action, developed her personality, discovered the exalting realm of responsibility. The freedom of the Algerian people from then on became identified with woman's liberation, with her entry into history. This woman who, in the avenues of Algiers or of Constantine, would carry the grenades or the submachine-gun chargers, this woman who tomorrow would be outraged, violated, tortured, could not put herself back into her former state of mind and relive her behaviour of the past; this woman who was writing the heroic pages of Algerian history was, in so doing, bursting the bounds of the narrow world in which she had lived without responsibility, and was at the same time participating in the destruction of colonialism and in the birth of a new woman.

The women in Algeria, from 1955, began to have models. In Algerian society stories were told of women who in ever greater number suffered death and imprisonment in order that an independent Algeria might be born. It was these militant women who constituted the points of reference around which the imagination of Algerian feminine society was to be stirred to the boiling point. The woman-for-marriage progressively disappeared, and gave way to the woman-for-action. The young girl was replaced by the militant, the woman by the *sister*.

The female cells of the FLN received mass memberships. The impatience of these new recruits was so great that it often endangered the traditions of complete secrecy. The leaders had to restrain the exceptional enthusiasm and radicalism that are always characteristic of any youth engaged in building a new world. As soon as they were enrolled, these women would ask to be given the most dangerous assignments. Only progressively did the political training that was given them lead them away from contemplating the struggle in an explosive form. The Algerian girl learned to contain her impatience and to show unexpected virtues of calm, composure and firmness.

It would happen that a girl would be sought after by the police or that several members of the group she belonged to would be arrested. The necessity to vanish, to make her getaway, would become urgent. The militant would first leave her family and take refuge with friends. But soon orders would come from the network leadership to join the nearest maquis. After all the previous shocks – the daughter relinquishing the veil, putting on makeup, going out at all hours heaven knew where, etc. – the parents no longer dared protest. The father himself no longer had any choice. His old fear of dishonour had become altogether absurd in the light of the immense tragedy being experienced by the people. But apart from this, the national authority that had decided that the girl should leave for the maquis would have no patience with such reticence on the father's part. Challenging the morality of a patriot had been ruled out long ago. Moreover, there was the overriding consideration of the combat – hard, intense, implacable. There was no time to lose. So the girl would go up into the maquis, alone with men. For months and months, the parents would be without news of a girl of eighteen who would sleep in the forest or in the grottoes, who would roam the *djebel* dressed as a man, with a gun in her hands.

Part 2

The Couple

The relations of wife and husband have likewise become modified in the course of the war of liberation. Whereas everyone in the house formerly had well-defined functions, the intensity of the struggle was to impose unanticipated types of behaviour.

Let us take the case of Mustapha. Mustapha has just come home. A little while ago, with another *fidaï*, he has thrown several grenades into the premises of the Judicial Police where patriots are being tortured night and day. He does not feel like talking. He lies down and shuts his eyes. His wife has seen him come in but has noticed nothing. An hour later, the news floods the district: two patriots have successfully carried out a spectacular coup. In the alleyway and in the court, the casualties of the adversary are estimated. The angry patrols that are already pouring into the streets are irrefutable proof that our people have dealt the colonists a hard blow. The woman comes back into the room, and seeing her husband slumbering, impervious to what has happened, gives vent to her contempt: 'You wouldn't be up to doing a thing like that! It's easier to sleep and eat.' And she goes on to mention a neighbour precarious nature of the present, of what could be rejected from one moment to the next, were strengthened, or at least changed character. What could formally be defined as mere cohabitation today includes a multiplicity of points of communication. First and foremost is the fact of incurring dangers together, of turning over in the same bed, each on his own side, each with his fragment of a secret. It is also the consciousness of collaborating in the immense work of destroying the world of oppression. The couple is no longer shut in upon itself. It no longer finds its end in itself. It is no longer the result of the natural instinct of perpetuation of the species, nor the institutionalised means of satisfying one's sexuality. The couple becomes the basic cell of the commonwealth, the fertile nucleus of the nation. The Algerian couple, in becoming the link in the revolutionary organisation, is transformed into a unit of existence. *The mingling of fighting experience with conjugal life deepens the relations between husband and wife and cements their union. There is a simultaneous and effervescent emergence of the citizen, the patriot, and the modern spouse.* The Algerian couple rids itself of its traditional weaknesses at the same time that the solidarity of the people becomes a part of history. This couple is no longer an accident but something rediscovered, willed, built. It is, as we can see, the very foundation of the sexual encounter that we are concerned with here.

Marriage and Divorce

In Algeria marriage is generally decided by the families. It is almost always at the wedding that the husband sees his wife's face for the first time. The social and economic reasons for this tradition are sufficiently well known and need not be explained here. Marriage in the underdeveloped countries is not an individual contract, but a contract between clan and clan, tribe and tribe, family and family.

With the Revolution, things were gradually to change. The presence of women in the maquis, the contact between unmarried men and women, created unexpected problems for the local FLN leaders. Men would go to their superior officer and ask to marry such and such a nurse. The FLN officer would hesitate for a long time. No one can give a girl away in marriage, except for her father, and in the father's absence, her uncle or her brother. The officer did not feel he had a right to entertain the *moudjahid's* request and sometimes found himself obliged to separate the two lovers. But love is an incontrovertible fact which must be reckoned with, and the leadership of the Revolution gave instructions that marriages could be contracted before a mayor or registry official.

Registry offices were opened. Marriages, births, and deaths could then be registered. Marriage in the maquis ceased to be an arrangement between families. All unions were voluntary. The future wife and husband had had time to know each other, to esteem, to love each other. Even the case of love at first sight had been anticipated by the directives. Whenever an application for marriage is presented, the instructions read, it is well to postpone any decision for three months. When the father learned of the marriage of his daughter in the maquis, the act would not be contested or condemned. On the contrary, pictures would be asked for, and the babies born in the maquis would be sent to the grandparents who would care for these children of the Revolution as they deserved.

Such innovations could not fail to have repercussions on the traditional modes of marriage that continued to be practised in the rest of the country. Algerian women began at first to demand guarantees of the future husband's patriotism. They would require that the young men who were being proposed to them be members of the FLN. The father's unchallengeable and massive authority let itself be shaken by this new requirement. Before the Revolution, a girl who had been asked for as a wife would leave the family circle for several days and take refuge with relatives. This is explained by the shame felt by the girl at being the object of a sexual pursuit. It was also usual for the young bride to avoid appearing before her father for one or two months after the consummation of the marriage. These modest, infantile patterns of behaviour disappeared with the Revolution and today the majority of young married women have themselves been present at the signature of their contract and have naturally been consulted as to their intended. Marriage in Algeria underwent this radical transformation in the very heart of the combat waged by the *Moudjahidines* and the *Moudjahidates*.

Under these conditions, divorce, the separation of husband and wife, was bound to undergo change. The husband's repudiation of his wife that could be immediately proclaimed at any time and that reflected the fragility of the conjugal bond is no longer automatically legalised. The husband must explain his reasons for wanting a divorce. There are attempts at reconciliation. In any case, the final decision rests with the local officer. The family emerges strengthened from this ordeal in which colonialism has resorted to every means to break the people's will. In the midst of the gravest dangers the Algerian adopts modern forms of existence and confers on the human person his maximum independence.

Feminine Society

The women who participate in the war and who marry in the maquis have initiated within Algerian feminine society radical changes in certain patterns of behaviour. A one-sided interpretation of the main changes observed must, however, be avoided. The war waged by French colonialism obliges the Algerian people to be constantly and wholly engaged in the battle. Confronted by an adversary who has sworn to keep Algeria, even without the Algerians, it is difficult to remain oneself, to maintain preferences or values intact. Feminine society undergoes change both through an organic solidarity with the Revolution, and more especially because the adversary cuts into the Algerian flesh with unheard-of violence.

The women, accustomed to going to the village cemetery or to visiting a local sanctuary on Fridays, interrupt this activity among others when they are regrouped along with tens of thousands of other families.[2]

In the camp they immediately organise themselves in FLN cells. They meet women from other regions, exchange their experiences of the repression – but also their experiences from before the Revolution, their hopes. The regrouped Algerian woman, cut off from her husband who has remained with the combatants, takes care of the old and the orphans, learns to read and to sew and often, in a group of several companions, leaves the camp and joins the Army of National Liberation.

With these considerable shifts in population, the whole social panorama and the perceptual framework are disturbed and restructured. A *mechta* evacuated is not a *mechta* that has migrated.[3] The chain of events of the operation must be patiently followed: bombardments of the region, multiple raids, able-bodied men taking to the mountains, the dead quickly buried, the hostages taken away by the French, certain members of the *mechta* taking refuge in a neighbouring town with relatives or friends.

The regrouped *mechta* is a broken, destroyed *mechta*. It is merely a group of men, women and children. Under these conditions, no gesture is kept intact. No previous rhythm is to be found unaltered. Caught in the meshes of the barbed wires, the members of regrouped Algerian families neither eat nor sleep as they did before. This can be seen, for example, on the occasion of a death. The lamentations, the wails, the grief-stricken faces, and the contortions of the body have today practically disappeared. The classic mourning tears are hardly any longer to be found in Algeria. All this began in 1955 when the French troops, for the fun of it, or in the course of a repression, would overrun a locality and machinegun five or ten men. These collective deaths, without warning, without a previous illness that had been treated and fought, abandoned in the ditch on the edge of the road, cannot set into motion emotional mechanisms that are homogeneous to a society. Lamentations and grief-stricken faces are part of a patterned, stable world. One does not weep, one does not do as before when one is faced with multiple murders. One grits one's teeth and one prays in silence. One further step, and it is cries of joy that salute the death of a *moudjahid* who has fallen on the field of honour. It must not be believed, however, that the traditional ceremonies are repeated in the case of natural deaths, resulting from illnesses or accidents. Even then, it seems virtually impossible to revive the habitual techniques of despair. The war has dislocated Algerian society to such a point that any death is conceived of as a direct or indirect consequence of colonialist repression. Today there is not a dead person in Algeria who is not the victim of French colonialism. It is impossible for an Algerian civilian to remain untouched by the war of colonial re-conquest. More than this, there is not a death of an Algerian outside of Algeria which is not attributed to French colonialism. The Algerian people have thus decided that, until independence, French colonialism will be innocent of none of the wounds inflicted upon its body and its consciousness.

Algeria Dispersed

The tactic adopted by French colonialism since the beginning of the Revolution has had the result of separating the people from each other, of fragmenting them, with the sole objective of making any cohesion impossible. This effort was at first concentrated on the men, who were interned by tens of thousands.

THE WRETCHED OF THE EARTH[1]

Chapter 1: Concerning Violence

National liberation, national renaissance, the restoration of nationhood to the people, commonwealth: whatever may be the headings used or the new formulas introduced, decolonisation is always a violent phenomenon. At whatever level we study it – relationships between individuals, new names for sports clubs, the human admixture at cocktail parties, in the police, on the directing boards of national or private banks – decolonisation is quite simply the replacing of a certain 'species' of men by another 'species' of men. Without any period of transition, there is a total, complete, and absolute substitution. It is true that we could equally well stress the rise of a new nation, the setting up of a new state, its diplomatic relations, and its economic and political trends. But we have precisely chosen to speak of that kind of tabula rasa which characterises at the outset all decolonisation. Its unusual importance is that it constitutes, from the very first day, the minimum demands of the colonised. To tell the truth, the proof of success lies in a whole social structure being changed from the bottom up. The extraordinary importance of this change is that it is willed, called for, demanded. The need for this change exists in its crude state, impetuous and compelling, in the consciousness and in the lives of the men and women who are colonised. But the possibility of this change is equally experienced in the form of a terrifying future in the consciousness of another 'species' of men and women: the colonisers.

Decolonisation, which sets out to change the order of the world, is, obviously, a programme of complete disorder. But it cannot come as a result of magical practices, nor of a natural shock, nor of a friendly understanding. Decolonisation, as we know, is a historical process: that is to say that it cannot be understood, it cannot become intelligible nor clear to itself except in the exact measure that we can discern the movements which give it historical form and content. Decolonisation is the meeting of two forces, opposed to each other by their very nature, which in fact owe their originality to that sort of substantification which results from and is nourished by the situation in the colonies. Their first encounter was marked by violence and their existence together – that is to say the exploitation of the native by the settler – was carried on by dint of a great array of bayonets and cannons. The settler and the native are old acquaintances. In fact, the settler is right when he speaks of knowing 'them' well. For it is the settler who has brought the native into existence and who perpetuates his existence. The settler owes the fact of his very existence, that is to say, his property, to the colonial system.

Decolonisation never takes place unnoticed, for it influences individuals and modifies them fundamentally. It transforms spectators crushed with their inessentiality into privileged actors, with the grandiose glare of history's floodlights upon them. It brings a natural rhythm into existence, introduced by new men, and with it a new language and a new humanity. Decolonisation is the veritable creation of new men. But this creation owes nothing of its legitimacy to any supernatural power; the 'thing' which has been colonised becomes man during the same process by which it frees itself.

In decolonisation there is, therefore, the need of a complete calling into question of the colonial situation. If we wish to describe it precisely, we might find it in the well-known words: 'The last shall be first and the first last.' Decolonisation is the putting into practice of this sentence. That is why, if we try to describe it, all decolonisation is successful.

The naked truth of decolonisation evokes for us the searing bullets and bloodstained knives which emanate from it. For if the last shall be first, this will only come to pass after a murderous and decisive struggle between the two protagonists. That affirmed intention to place the last at the head of things, and to make them climb at a pace (too quickly, some say) the well-known steps, which characterise an organised society, can only triumph if we use all means to turn the scale, including, of course, that of violence.

You do not turn any society, however primitive it may be, upside down with such a programme, if you have not decided from the very beginning, that is to say from the actual formulation of that programme, to overcome all the obstacles that you will come across in so doing. The native who decides to put the programme into practice, and to become its moving force, is ready for violence at all times. From birth it is clear to him that this narrow world, strewn with prohibitions, can only be called into question by absolute violence.

The colonial world is a world divided into compartments. It is probably unnecessary to recall the existence of native quarters and European quarters, of schools for natives and schools for Europeans; in the same way we need not recall apartheid in South Africa. Yet, if we examine closely this system of compartments, we will at least be able to reveal the lines of force it implies. This approach to the colonial world, its ordering and its geographical layout, will allow us to mark out the lines on which a decolonised society will be reorganised.

The colonial world is a world cut in two. The dividing line, the frontiers are shown by barracks and police stations. In the colonies it is the policeman and the soldier who are the official, instituted go-betweens, the spokesmen of the settler and his rule of oppression. In capitalist societies, the educational system, whether lay or clerical, the structure of moral reflexes handed down from father to son, the exemplary honesty of workers who are given a medal after fifty years of good and loyal service, and the affection which springs from harmonious relations and good behaviour – all these aesthetic expressions of respect for the established order serve to create around the exploited person an atmosphere of submission and of inhibition which lightens the task of policing considerably. In the capitalist countries, a multitude of moral teachers, counsellors and 'bewilderers' separate the exploited from those in power. In the colonial countries, on the contrary, the policeman and the soldier, by their immediate presence and their frequent and direct action, maintain contact with the native and advise him by means of rifle butts and napalm not to budge. It is obvious here that the agents of government speak the language of pure force. The intermediary does not lighten the oppression, nor seek to hide the domination; he shows them up and puts them into practice with the clear conscience of an upholder of the peace; yet he is the bringer of violence into the home and into the mind of the native.

The zone where the natives live is not complementary to the zone inhabited by the settlers. The two zones are opposed, but not in the service of a higher unity. Obedient to the rules of pure Aristotelian logic, they both follow the principle of reciprocal exclusivity. No conciliation is possible, for of the two terms, one is superfluous. The settler's town is a strongly built town, all made of stone and steel. It is a brightly lit town; the streets are covered with asphalt, and the garbage cans swallow all the leavings, unseen, unknown and hardly thought about. The settler's feet are never visible, except perhaps in the sea; but there you're never close enough to see them. His feet are protected by strong shoes although the streets of his town are clean and even, with no holes or stones. The settler's town is a well-fed town, an easygoing town; its belly is always full of good things. The settler's town is a town of white people, of foreigners.

The town belonging to the colonised people, or at least the native town, the Negro village, the medina, the reservation, is a place of ill fame, peopled by men of evil repute. They are born there, it matters little where or how; they die there, it matters not where nor how. It is a world without spaciousness; men live there on top of each other, and their huts are built one on top of the other. The native town is a hungry town, starved of bread, of meat, of shoes, of coal, of light. The native town is a crouching village, a town on its knees, a town wallowing in the mire. It is a town of niggers and dirty Arabs. The look that the native turns on the settler's town is a look of lust, a look of envy; it expresses his dreams of possession – all manner of possession: to sit at the settler's table, to sleep in the settler's bed, with his wife if possible. The colonised man is an envious man. And this the settler knows very well; when their glances meet he ascertains bitterly, always on the defensive, 'They want to take our place.' It is true, for there is no native who does not dream at least once a day of setting himself up in the settler's place.

This world divided into compartments, this world cut in two, is inhabited by two different species. The originality of the colonial context is that economic reality, inequality, and the immense difference of ways of life never come to mask the human realities. When you examine at close quarters the colonial context, it is evident that what parcels out the world is to begin with the fact of belonging to or not belonging to a given race, a given species. In the colonies the economic substructure is also a superstructure. The cause is the consequence; you are rich because you are white, you are white because you are rich. This is why Marxist analysis should always be slightly stretched every time we have to do with the colonial problem.

Everything up to and including the very nature of pre-capitalist society, so well explained by Marx, must here be thought out again. The serf is in essence different from the knight, but a reference to divine right is necessary to legitimise this statutory difference. In the colonies, the foreigner coming from another country imposed his rule by means of guns and machines. In defiance of his successful transplantation, in spite of his appropriation, the settler still remains a foreigner. It is neither the act of owning factories, nor estates, nor a

sort of stiffening or muscular lockjaw. During the period of decolonisation, the native's reason is appealed to. He is offered definite values, he is told frequently that decolonisation need not mean regression, and that he must put his trust in qualities which are well tried, solid, and highly esteemed. But it so happens that when the native hears a speech about Western culture he pulls out his knife – or at least he makes sure it is within reach. The violence with which the supremacy of white values is affirmed and the aggressiveness which has permeated the victory of these values over the ways of life and of thought of the native mean that, in revenge, the native laughs in mockery when Western values are mentioned in front of him. In the colonial context the settler only ends his work of breaking in the native when the latter admits loudly and intelligibly the supremacy of the white man's values. In the period of decolonisation, the colonised masses mock at these very values, insult them, and vomit them up.

This phenomenon is ordinarily masked because, during the period of decolonisation, certain colonised intellectuals have begun a dialogue with the bourgeoisie of the colonialist country. During this phase, the indigenous population is discerned only as an indistinct mass. The few native personalities whom the colonialist bourgeoisie have come to know here and there have not sufficient influence on that immediate discernment to give rise to nuances. On the other hand, during the period of liberation, the colonialist bourgeoisie looks feverishly for contacts with the elite and it is with these elite that the familiar dialogue concerning values is carried on. The colonialist bourgeoisie, when it realises that it is impossible for it to maintain its domination over the colonial countries, decides to carry out a rearguard action with regard to culture, values, techniques, and so on.

Now what we must never forget is that the immense majority of colonised peoples is oblivious to these problems. For a colonised people the most essential value, because the most concrete, is first and foremost the land: the land which will bring them bread and, above all, dignity. But this dignity has nothing to do with the dignity of the human individual: for that human individual has never heard tell of it. All that the native has seen in his country is that they can freely arrest him, beat him, starve him: and no professor of ethics, no priest has ever come to be beaten in his place, nor to share their bread with him. As far as the native is concerned, morality is very concrete; it is to silence the settler's defiance, to break his flaunting violence – in a word, to put him out of the picture. The well-known principle that all men are equal will be illustrated in the colonies from the moment that the native claims that he is the equal of the settler. One step more, and he is ready to fight to be more than the settler. In fact, he has already decided to eject him and to take his place; as we see it, it is a whole material and moral universe which is breaking up. The intellectual who for his part has followed the colonialist with regard to the universal abstract will fight in order that the settler and the native may live together in peace in a new world. But the thing he does not see, precisely because he is permeated by colonialism and all its ways of thinking, is that the settler, from the moment that the colonial context disappears, has no longer any interest in remaining or in co-existing. It is not by chance that, even before any negotiation[3] between the Algerian and French governments has taken place, the European minority which calls itself 'liberal' has already made its position clear: it demands nothing more nor less than twofold citizenship. By setting themselves apart in an abstract manner, the liberals try to force the settler into taking a very concrete jump into the unknown. Let us admit it, the settler knows perfectly well that no phraseology can be a substitute for reality.

Thus the native discovers that his life, his breath, his beating heart are the same as those of the settler. He finds out that the settler's skin is not of any more value than a native's skin; and it must be said that this discovery shakes the world in a very necessary manner. All the new, revolutionary assurance of the native stems from it. For if, in fact, my life is worth as much as the settler's, his glance no longer shrivels me up nor freezes me, and his voice no longer turns me into stone. I am no longer on tenterhooks in his presence; in fact, I don't give a damn for him. Not only does his presence no longer trouble me, but I am already preparing such efficient ambushes for him that soon there will be no way out but that of flight.

We have said that the colonial context is characterised by the dichotomy which it imposes upon the whole people. Decolonisation unifies that people by the radical decision to remove from it its heterogeneity, and by unifying it on a national, sometimes a racial, basis. We know the fierce words of the Senegalese patriots, referring to the manoeuvres of their president, Senghor: 'We have demanded that the higher posts should be given to Africans; and now Senghor is Africanising the Europeans.' That is to say that the native can see clearly and immediately if decolonisation has come to pass or not, for his minimum demands are simply that the last shall be first.

But the native intellectual brings variants to this petition, and, in fact, he seems to have good reasons: higher civil servants, technicians, specialists – all seem to be needed. Now, the ordinary native interprets these unfair promotions as so many acts of sabotage, and he is often heard to declare: 'It wasn't worth while, then, our becoming independent ...'

In the colonial countries where a real struggle for freedom has taken place, where the blood of the people has flowed and where the length of the period of armed warfare has favoured the backward surge of intellectuals toward bases grounded in the people, we can observe a genuine eradication of the superstructure built by these intellectuals from the bourgeois colonialist environment. The colonialist bourgeoisie, in its narcissistic dialogue, expounded by the members of its universities, had in fact deeply implanted in the minds of the colonised intellectual that the essential qualities remain eternal in spite of all the blunders men may make: the essential qualities of the West, of course. The native intellectual accepted the cogency of these ideas, and deep down in his brain you could always find a vigilant sentinel ready to defend the Greco-Latin pedestal. Now it so happens that during the struggle for liberation, at the moment that the native intellectual comes into touch again with his people, this artificial sentinel is turned into dust. All the Mediterranean values – the triumph of the human individual, of clarity, and of beauty – become lifeless, colourless knickknacks. All those speeches seem like collections of dead words; those values which seemed to uplift the soul are revealed as worthless, simply because they have nothing to do with the concrete conflict in which the people is engaged.

Individualism is the first to disappear. The native intellectual had learned from his masters that the individual ought to express himself fully. The colonialist bourgeoisie had hammered into the native's mind the idea of a society of individuals where each person shuts himself up in his own subjectivity, and whose only wealth is individual thought. Now the native who has the opportunity to return to the people during the struggle for freedom will discover the falseness of this theory. The very forms of organisation of the struggle will suggest to him a different vocabulary. Brother, sister, friend – these are words outlawed by the colonialist bourgeoisie, because for them my brother is my purse, my friend is part of my scheme for getting on. The native intellectual takes part, in a sort of auto-da-fé, in the destruction of all his idols: egoism, recrimination that springs from pride, and the childish stupidity of those who always want to have the last word. Such a colonised intellectual, dusted over by colonial culture, will in the same way discover the substance of village assemblies, the cohesion of people's committees, and the extraordinary fruitfulness of local meetings and groupments. Henceforward, the interests of one will be the interests of all, for in concrete fact *everyone* will be discovered by the troops, *everyone* will be massacred – or *everyone* will be saved. The motto 'look out for yourself', the atheist's method of salvation, is in this context forbidden.

Self-criticism has been much talked about of late, but few people realise that it is an African institution. Whether in the *djemaas*[4] of northern Africa or in the meetings of western Africa, tradition demands that the quarrels which occur in a village should be settled in public. It is communal self-criticism, of course, and with a note of humour, because everybody is relaxed, and because in the last resort we all want the same things. But the more the intellectual imbibes the atmosphere of the people, the more completely he abandons the habits of calculation, of unwonted silence, of mental reservations, and shakes off the spirit of concealment. And it is true that already at that level we can say that the community triumphs, and that it spreads its own light and its own reason.

But it so happens sometimes that decolonisation occurs in areas which have not been sufficiently shaken by the struggle for liberation, and there may be found those same know-all, smart, wily intellectuals. We find intact in them the manners and forms of thought picked up during their association with the colonialist bourgeoisie. Spoilt children of yesterday's colonialism and of today's national governments, they organise the loot of whatever national resources exist. Without pity, they use today's national distress as a means of getting on through scheming and legal robbery, by import-export combines, limited liability companies, gambling on the stock exchange, or unfair promotion. They are insistent in their demands for the nationalisation of commerce, that is to say the reservation of markets and advantageous bargains for nationals only. As far as doctrine is concerned, they proclaim the pressing necessity of nationalising the robbery of the nation. In this arid

he himself is the extension of that mother country. Thus the history which he writes is not the history of the country which he plunders but the history of his own nation in regard to all that she skims off, all that she violates and starves.

The immobility to which the native is condemned can only be called in question if the native decides to put an end to the history of colonisation – the history of pillage – and to bring into existence the history of the nation – the history of decolonisation.

A world divided into compartments, a motionless, Manicheistic world, a world of statues: the statue of the general who carried out the conquest, the statue of the engineer who built the bridge; a world which is sure of itself, which crushes with its stones the backs flayed by whips: this is the colonial world. The native is a being hemmed in; apartheid is simply one form of the division into compartments of the colonial world. The first thing which the native learns is to stay in his place, and not to go beyond certain limits. This is why the dreams of the native are always of muscular prowess; his dreams are of action and of aggression. I dream I am jumping, swimming, running, climbing; I dream that I burst out laughing, that I span a river in one stride, or that I am followed by a flood of motorcars which never catch up with me. During the period of colonisation, the native never stops achieving his freedom from nine in the evening until six in the morning.

The colonised man will first manifest this aggressiveness which has been deposited in his bones against his own people. This is the period when the niggers beat each other up, and the police and magistrates do not know which way to turn when faced with the astonishing waves of crime in North Africa. We shall see later how this phenomenon should be judged. When the native is confronted with the colonial order of things, he finds he is in a state of permanent tension. The settler's world is a hostile world, which spurns the native, but at the same time it is a world of which he is envious. We have seen that the native never ceases to dream of putting himself in the place of the settler – not of becoming the settler but of substituting himself for the settler. This hostile world, ponderous and aggressive because it fends off the colonised masses with all the harshness it is capable of, represents not merely a hell from which the swiftest flight possible is desirable, but also a paradise close at hand which is guarded by terrible watchdogs.

The native is always on the alert, for since he can only make out with difficulty the many symbols of the colonial world, he is never sure whether or not he has crossed the frontier. Confronted with a world ruled by the settler, the native is always presumed guilty. But the native's guilt is never a guilt which he accepts; it is rather a kind of curse, a sort of sword of Damocles, for, in his innermost spirit, the native admits no accusation. He is overpowered but not tamed; he is treated as an inferior but he is not convinced of his inferiority. He is patiently waiting until the settler is off his guard to fly at him. The native's muscles are always tensed. You can't say that he is terrorised, or even apprehensive. He is in fact ready at a moment's notice to exchange the role of the quarry for that of the hunter. The native is an oppressed person whose permanent dream is to become the persecutor. The symbols of social order – the police, the bugle calls in the barracks, military parades and the waving flags – are at one and the same time inhibitory and stimulating: for they do not convey the message 'Don't dare to budge'; rather, they cry out 'Get ready to attack.' And, in fact, if the native had any tendency to fall asleep and to forget, the settler's hauteur and the settler's anxiety to test the strength of the colonial system would remind him at every turn that the great showdown cannot be put off indefinitely. That impulse to take the settler's place implies a tonicity of muscles the whole time; and in fact we know that in certain emotional conditions the presence of an obstacle accentuates the tendency toward motion.

The settler-native relationship is a mass relationship. The settler pits brute force against the weight of numbers. He is an exhibitionist. His preoccupation with security makes him remind the native out loud that there he alone is master. The settler keeps alive in the native an anger which he deprives of outlet; the native is trapped in the tight links of the chains of colonialism. But we have seen that inwardly the settler can only achieve a pseudo petrification. The native's muscular tension finds outlet regularly in bloodthirsty explosions – in tribal warfare, in feuds between septs, and in quarrels between individuals.

Where individuals are concerned, a positive negation of common sense is evident. While the settler or the policeman has the right the livelong day to strike the native, to insult him and to make him crawl to them, you will see the native reaching for his knife at the slightest hostile or aggressive glance cast on him by another native; for the last resort of the native is to defend his personality vis-à-vis his brother. Tribal feuds only serve to perpetuate old grudges buried deep in the memory. By throwing himself with all his force into the vendetta, the native tries to persuade himself that colonialism does not exist, that everything is going on as before, that history continues. Here on the level of communal organisations we clearly discern the well-known behaviour patterns of avoidance. It is as if plunging into a fraternal bloodbath allowed them to ignore the obstacle, and to put off till later the choice, nevertheless inevitable, which opens up the question of armed resistance to colonialism. Thus collective autodestruction in a very concrete form is one of the ways in which the native's muscular tension is set free. All these patterns of conduct are those of the death reflex when faced with danger, a suicidal behaviour which proves to the settler (whose existence and domination is by them all the more justified) that these men are not reasonable human beings. In the same way the native manages to by-pass the settler. A belief in fatality removes all blame from the oppressor; the cause of misfortunes and of poverty is attributed to God: He is Fate. In this way the individual accepts the disintegration ordained by God, bows down before the settler and his lot, and by a kind of interior restabilisation acquires a stony calm.

Meanwhile, however, life goes on, and the native will strengthen the inhibitions which contain his aggressiveness by drawing on the terrifying myths which are so frequently found in underdeveloped communities. There are maleficent spirits which intervene every time a step is taken in the wrong direction, leopard-men, serpent-men, six-legged dogs, zombies – a whole series of tiny animals or giants which create around the native a world of prohibitions, of barriers and of inhibitions far more terrifying than the world of the settler. This magical superstructure which permeates native society fulfils certain well-defined functions in the dynamism of the libido. One of the characteristics of underdeveloped societies is in fact that the libido is first and foremost the concern of a group, or of the family. The feature of communities whereby a man who dreams that he has sexual relations with a woman other than his own must confess it in public and pay a fine in kind or in working days to the injured husband or family is fully described by ethnologists. We may note in passing that this proves that the so-called prehistoric societies attach great importance to the unconscious.

The atmosphere of myth and magic frightens me and so takes on an undoubted reality. By terrifying me, it integrates me in the traditions and the history of my district or of my tribe, and at the same time it reassures me, it gives me a status, as it were an identification paper. In underdeveloped countries the occult sphere is a sphere belonging to the community which is entirely under magical jurisdiction. By entangling myself in this inextricable network where actions are repeated with crystalline inevitability, I find the everlasting world which belongs to me, and the perenniality which is thereby affirmed of the world belonging to us. Believe me, the zombies are more terrifying than the settlers; and in consequence the problem is no longer that of keeping oneself right with the colonial world and its barbed-wire entanglements, but of considering three times before urinating, spitting, or going out into the night.

The supernatural, magical powers reveal themselves as essentially personal; the settler's powers are infinitely shrunken, stamped with their alien origin. We no longer really need to fight against them since what counts is the frightening enemy created by myths. We perceive that all is settled by a permanent confrontation on the phantasmic plane.

It has always happened in the struggle for freedom that such a people, formerly lost in an imaginary maze, a prey to unspeakable terrors yet happy to lose themselves in a dreamlike torment, such a people becomes unhinged, reorganises itself, and in blood and tears gives birth to very real and immediate action. Feeding the *moudjahidines*,[5] posting sentinels, coming to the help of families which lack the bare necessities, or taking the place of a husband who has been killed or imprisoned: such are the concrete tasks to which the people is called during the struggle for freedom.

In the colonial world, the emotional sensitivity of the native is kept on the surface of his skin like an open sore which flinches from the caustic agent; and the psyche shrinks back, obliterates itself and finds outlet in muscular demonstrations which have caused certain very wise men to say that the native is a hysterical type. This sensitive emotionalism, watched by invisible keepers who are however in unbroken contact with the core of the personality, will find its fulfilment through eroticism in the driving forces behind the dissolution of the crisis.

On another level we see the native's emotional sensibility exhausting itself in dances which are more or less ecstatic. This is why any study of the colonial world should take into consideration the phenomena of the dance and of possession. The native's relaxation takes precisely the form of a muscular orgy in which the most acute aggressivity and the most impelling violence

When the nationalist political leaders *say* something, they make quite clear that they do not really *think* it.

This characteristic on the part of the nationalist political parties should be interpreted in the light both of the make-up of their leaders and the nature of their followings. The rank-and-file of a nationalist party is urban. The workers, primary schoolteachers, artisans, and small shopkeepers who have begun to profit – at a discount, to be sure – from the colonial setup, have special interests at heart. What this sort of following demands is the betterment of their particular lot: increased salaries, for example. The dialogue between these political parties and colonialism is never broken off. Improvements are discussed, such as full electoral representation, the liberty of the press, and liberty of association. Reforms are debated. Thus it need not astonish anyone to notice that a large number of natives are militant members of the branches of political parties which stem from the mother country. These natives fight under an abstract watchword: 'Government by the workers', and they forget that in their country it should be *nationalist* watchwords which are first in the field. The native intellectual has clothed his aggressiveness in his barely veiled desire to assimilate himself to the colonial world. He has used his aggressiveness to serve his own individual interests.

Thus there is very easily brought into being a kind of class of affranchised slaves, or slaves who are individually free. What the intellectual demands is the right to multiply the emancipated, and the opportunity to organise a genuine class of emancipated citizens. On the other hand, the mass of the people has no intention of standing by and watching individuals increase their chances of success. What they demand is not the settler's position of status, but the settler's place. The immense majority of natives want the settler's farm. For them, there is no question of entering into competition with the settler. They want to take his place.

The peasantry is systematically disregarded for the most part by the propaganda put out by the nationalist parties. And it is clear that in the colonial countries the peasants alone are revolutionary, for they have nothing to lose and everything to gain. The starving peasant, outside the class system, is the first among the exploited to discover that only violence pays. For him there is no compromise, no possible coming to terms; colonisation and decolonisation are simply a question of relative strength. The exploited man sees that his liberation implies the use of all means, and that of force first and foremost. When in 1956, after the capitulation of Monsieur Guy Mollet to the settlers in Algeria, the Front de Libération Nationale, in a famous leaflet, stated that colonialism only loosens its hold when the knife is at its throat, no Algerian really found these terms too violent. The leaflet only expressed what every Algerian felt at heart: colonialism is not a thinking machine, nor a body endowed with reasoning faculties. It is violence in its natural state, and it will only yield when confronted with greater violence.

At the decisive moment, the colonialist bourgeoisie, which up till then has remained inactive, comes into the field. It introduces that new idea which is in proper parlance a creation of the colonial situation: non-violence. In its simplest form this non-violence signifies to the intellectual and economic elite of the colonised country that the bourgeoisie has the same interests as they and that it is therefore urgent and indispensable to come to terms for the public good. Non-violence is an attempt to settle the colonial problem around a green baize table, before any regrettable act has been performed or irreparable gesture made, before any blood has been shed. But if the masses, without, waiting for the chairs to be arranged around the baize table, listen to their own voice and begin committing outrages and setting fire to buildings, the elite and the nationalist bourgeois parties will be seen rushing to the colonialists to exclaim, 'This is very serious! We do not know how it will end; we must find a solution – some sort of compromise.'

This idea of compromise is very important in the phenomenon of decolonisation, for it is very far from being a simple one. Compromise involves the colonial system and the young nationalist bourgeoisie at one and the same time. The partisans of the colonial system discover that the masses may destroy everything. Blown-up bridges, ravaged farms, repressions, and fighting harshly disrupt the economy. Compromise is equally attractive to the nationalist bourgeoisie, who since they are not clearly aware of the possible consequences of the rising storm, are genuinely afraid of being swept away by this huge hurricane and never stop saying to the settlers: 'We are still capable of stopping the slaughter; the masses still have confidence in us; act quickly if you do not want to put everything in jeopardy.' One step more, and the leader of the nationalist party keeps his distance with regard to that violence. He loudly proclaims that he has nothing to do with these Mau-Mau, these terrorists, these throat-slitters. At best, he shuts himself off in a no man's land between the terrorists and the settlers and willingly offers his services as go-between; that is to say, that as the settlers cannot discuss terms with these Mau-Mau, he himself will be quite willing to begin negotiations. Thus it is that the rearguard of the national struggle, that very party of people who have never ceased to be on the other side in the fight, find themselves somersaulted into the van of negotiations and compromise – precisely because that party has taken very good care never to break contact with colonialism.

Before negotiations have been set afoot, the majority of nationalist parties confine themselves for the most part to explaining and excusing this 'savagery'. They do not assert that the people have to use physical force, and it sometimes even happens that they go so far as to condemn, in private, the spectacular deeds which are declared to be hateful by the press and public opinion in the mother country. The legitimate excuse for this ultra-conservative policy is the desire to see things in an objective light; but this traditional attitude of the native intellectual and of the leaders of the nationalist parties is not, in reality, in the least objective. For in fact they are not at all convinced that this impatient violence of the masses is the most efficient means of defending their own interests. Moreover, there are some individuals who are convinced of the ineffectiveness of violent methods; for them, there is no doubt about it, every attempt to break colonial oppression by force is a hopeless effort, an attempt at suicide, because in the innermost recesses of their brains the settler's tanks and airplanes occupy a huge place. When they are told 'Action must be taken,' they see bombs raining down on them, armoured cars coming at them on every path, machine-gunning and police action ... and they sit quiet. They are beaten from the start. There is no need to demonstrate their incapacity to triumph by violent methods; they take it for granted in their everyday life and in their political manoeuvres. They have remained in the same childish position as Engels took up in his famous polemic with that monument of puerility, Monsieur Duhring:

> In the same way that Robinson [Crusoe] was able to obtain a sword, we can just as well suppose that [Man] Friday might appear one fine morning with a loaded revolver in his hand, and from then on the whole relationship of violence is reversed: Man Friday gives the orders

and Crusoe is obliged to work ... Thus, the revolver triumphs over the sword, and even the most childish believer in axioms will doubtless form the conclusion that violence is not a simple act of will, but needs for its realisation certain very concrete preliminary conditions, and in particular the implements of violence; and the more highly developed of these implements will carry the day against primitive ones. Moreover, the very fact of the ability to produce such weapons signifies that the producer of highly developed weapons, in everyday speech the arms manufacturer, triumphs over the producer of primitive weapons. To put it briefly, the triumph of violence depends upon the production of armaments, and this in its turn depends on production in general, and thus ... on economic strength, on the economy of the State, and in the last resort on the material means which that violence commands.[6]

In fact, the leaders of reform have nothing else to say than: 'With what are you going to fight the settlers? With your knives? Your shotguns?'

It is true that weapons are important when violence comes into play, since all finally depends on the distribution of these implements. But it so happens that the liberation of colonial countries throws new light on the subject. For example, we have seen that during the Spanish campaign, which was a very genuine colonial war, Napoleon, in spite of an army which reached in the offensives of the spring of 1810 the huge figure of 400 000 men, was forced to retreat. Yet the French army made the whole of Europe tremble by its weapons of war, by the bravery of its soldiers, and by the military genius of its leaders. Face to face with the enormous potentials of the Napoleonic troops, the Spaniards, inspired by an unshakeable national ardour, rediscovered the famous methods of guerilla warfare which, twenty-five years before, the American militia had tried out on the English forces. But the native's guerilla warfare would be of no value as opposed to other means of violence if it did not form a new element in the worldwide process of competition between trusts and monopolies.

In the early days of colonisation, a single column could occupy immense stretches of country: the Congo, Nigeria, the Ivory Coast, and so on. Today, however, the colonised countries' national struggle crops up in a completely new international situation. Capitalism, in its early days, saw in the colonies a

former party and rejected by its leaders, these undesirable firebrands will be stranded in county districts. Then it is that they will realise bewilderedly that the peasant masses catch on to what they have to say immediately, and without delay ask them the question to which they have not yet prepared the answer: 'When do we start?'

This meeting of revolutionaries coming from the towns and country dwellers will be dealt with later on. For the moment we must go back to the political parties, in order to show the nature of their action, which is all the same progressive. In their speeches the political leaders give a name to the nation. In this way the native's demands are given shape.

There is however no definite subject matter and no political or social programme. There is a vague outline or skeleton, which is nevertheless national in form, what we describe as 'minimum requirements'. The politicians who make speeches and who write in the nationalist newspapers make the people dream dreams. They avoid the actual overthrowing of the state, but in fact they introduce into their readers' or hearers' consciousness the terrible ferment of subversion. The national or tribal language is often used. Here, once again, dreams are encouraged, and the imagination is let loose outside the bounds of the colonial order; and sometimes these politicians speak of 'We Negroes, we Arabs,' and these terms which are so profoundly ambivalent take on during the colonial epoch a sacramental signification. The nationalist politicians are playing with fire: for, as an African leader recently warned a group of young intellectuals, 'Think well before you speak to the masses, for they flare up quickly.' This is one of the terrible tricks that destiny plays in the colonies.

When a political leader calls a mass meeting, we may say that there is blood in the air. Yet the same leader very often is above all anxious to 'make a show' of force, so that in fact he need not use it. But the agitation which ensues, the coming and going, the listening to speeches, seeing the people assembled in one place, with the police all around, the military demonstrations, arrests, and the deportation of the leaders – all this hubbub makes the people think that the moment has come for them to take action. In these times of instability the political parties multiply their appeals to the left for calm, while on their right they scan the horizon, trying to make out the liberal intentions of colonialism.

In the same way the people make use of certain episodes in the life of the community in order to hold themselves ready and to keep alive their revolutionary zeal. For example, the gangster who holds up the police set on to track him down for days on end, or who dies in single combat after having killed four or five policemen, or who commits suicide in order not to give away his accomplices – these types light the way for the people, form the blueprints for action and become heroes. Obviously, it's a waste of breath to say that such-and-such a hero is a thief, a scoundrel, or a reprobate. If the act for which he is prosecuted by the colonial authorities is an act exclusively directed against a colonialist person or colonialist property, the demarcation line is definite and manifest. The process of identification is automatic.

We must also notice in this ripening process the role played by the history of the resistance at the time of the conquest. The great figures of the colonised people are always those who led the national resistance to invasion. Behanzin, Soundiata, Samory, Abdel Kader – all spring again to life with peculiar intensity in the period which comes directly before action. This is the proof that the people are getting ready to begin to go forward again, to put an end to the static period begun by colonisation, and to make history.

The uprising of the new nation and the breaking down of colonial structures are the result of one of two causes: either of a violent struggle of the people in their own right, or of action on the part of surrounding colonised peoples which acts as a brake on the colonial regime in question.

A colonised people is not alone. In spite of all that colonialism can do, its frontiers remain open to new ideas and echoes from the world outside. It discovers that violence is in the atmosphere, that it here and there bursts out, and here and there sweeps away the colonial regime – that same violence which fulfils for the native a role that is not simply informatory, but also operative. The great victory of the Vietnamese people at Dien Bien Phu is no longer, strictly speaking, a Vietnamese victory. Since July 1954, the question which the colonised peoples have asked themselves has been, 'What must be done to bring about another Dien Bien Phu? How can we manage it?' Not a single colonised individual could ever again doubt the possibility of a Dien Bien Phu; the only problem was how best to use the forces at their disposal, how to organise them, and when to bring them into action. This encompassing violence does not work upon the colonised people only; it modifies the attitude of the colonialists who become aware of manifold Dien Bien Phus. This is why a veritable panic takes hold of the colonialist governments in turn. Their purpose is to capture the vanguard, to turn the movement of liberation toward the right, and to disarm the people: quick, quick, let's decolonise. Decolonise the Congo before it turns into another Algeria. Vote the constitutional framework for all Africa, create the French *Communauté*, renovate that same *Communauté*, but for God's sake let's decolonise quick … And they decolonise at such a rate that they impose independence on Houphouët-Boigny. To the strategy of Dien Bien Phu, defined by the colonised peoples, the colonialist replies by the strategy of encirclement – based on the respect of the sovereignty of states.

But let us return to that atmosphere of violence, that violence which is just under the skin. We have seen that in its process toward maturity many leads are attached to it, to control it and show it the way out. Yet in spite of the metamorphoses which the colonial regime imposes upon it in the way of tribal or regional quarrels, that violence makes its way forward, and the native identifies his enemy and recognises all his misfortunes, throwing all the exacerbated might of his hate and anger into this new channel. But how do we pass from the atmosphere of violence to violence in action? What makes the lid blow off? There is first of all the fact that this development does not leave the settler's blissful existence intact. The settler who 'understands' the natives is made aware by several straws in the wind showing that something is afoot. 'Good' natives become scarce; silence falls when the oppressor approaches; sometimes looks are black, and attitudes and remarks openly aggressive. The nationalist parties are astir, they hold a great many meetings, the police are increased and reinforcements of soldiers are brought in. The settlers, above all the farmers isolated on their land, are the first to become alarmed. They call for energetic measures.

The authorities do in fact take some spectacular measures. They arrest one or two leaders, they organise military parades and manoeuvres, and air force displays. But the demonstrations and warlike exercises, the smell of gunpowder which now fills the atmosphere, these things do not make the people draw back. Those bayonets and cannonades only serve to reinforce their aggressiveness. The atmosphere becomes dramatic, and everyone wishes to show that he is ready for anything. And it is in these circumstances that the guns go off by themselves, for nerves are jangled, fear reigns and everyone is trigger-happy. A single commonplace incident is enough to start the machine-gunning: Sétif in Algeria, the Central Quarries in Morocco, Moramanga in Madagascar.

The repressions, far from calling a halt to the forward rush of national consciousness, urge it on. Mass slaughter in the colonies at a certain stage of the embryonic development of consciousness increases that consciousness, for the hecatombs are an indication that between oppressors and oppressed everything can be solved by force. It must be remarked here that the political parties have not called for armed insurrection, and have made no preparations for such an insurrection. All these repressive measures, all those actions which are a result of fear are not within the leaders' intentions: they are overtaken by events. At this moment, then, colonialism may decide to arrest the nationalist leaders. But today the governments of colonised countries know very well that it is extremely dangerous to deprive the masses of their leaders; for then the people, unbridled, fling themselves into *jacqueries*, mutinies, and 'brutish murders'. The masses give free rein to their 'bloodthirsty instincts' and force colonialism to free their leaders, to whom falls the difficult task of bringing them back to order. The colonised people, who have spontaneously brought their violence to the colossal task of destroying the colonial system, will very soon find themselves with the barren, inert slogan 'Release X or Y'.[7] Then colonialism will release these men, and hold discussions with them. The time for dancing in the streets has come.

In certain circumstances, the party political machine may remain intact. But as a result of the colonialist repression and of the spontaneous reaction of the people the parties find themselves out-distanced by their militants.

The violence of the masses is vigorously pitted against the military forces of the occupying power, and the situation deteriorates and comes to a head. Those leaders who are free remain, therefore, on the touchline. They have suddenly become useless, with their bureaucracy and their reasonable demands; yet we see them, far removed from events, attempting the crowning imposture – that of 'speaking in the name of the silenced nation.' As a general rule, colonialism welcomes this godsend with open arms, transforms these 'blind mouths' into spokesmen, and in two minutes endows them with independence, on condition that they restore order.

So we see that all parties are aware of the power of such violence and that the question is not always to reply to it by a greater violence, but rather to see how to relax the tension.

the local weaknesses of its system. Thus the colonised peoples realise that neither clan remains outside local incidents. They no longer limit themselves to regional horizons, for they have caught on to the fact that they live in an atmosphere of international stress.

When every three months or so we hear that the Sixth or Seventh Fleet is moving toward such-and-such a coast; when Khrushchev threatens to come to Castro's aid with rockets; when Kennedy decides upon some desperate solution for the Laos question, the colonised person or the newly independent native has the impression that whether he wills it or not he is being carried away in a kind of frantic cavalcade. In fact, he is marching in it already. Let us take, for example, the case of the governments of recently liberated countries. The men at the head of affairs spend two-thirds of their time in watching the approaches and trying to anticipate the dangers which threaten them, and the remaining one-third of their time in working for their country. At the same time, they search for allies. Obedient to the same dialectic, the national parties of opposition leave the paths of parliamentary behaviour. They also look for allies to support them in their ruthless ventures into sedition. The atmosphere of violence, after having coloured all the colonial phase, continues to dominate national life, for as we have already said, the Third World is not cut off from the rest. Quite the contrary, it is at the middle of the whirlpool. This is why the statesmen of underdeveloped countries keep up indefinitely the tone of aggressiveness and exasperation in their public speeches which in the normal way ought to have disappeared. Herein, also, may be found the reasons for that lack of politeness so often spoken of in connection with newly established rulers. But what is less visible is the extreme courtesy of these same rulers in their contacts with their brothers or their comrades. Discourtesy is first and foremost a manner to be used in dealings with the others, with the former colonists who come to observe and to investigate. The 'ex-native' too often gets the impression that these reports are already written. The photos which illustrate the article are simply a proof that one knows what one is talking about, and that one has visited the country. The report intends to verify the evidence: everything's going badly out there since we left. Frequently reporters complain of being badly received, of being forced to work under bad conditions and of being fenced round by indifference or hostility: all this is quite normal. The nationalist leaders know that international opinion is formed solely by the Western press. Now, when a journalist from the West asks us questions, it is seldom in order to help us. In the Algerian war, for example, even the most liberal of the French reporters never ceased to use ambiguous terms in describing our struggle. When we reproached them for this, they replied in all good faith that they were being objective. For the native, objectivity is always directed against him. We may in the same way come to understand the new tone which swamped international diplomacy at the United Nations General Assembly in September, 1960. The representatives of the colonial countries were aggressive and violent, and carried things to extremes, but the colonial peoples did not find that they exaggerated. The radicalism of the African spokesmen brought the abscess to a head and showed up the inadmissible nature of the veto and of the dialogue between the great powers, and above all the tiny role reserved for the Third World.

Diplomacy, as inaugurated by the newly independent peoples, is no longer an affair of nuances, of implications, and of hypnotic passes. For the nation's spokesmen are responsible at one and the same time for safeguarding the unity of the nation, the progress of the masses toward a state of well-being and the right of all peoples to bread and liberty. Thus it is a diplomacy which never stops moving, a diplomacy which leaps ahead, in strange contrast to the motionless, petrified world of colonisation. And when Mr Khrushchev brandishes his shoe at the United Nations, or thumps the table with it, there's not a single ex-native, nor any representative of an underdeveloped country, who laughs. For what Mr Khrushchev shows the colonised countries which are looking on is that he, the *moujik*, who moreover is the possessor of space rockets, treats these miserable capitalists in the way that they deserve. In the same way, Castro sitting in military uniform in the United Nations Organisation does not scandalise the underdeveloped countries. What Castro demonstrates is the consciousness he has of the continuing existence of the rule of violence. The astonishing thing is that he did not come into the UNO with a machinegun; but if he had, would anyone have minded? All the *jacqueries* and desperate deeds, all those bands armed with cutlasses or axes find their nationality in the implacable struggle which opposes socialism and capitalism.

In 1945, the 45 000 dead at Sétif could pass unnoticed; in 1947, the 90 000 dead in Madagascar could be the subject of a simple paragraph in the papers; in 1952, the 200 000 victims of the repression in Kenya could meet with relative indifference. This was because the international contradictions were not sufficiently distinct. Already the Korean and Indo-Chinese wars had begun a new phase. But it is above all Budapest and Suez which constitute the decisive moments of this confrontation.

Strengthened by the unconditional support of the socialist countries, the colonised peoples fling themselves with whatever arms they have against the impregnable citadel of colonialism. If this citadel is invulnerable to knives and naked fists, it is no longer so when we decide to take into account the context of the Cold War.

In this fresh juncture, the Americans take their role of patron of international capitalism very seriously. Early on, they advise the European countries to decolonise in a friendly fashion. Later on, they do not hesitate to proclaim first the respect for and then the support of the principle of 'Africa for the Africans'. The United States is not afraid today of stating officially that they are the defenders of the right of all peoples to self-determination. Mr Mennen Williams' last journey is only the illustration of the consciousness which the Americans have that the Third World ought not to be sacrificed. From then on we understand why the violence of the native is only hopeless if we compare it in the abstract to the military machine of the oppressor. On the other hand, if we situate that violence in the dynamics of the international situation, we see at once that it constitutes a terrible menace for the oppressor. Persistent *jacqueries* and Mau-Mau disturbance unbalance the colony's economic life but do not endanger the mother country. What is more important in the eyes of imperialism is the opportunity for socialist propaganda to infiltrate among the masses and to contaminate them. This is already a serious danger in the Cold War; but what would happen to that colony in case of real war, riddled as it is by murderous guerillas?

Thus capitalism realises that its military strategy has everything to lose by the outbreak of nationalist wars.

Again, within the framework of peaceful co-existence, all colonies are destined to disappear, and in the long run neutralism is destined to be respected by capitalism. What must at all costs be avoided is strategic insecurity: the breakthrough of enemy doctrine into the masses and the deeprooted hatred of millions of men. The colonised peoples are very well aware of these imperatives which rule international political life; for this reason even those who thunder denunciations of violence take their decisions and act in terms of this universal violence. Today, peaceful coexistence between the two blocs provokes and feeds violence in the colonial countries. Tomorrow, perhaps we shall see the shifting of that violence after the complete liberation of the colonial territories. Perhaps we will see the question of minorities cropping up. Already certain minority groups do not hesitate to preach violent methods for resolving their problems and it is not by chance (so the story runs) that in consequence Negro extremists in the United States organise a militia and arm themselves. It is not by chance, either, that in the so-called free world there exist committees for the defence of Jewish minorities in the USSR, nor an accident if General de Gaulle in one of his orations sheds tears over the millions of Moslems oppressed by Communist dictatorship. Both capitalism and imperialism are convinced that the struggle against racialism and the movements toward national freedom are purely and simply directed by remote control, fomented from outside. So they decide to use that very efficacious tactic, the Radio Free Europe station, voice of the committee for the aid of overruled minorities ... They practise anti-colonialism, as did the French colonels in Algeria when they carried on subversive warfare with the SAS[8] or the psychological services. They 'use the people against the people.' We have seen with what results.

This atmosphere of violence and menaces, these rockets brandished by both sides, do not frighten nor deflect the colonised peoples. We have seen that all their recent history has prepared them to understand and grasp the situation. Between the violence of the colonies and that peaceful violence that the world is steeped in, there is a kind of complicit agreement, a sort of homogeneity. The colonised peoples are well adapted to this atmosphere; for once, they are up to date. Sometimes people wonder that the native, rather than give his wife a dress, buys instead a transistor radio. There is no reason to be astonished. The natives are convinced that their fate is in the balance, here and now. They live in the atmosphere of doomsday, and they consider that nothing ought to be let pass unnoticed. That is why they understand very well Phouma and Phoumi, Lumumba and Tshombe, Ahidjo and Moumie, Kenyatta, and the men who are pushed forward regularly to replace him. They understand all these figures very well, for they can unmask the forces working behind them. The native and the underdeveloped man are today political animals in the most universal sense of the word.

THE MOTHER:

And I had dreamed of a son to close his mother's eyes.

THE REBEL:

But I chose to open my son's eyes upon another sun.

THE MOTHER:

O my son, son of evil and unlucky death –

THE REBEL:

Mother of living and splendid death,

THE MOTHER:

Because he has hated too much,

THE REBEL:

Because he has too much loved.

THE MOTHER:

Spare me, I am choking in your bonds. I bleed from your wounds.

THE REBEL:

And the world does not spare me ... There is not anywhere in the world a poor creature who's been lynched or tortured in whom I am not murdered and humiliated ...

THE MOTHER:

God of Heaven, deliver him!

THE REBEL:

My heart, thou wilt not deliver me from all that I remember ...

It was an evening in November ...

And suddenly shouts lit up the silence;

We had attacked, we the slaves; we, the dung underfoot, we the animals with patient hooves,

We were running like madmen; shots rang out ... We were striking. Blood and sweat cooled and refreshed us. We were striking where the shouts came from, and the shouts became more strident and a great clamour rose from the east: it was the outhouses burning and the flames flickered sweetly on our cheeks.

Then was the assault made on the master's house.

They were firing from the windows.

We broke in the doors.

The master's room was wide open. The master's room was brilliantly lighted, and the master was there, very calm ... and our people stopped dead ... it was the master ... I went in. 'It's you,' he said, very calm.

It was I, even I, and I told him so, the good slave, the faithful slave, the slave of slaves, and suddenly his eyes were like two cockroaches, frightened in the rainy season ... I struck, and the blood spurted; that is the only baptism that I remember today.[11]

It is understandable that in this atmosphere, daily life becomes quite simply impossible. You can no longer be a fellah, a pimp, or an alcoholic as before. The violence of the colonial regime and the counter-violence of the native balance each other and respond to each other in an extraordinary reciprocal homogeneity. This reign of violence will be the more terrible in proportion to the size of the implantation from the mother country. The development of violence among the colonised people will be proportionate to the violence exercised by the threatened colonial regime. In the first phase of this insurrectional period, the home governments are the slaves of the settlers, and these settlers seek to intimidate the natives and their home governments at one and the same time. They use the same methods against both of them. The assassination of the Mayor of Evian, in its method and motivation, is identifiable with the assassination of Ali Boumendjel. For the settlers, the alternative is not between *Algérie algérienne* and *Algérie française* but between an independent Algeria and a colonial Algeria, and anything else is mere talk or attempts at treason. The settler's logic is implacable and one is only staggered by the counter-logic visible in the behaviour of the native insofar as one has not clearly understood beforehand the mechanisms of the settler's ideas. From the moment that the native has chosen the methods of counter-violence, police reprisals automatically call forth reprisals on the side of the nationalists. However, the results are not equivalent, for machine-gunning from airplanes and bombardments from the fleet go far beyond in horror and magnitude any answer the natives can make. This recurring terror de-mystifies once and for all the most estranged members of the colonised race. They find out on the spot that all the piles of speeches on the equality of human beings do not hide the commonplace fact that the seven Frenchmen killed or wounded at the Col de Sakamody kindles the indignation of all civilised consciences, whereas the sack of the douars[12] of Guergour and of the dechras of Djerah and the massacre destiny, or the fate of their country in the hands of a living god. Yesterday they were completely irresponsible; today they mean to understand everything and make all decisions. Illuminated by violence, the consciousness of the people rebels against any pacification. From now on the demagogues, the opportunists, and the magicians have a difficult task. The action which has thrown them into a hand-to-hand struggle confers upon the masses a voracious taste for the concrete. The attempt at mystification becomes, in the long run, practically impossible.

Violence in the International Context

We have pointed out many times in the preceding pages that in underdeveloped regions the political leader is forever calling on his people to fight: to fight against colonialism, to fight against poverty and underdevelopment, and to fight against sterile traditions. The vocabulary which he uses in his appeals is that of a chief of staff: 'mass mobilisation'; 'agricultural front'; 'fight against illiteracy'; 'defeats we have undergone'; 'victories won'. The young independent nation evolves during the first years in an atmosphere of the battlefield, for the political leader of an underdeveloped country looks fearfully at the huge distance his country will have to cover. He calls to the people and says to them: 'Let us gird up our loins and set to work,' and the country, possessed by a kind of creative madness, throws itself into a gigantic and disproportionate effort. The programme consists not only of climbing out of the morass but also of catching up with the other nations using the only means at hand. They reason that if the European nations have reached that stage of development, it is on account of their efforts: 'Let us therefore,' they seem to say, 'prove to ourselves and to the whole world that we are capable of the same achievements.' This manner of setting out the problem of the evolution of underdeveloped countries seems to us to be neither correct nor reasonable.

The European states achieved national unity at a moment when the national middle classes had concentrated most of the wealth in their hands. Shopkeepers and artisans, clerks and bankers monopolised finance, trade, and science in the national framework. The middle class was the most dynamic and prosperous of all classes. Its coming to power enabled it to undertake certain very important speculations: industrialisation, the development of communications, and soon the search for outlets overseas.

In Europe, apart from certain slight differences (England, for example, was some way ahead) the various states were at a more or less uniform stage economically when they achieved national unity. There was no nation which by reason of the character of its development and evolution caused affront to the others.

Today, national independence and the growth of national feeling in underdeveloped regions take on totally new aspects. In these regions, with the exception of certain spectacular advances, the different countries show the same absence of infrastructure. The mass of the people struggle against the same poverty, flounder about making the same gestures and with their shrunken bellies outline what has been called the geography of hunger. It is an underdeveloped world, a world inhuman in its poverty; but also it is a world without doctors, without engineers, and without administrators. Confronting this world, the European nations sprawl, ostentatiously opulent. This European opulence is literally scandalous, for it has been founded on slavery, it has been nourished with the blood of slaves and it comes directly from the soil and from the subsoil of that underdeveloped world. The well-being and the progress of Europe have been built up with the sweat and the dead bodies of Negroes, Arabs, Indians, and the yellow races. We have decided not to overlook this any longer. When a colonialist country, embarrassed by the claims for independence made by a colony, proclaims to the nationalist leaders: 'If you wish for independence, take it, and go back to the Middle Ages,' the newly independent people tend to acquiesce and to accept the challenge; in fact you may see colonialism withdrawing its capital and its technicians and setting up around the young State the apparatus of economic pressure.[15] The apotheosis of independence is transformed into the curse of independence, and the colonial power through its immense resources of coercion condemns the young nation to regression. In plain words, the colonial power says: 'Since you want independence, take it and starve.' The nationalist leaders have no other choice but to turn to their people and ask from them a gigantic effort. A regime of austerity is imposed on these starving men; a disproportionate amount of work is required from their atrophied muscles. An autarkic regime is set up and each state, with the miserable resources it has in hand, tries to find an answer to the nation's great hunger and poverty. We see the mobilisation of a people which toils to exhaustion in front of a suspicious and bloated Europe.

Other countries of the Third World refuse to undergo this ordeal and agree to get over it by accepting the conditions of the former guardian power. These countries use their strategic position – a position which accords them privileged treatment in the struggle between the two blocs – to conclude treaties and give undertakings. The former dominated country becomes an economically dependent country. The ex-colonial power, which has kept intact and sometimes even reinforced its colonialist trade channels, agrees to provision the budget of the independent nation by small injections. Thus we see that the accession to independence of the colonial countries places an important question before the world, for the national liberation of colonised countries unveils their true economic state and makes it seem even more unendurable. The fundamental duel which seemed to be that between colonialism and anticolonialism, and indeed between capitalism and socialism, is already losing some of its importance. What counts today, the question which is looming on the horizon, is the need for a redistribution of wealth. Humanity must reply to this question, or be shaken to pieces by it.

It might have been generally thought that the time had come for the world, and particularly for the Third World, to choose between the capitalist and socialist systems. The underdeveloped countries, which have used the fierce competition which exists between the two systems in order to assure the triumph of their struggle for national liberation, should however refuse to become a factor in that competition. The Third World ought not to be content to define itself in the terms of values which have preceded it. On the contrary, the underdeveloped countries ought to do their utmost to find their own particular values and methods and a style which shall be peculiar to them. The concrete problem we find ourselves up against is not that of a choice, cost what it may, between socialism and capitalism as they have been defined by men of other continents and of other ages. Of course we know that the capitalist regime, in so far as it is a way of life, cannot leave us free to perform our work at home, nor our duty in the world. Capitalist exploitation and cartels and monopolies are the enemies of underdeveloped countries. On the other hand the choice of a socialist regime, a regime which is completely orientated toward the people as a whole and based on the principle that man is the most precious of all possessions, will allow us to go forward more quickly and more harmoniously, and thus make impossible that caricature of society where all economic and political power is held in the hands of a few who regard the nation as a whole with scorn and contempt.

But in order that this regime may work to good effect so that we can in every instance respect those principles which were our inspiration, we need something more than human output. Certain underdeveloped countries expend a huge amount of energy in this way. Men and women, young and old undertake enthusiastically what is in fact forced labour, and proclaim themselves the slaves of the nation. The gift of oneself, and the contempt for every preoccupation which is not in the common interest, bring into being a national morale which comforts the heart of man, gives him fresh confidence in the destiny of mankind and disarms the most reserved observers. But we cannot believe that such an effort can be kept up at the same frenzied pace for very long. These young countries have agreed to take up the challenge after the unconditional withdrawal of the ex-colonial countries. The country finds itself in the hands of new managers; but the fact is that everything needs to be reformed and everything thought out anew. In reality the colonial system was concerned with certain forms of wealth and certain resources only – precisely those which provisioned her own industries. Up to the present no serious effort had been made to estimate the riches of the soil or of mineral resources. Thus the young independent nation sees itself obliged to use the economic channels created by the colonial regime. It can, obviously, export to other countries and other currency areas, but the basis of its exports is not fundamentally modified. The colonial regime has carved out certain channels and they must be maintained or catastrophe will threaten. Perhaps it is necessary to begin everything all over again: to change the nature of the country's exports, and not simply their destination, to re-examine the soil and mineral resources, the rivers, and – why not? – the sun's productivity. Now, in order to do all this other things are needed over and above human output – capital of all kinds, technicians, engineers, skilled mechanics, and so on. Let's be frank: we do not believe that the colossal effort which the underdeveloped peoples are called upon to make by their leaders will give the desired results. If conditions of work are not modified, centuries will be needed to humanise this world which has been forced down to animal level by imperial powers.[16]

The truth is that we ought not to accept these conditions. We should flatly refuse the situation to which the Western countries wish to condemn us.

Colonialism and imperialism have not paid their score when they withdraw their flags and their police forces from our territories. For centuries the capitalists have behaved in the underdeveloped world like nothing more than war criminals. Deportations, massacres, forced labour, and slavery have been the main methods used by capitalism to increase its wealth, its gold or diamond reserves, and to establish its power. Not long ago Nazism transformed the whole of Europe into a veritable colony. The governments of the various European nations called for reparations and demanded the restitution in kind and money of the wealth which had been stolen from them: cultural treasures, pictures, sculptures, and stained glass have been given back to their owners. There was only one slogan in the mouths of Europeans on the morrow of the 1945 V-day: 'Germany must pay.' Herr Adenauer, it must be said, at the opening of the Eichmann trial, and in the name of the German people, asked once more for forgiveness from the Jewish people. Herr Adenauer has renewed the promise of his people to go on paying to the state of Israel the enormous sums which are supposed to be compensation for the crimes of the Nazis.[17]

In the same way we may say that the imperialist states would make a great mistake and commit an unspeakable injustice if they contented themselves with withdrawing from our soil the military cohorts, and the administrative and managerial services whose function it was to discover the wealth of the country, to extract it and to send it off to the mother countries. We are not blinded by the moral reparation of national independence; nor are we fed by it. The wealth of the imperial countries is our wealth too. On the universal plane this affirmation, you may be sure, should on no account be taken to signify that we feel ourselves affected by the creations of Western arts or techniques. For in a very concrete way Europe has stuffed herself inordinately with the gold and raw materials of the colonial countries: Latin America, China, and Africa. From all these continents, under whose eyes Europe today raises up her tower of opulence, there has flowed out for centuries toward that same Europe diamonds and oil, silk and cotton, wood and exotic products. Europe is literally the creation of the Third World. The wealth which smothers her is that which was stolen from the underdeveloped peoples. The ports of Holland, the docks of Bordeaux and Liverpool were specialised in the Negro slave trade, and owe their renown to millions of deported slaves. So when we hear the head of a European state declare with his hand on his heart that he must come to the aid of the poor underdeveloped peoples, we do not tremble with gratitude. Quite the contrary; we say to ourselves: 'It's a just reparation which will be paid to us.' Nor will we acquiesce in the help for underdeveloped countries being a programme of 'sisters of charity'. This help should be the ratification of a double realisation: the realisation by the colonised peoples that it is their due, and the realisation by the capitalist powers that in fact they must pay.[18] For if, through lack of intelligence (we won't speak of lack of gratitude) the capitalist countries refuse to pay, then the relentless dialectic of their own system will smother them. It is fact that young nations do not attract much private capital. There are many reasons which explain and render legitimate this reserve on the part of the monopolies. As soon as the capitalists know – and of course they are the first to know – that their government is getting ready to decolonise, they hasten to withdraw all their capital from the colony in question. The spectacular flight of capital is one of the most constant phenomena of decolonisation.

Private companies, when asked to invest in independent countries, lay down conditions which are shown in practice to be inacceptable or unrealisable. Faithful to the principle of immediate returns which is theirs as soon as they go 'overseas', the capitalists are very chary concerning all long-term investments. They are unamenable and often openly hostile to the prospective programmes of planning laid down by the young teams which form the new government. At a pinch they willingly agree to lend money to the young states, but only on condition that this money is used to buy manufactured products and machines: in other words, that it serves to keep the factories in the mother country going.

In fact the cautiousness of the Western financial groups may be explained by their fear of taking any risk. They also demand political stability and a calm social climate which are impossible to obtain when account is taken of the appalling state of the population as a whole immediately after independence. Therefore, vainly looking for some guarantee which the former colony cannot give, they insist on garrisons being maintained or the inclusion of the young state in military or economic pacts. The private companies put pressure on their own governments to at least set up military bases in these countries for the purpose of assuring the protection of their interests. In the last resort these companies ask their government to guarantee the investments which they decide to make in such-and-such an underdeveloped region.

It happens that few countries fulfil the conditions demanded by the trusts and monopolies. Thus capital, failing to find a safe outlet, remains blocked in Europe, and is frozen. It is all the more frozen because the capitalists refuse to invest in their own countries. The returns in this case are in fact negligible and treasury control is the despair of even the boldest spirits.

In the long run the situation is catastrophic. Capital no longer circulates, or else its circulation is considerably diminished. In spite of the huge sums swallowed up by military budgets, international capitalism is in desperate straits.

But another danger threatens it as well. Insofar as the Third World is in fact abandoned and condemned to regression or at least to stagnation by the selfishness and wickedness of Western nations, the underdeveloped peoples will decide to continue their evolution inside a collective autarky. Thus the Western industries will quickly be deprived of their overseas markets. The machines will pile up their products in the warehouses and a merciless struggle will ensue on the European market between the trusts and the financial groups. The closing of factories, the paying off of workers and unemployment will force the European working class to engage in an open struggle against the capitalist regime. Then the monopolies will realise that their true interests lie in giving aid to the underdeveloped countries – unstinted aid with not too many conditions. So we see that the young nations of the Third World are wrong in trying to make up to the capitalist countries. We are strong in our own right, and in the justice of our point of view. We ought on the contrary to emphasise and explain to the capitalist countries that the fundamental problem of our time is not the struggle between the socialist regime and them. The Cold War must be ended, for it leads nowhere. The plans for nuclearising the world must stop, and large-scale investments and technical aid must be given to underdeveloped regions. The fate of the world depends on the answer that is given to this question.

Moreover, the capitalist regime must not try to enlist the aid of the socialist regime over 'the fate of Europe' in face of the starving multitudes of coloured peoples. The exploit of Colonial Gargarin doesn't seem to displease General de Gaulle, for is it not a triumph which brings honour to Europe? For some time past the statesmen of the capitalist countries have adopted an equivocal attitude toward the Soviet Union. After having united all their forces to abolish the socialist regime, they now realise that they'll have to reckon with it. So they look as pleasant as they can, they make all kinds of advances, and they remind the Soviet people the whole time that they 'belong to Europe'.

They will not manage to divide the progressive forces which mean to lead mankind toward happiness by brandishing the threat of a Third World which is rising like the tide to swallow up all Europe. The Third World does not mean to organise a great crusade of hunger against the whole of Europe. What it expects from those who for centuries have kept it in slavery is that they will help it to rehabilitate mankind, and make man victorious everywhere, once and for all. But it is clear that we are not so naive as to think that this will come about with the cooperation and the good will of the European governments. This huge task which consists of reintroducing mankind into the world, the whole of mankind, will be carried out with the indispensable help of the European peoples, who themselves must realise that in the past they have often joined the ranks of our common masters where colonial questions were concerned. To achieve this, the European peoples must first decide to wake up and shake themselves, use their brains, and stop playing the stupid game of the Sleeping Beauty.

NOTES

1 Preface by Jean-Paul Sartre; translated by Constance Farrington (New York: Grove Weidenfeld, 1963).

2 We have demonstrated the mechanism of this Manichean world in *Black Skin, White Masks* (New York: Grove Press, 1967).

3 Fanon is writing in 1961. (Translator's note)

4 Village assemblies. (Translator's note)

5 Highly trained soldiers who are completely dedicated to the Moslem cause – *Translator*.

6 F. Engels, 'Theory of Violence' in *Anti-Dühring* (New York: International Publishers, 1983), p. 199.

7 It may happen that the arrested leader is in fact the authentic mouthpiece of the colonised masses. In this case colonialism will make use of his period of detention to try to launch new leaders.

8 Section Administrative Spéciale: An officers' corps whose task was to strengthen contact with the Algerians in non-military matters.

9 This refers to Mirabeau's famous saying: 'I am here by the will of the People; I shall leave only by the force of bayonets.' (Translator's note)

10 It is evident that this vacuum cleaning destroys the very thing that they want to preserve. Sartre points this out when he says: 'In short by the very fact of repeating them [concerning racist ideas] it is revealed that the simultaneous union of all against the natives is unrealisable. Such union

only recurs from time to time and moreover it can only come into being as an active groupment in order to massacre the natives – an absurd though perpetual temptation to the settlers, which even if it was feasible would only succeed in abolishing colonisation at one blow.' (*Critique de la Raison Dialectique*, p. 346.)

11 A. Césaire, *Les Armes Miraculeuss* (*Et les chiens se taisaient*), pp. 133–37.

12 Temporary village for the use of shepherds. (Translator's note)

13 We must go back to this period in order to judge the importance of this decision on the part of the French government in Algeria. Thus we may read in *Résistance Algérienne* No. 4 (28 March 1957) the following:

'In reply to the wish expressed by the General Assembly of the United Nations, the French Government has now decided to create urban militias in Algeria. "Enough blood has been spilled" was what the United Nations said; Lacoste replies "Let us form militias." "Cease fire," advised UNO; Lacoste vociferates, "We must arm the civilians." Whereas the two parties face-to-face with each other were on the recommendation of the United Nations invited to contact each other with a view to coming to an agreement and finding a peaceful and democratic solution, Lacoste decrees that henceforward every European will be armed and should open fire on any person who seems to him suspect. It was then agreed (in the Assembly) that savage and iniquitous repression verging on genocide ought at all costs to be opposed by the authorities: but Lacoste replies "Let us systematise the repression and organise the Algerian manhunt." And, symbolically, he entrusts the military with civil powers, and gives military powers to civilians. The ring is closed. In the middle, the Algerian, disarmed, famished, tracked down, jostled, struck, lynched, will soon be slaughtered as a suspect. Today, in Algeria, there is not a single Frenchman who is not authorised and even invited to use his weapons. There is not a single Frenchman, in Algeria, one month after the appeal for calm made by UNO, who is not permitted, and obliged to search out, investigate and pursue suspects.

'One month after the vote on the final motion of the General Assembly of the United Nations, there is not one European in Algeria who is not party to the most frightful work of extermination of modern times. A democratic solution? Right, Lacoste concedes; let's begin by exterminating the Algerians, and to do that, let's arm the civilians and give them *carte blanche*. The Paris press, on the whole, has welcomed the creation of these armed groups with reserve. Fascist militias, they've been called. Yes; but on the individual level, on the plane of human rights, what is fascism if not colonialism when rooted in a traditionally colonialist country? The opinion has been advanced that they are systematically legalised and commended; but does not the body of Algeria bear for the last one hundred and thirty years wounds which gape still wider, more numerous and more deepseated than ever? "Take care," advises Monsieur Kenne-Vignes, member of parliament for the MRP, "do we not by the creation of these militias risk seeing the gap widen between the two communities in Algeria?" Yes; but is not colonial status simply the organised reduction to slavery of a whole people? The Algerian revolution is precisely the affirmed contestation of that slavery and that abyss. The Algerian revolution speaks to the occupying nation and says: "Take your fangs out of the bleeding flesh of Algeria! Let the people of Algeria speak!"

'The creation of militias, they say, will lighten the tasks of the Army. It will free certain units whose mission will be to protect the Moroccan and Tunisian borders. In Algeria, the Army is six hundred thousand strong. Almost all the Navy and the Air Force are based there. There is an enormous, speedy police force with a horribly good record since it has absorbed the ex-torturers from Morocco and Tunisia. The territorial units are one hundred thousand strong. The task of the Army, all the same, must be lightened. So let us create urban militias. The fact remains that the hysterical and criminal frenzy of Lacoste imposes them even on clearsighted French people. The truth is that the creation of militias carries its contradiction even in its justification. The task of the French Army is neverending. Consequently, when it is given as an objective the gagging of the Algerian people, the door is closed on the future forever. Above all, it is forbidden to analyse, to understand, or to measure the depth and the density of the Algerian revolution: departmental leaders, housing-estate leaders, street leaders, house leaders, leaders who control each landing ... Today, to the surface checker-board is added an underground network.

'In 48 hours two thousand volunteers were enrolled. The Europeans of Algeria responded immediately to Lacoste's call to kill. From now on, each European must check up on all surviving Algerians in his sector; and in addition he will be responsible for information, for a "quick response" to acts of terrorism, for the detection of suspects, for the liquidation of runaways and for the reinforcement of police services. Certainly, the tasks of the Army must be lightened. Today, to the surface mopping-up is added a deeper harrowing. Today, to the killing which is all in the day's work is added planified murder. "Stop the bloodshed," was the advice given by UNO. "The best way of doing this," replied Lacoste, "is to make sure there remains no blood to shed." The Algerian people, after having been delivered up to Massu's hordes, is put under the protection of the urban militias. By his decision to create these militias, Lacoste shows quite plainly that he will brook no interference with HIS war. It is a proof that there are no limits once the rot has set in. True, he is at the moment a prisoner of the situation; but what a consolation to drag everyone down in one's fall!

'After each of these decisions, the Algerian people tense their muscles still more and fight still harder. After each of these organised, deliberately sought after assassinations, the Algerian people builds up its awareness of self, and consolidates its resistance. Yes; the tasks of the French Army are infinite: for oh, how infinite is the unity of the people of Algeria!'

14 This is why there are no prisoners when the fighting first starts. It is only through educating the local leaders politically that those at the head of the movement can make the masses accept 1) that people coming from the mother country do not always act of their own free will and are sometimes even disgusted by the war; 2) that it is of immediate advantage to the movement that its supporters should show by their actions that they respect certain international conventions; 3) that an army which takes prisoners is an army, and ceases to be considered as a group of wayside bandits; 4) that whatever the circumstances, the possession of prisoners constitutes a means of exerting pressure which must not be overlooked in order to protect our men who are in enemy hands.

15 In the present international context, capitalism does not merely operate an economic blockade against African or Asiatic colonies. The United States with its anti-Castro operations is opening a new chapter in the long story of man's toiling advance toward freedom. Latin America, made up of new independent countries which sit at the United Nations and raise the wind there, ought to be an object lesson for Africa. These former colonies since their liberation have suffered the brazenfaced rule of Western capitalism in terror and destitution.

The liberation of Africa and the growth of consciousness among mankind have made it possible for the Latin American peoples to break with the old merry-go-round of dictatorships where each succeeding regime exactly resembled the preceding one. Castro took over power in Cuba, and gave it to the people. This heresy is felt to be a national scourge by the Yankees, and the United States now organises counterrevolutionary brigades, puts together a provisional government, burns the sugar-cane crops, and generally has decided to strangle the Cuban people mercilessly. But this will be difficult. The people of Cuba will suffer, but they will conquer. The Brazilian president Janio Quadros has just announced in a declaration of historic importance that his country will defend the Cuban Revolution by all means. Perhaps even the United States may draw back when faced with the declared will of the peoples. When that day comes, we'll hang out the flags, for it will be a decisive moment for the men and women of the whole world. The almighty dollar, which when all is said or done is only guaranteed by slaves scattered all over the globe, in the oil wells of the Middle East, the mines of Peru or of the Congo, and the United Fruit or Firestone plantations, will then cease to dominate with all its force these slaves which it has created and who continue, empty-headed and empty-bellied, to feed it from their substance.

16 Certain countries which have benefitted by a large European settlement come to independence with houses and wide streets, and these tend to forget the poverty-stricken, starving hinterland. By the irony of fate, they give the impression by a kind of complicit silence that their towns are contemporaneous with independence.

17 It is true that Germany has not paid all her reparations. The indemnities imposed on the vanquished nation have not been claimed in full, for the injured nations have included Germany in their anti-communist system of defence. This same preoccupation is the permanent motivation of the colonialist countries when they try to obtain from their former colonies, if not their inclusion in the Western system, at least military bases and enclaves. On the other hand they have decided unanimously to forget their demands for the sake of NATO strategy and to preserve the free world; and we have seen Germany receiving floods of dollars and machines. A Germany once more standing on its feet, strong and powerful, was a necessity for the Western camp. It was in the understood interests of so-called free Europe to have a prosperous and reconstructed Germany which would be capable of serving as a first rampart against the eventual Red hordes. Germany has made admirable use of the European crisis. At the same time the United States and other European states feel a legitimate bitterness when confronted with this Germany, yesterday at their feet, which today metes out to them cutthroat competition in the economic field.

18 'To make a radical difference between the building up of socialism in Europe and our relations with the Third World (as if our only relations with it were external ones) is, whether we know it or not, to set the pace for the distribution of the colonial inheritance over and above the liberation of the underdeveloped countries. It is to wish to build up a luxury socialism upon the fruits of imperialist robbery – as if, inside the gang, the swag is more or less shared out equally, and even a little of it is given to the poor in the form of charity, since it's been forgotten that they were the people it was stolen from.' M. Péju, 'To die for De Gaulle?' *Temps Modernes*, No. 175–6 (October–November 1960).

Chapter 3: The Pitfalls of National Consciousness

History teaches us clearly that the battle against colonialism does not run straight away along the lines of nationalism. For a very long time the native devotes his energies to ending certain definite abuses: forced labour, corporal punishment, inequality of salaries, limitation of political rights, etc. This fight for democracy against the oppression of mankind will slowly leave the confusion of neo-liberal universalism to emerge, sometimes laboriously, as a claim to nationhood. It so happens that the unpreparedness of the educated classes, the lack of practical links between them and the mass of the people, their laziness, and, let it be said, their cowardice at the decisive moment of the struggle will give rise to tragic mishaps.

National consciousness, instead of being the all-embracing crystallisation of the innermost hopes of the whole people, instead of being the immediate and most obvious result of the mobilisation of the people, will be in any case only an empty shell, a crude and fragile travesty of what it might have been. The faults that we find in it are quite sufficient explanation of the facility with which, when dealing with young and independent nations, the nation is passed over for the race, and the tribe is preferred to the state. These are the cracks in the edifice which show the process of retrogression that is so harmful and prejudicial to national effort and national unity. We shall see that such retrograde steps with all the weaknesses and serious dangers that they entail are the historical result of the incapacity of the national middle class to rationalise popular action, that is to say their incapacity to see into the reasons for that action.

This traditional weakness, which is almost congenital to the national consciousness of underdeveloped countries, is not solely the result of the mutilation of the colonised people by the colonial regime. It is also the result of the intellectual laziness of the national middle class, of its spiritual penury, and of the profoundly cosmopolitan mould that its mind is set in.

The national middle class which takes over power at the end of the colonial regime is an underdeveloped middle class. It has practically no economic power, and in any case it is in no way commensurate with the bourgeoisie of the mother country which it hopes to replace. In its wilful narcissism, the national middle class is easily convinced that it can advantageously replace the middle class of the mother country. But that same independence which literally drives it into a corner will give rise within its ranks to catastrophic reactions, and will oblige it to send out frenzied appeals for help to the former mother country. The university and merchant classes which make up the most enlightened section of the new state are in fact characterised by the smallness of their number and their being concentrated in the capital, and the type of activities in which they are engaged: business, agriculture and the liberal professions. Neither financiers nor industrial magnates are to be found within this national middle class. The national bourgeoisie of underdeveloped countries is not engaged in production, nor in invention, nor building, nor labour; it is completely canalised into activities of the intermediary type. Its innermost vocation seems to be to keep in the running and to be part of the racket. The psychology of the national bourgeoisie is that of the businessman, not that of a captain of industry; and it is only too true that the greed of the settlers and the system of embargoes set up by colonialism have hardly left them any other choice.

Under the colonial system, a middle class which accumulates capital is an impossible phenomenon. Now, precisely, it would seem that the historical vocation of an authentic national middle class in an underdeveloped country is to repudiate its own nature in so far as it is bourgeois, that is to say in so far as it is the tool of capitalism, and to make itself the willing slave of that revolutionary capital which is the people.

In an underdeveloped country an authentic national middle class ought to consider as its bounden duty to betray the calling fate has marked out for it, and to put itself to school with the people: in other words to put at the people's disposal the intellectual and technical capital that it has snatched when going through the colonial universities. But unhappily we shall see that very often the national middle class does not follow this heroic, positive, fruitful and just path; rather, it disappears with its soul set at peace into the shocking ways – shocking because anti-national – of a traditional bourgeoisie, of a bourgeoisie which is stupidly, contemptibly, cynically bourgeois.

The objective of nationalist parties as from a certain given period is, we have seen, strictly national. They mobilise the people with slogans of independence, and for the rest leave it to future events. When such parties are questioned on the economic programme of the state that they are clamouring for, or on the nature of the regime which they propose to install, they are incapable of replying, because, precisely, they are completely ignorant of the economy of their own country.

This economy has always developed outside the limits of their knowledge. They have nothing more than an approximate, bookish acquaintance with the actual and potential resources of their country's soil and mineral deposits; and therefore they can only speak of these resources on a general and abstract plane. After independence this underdeveloped middle class, reduced in numbers and without capital, which refuses to follow the path of revolution, will fall into deplorable stagnation. It is unable to give free rein to its genius, which formerly it was wont to lament, though rather too glibly, was held in check by colonial domination. The precariousness of its resources and the paucity of its managerial class force it back for years into an artisan economy. From its point of view, which is inevitably a very limited one, a national economy is an economy based on what may be called local products. Long speeches will be made about the artisan class. Since the middle classes find it impossible to set up factories that would be more profit-earning both for themselves and for the country as a whole, they will surround the artisan class with a chauvinistic tenderness in keeping with the new awareness of national dignity, and which moreover will bring them in quite a lot of money. This cult of local products and this incapability to seek out new systems of management will be equally manifested by the bogging down of the national middle class in the methods of agricultural production which were characteristic of the colonial period.

The national economy of the period of independence is not set on a new footing. It is still concerned with the groundnut harvest, with the cocoa crop and the olive yield. In the same way there is no change in the marketing of basic products, and not a single industry is set up in the country. We go on sending out raw materials; we go on being Europe's small farmers who specialise in unfinished products.

Yet the national middle class constantly demands the nationalisation of the economy and of the trading sectors. This is because, from their point of view, nationalisation does not mean placing the whole economy at the service of the nation and deciding to satisfy the needs of the nation. For them, nationalisation does not mean governing the state with regard to the new social relations whose growth it has been decided to encourage. To them, nationalisation quite simply means the transfer into native hands of those unfair advantages which are a legacy of the colonial period.

Since the middle class has neither sufficient material nor intellectual resources (by intellectual resources we mean engineers and technicians) it limits its claims to the taking over of business offices and commercial houses formerly occupied by the settlers. The national bourgeoisie steps into the shoes of the former European settlement: doctors, barristers, traders, commercial travellers, general agents and transport agents. It considers that the dignity of the country and its own welfare require that it should occupy all these posts. From now on it will insist that all the big foreign companies should pass through its hands, whether these companies wish to keep on their connections with the country, or to open it up. The national middle class discovers its historic mission: that of intermediary.

Seen through its eyes, its mission has nothing to do with transforming the nation; it consists, prosaically, of being the transmission line between the nation and a capitalism, rampant though camouflaged, which today puts on the mask of neo-colonialism. The national bourgeoisie will be quite content with the role of the Western bourgeoisie's business agent, and it will play its part without any complexes in a most dignified manner. But this same lucrative role, this cheap-Jack's function, this meanness of outlook and this absence of all ambition symbolise the incapability of the national middle class to fulfil its historic role of bourgeoisie. Here, the dynamic, pioneer aspect, the characteristics of the inventor and of the discoverer of new worlds which are found in all national bourgeoisies are lamentably absent. In the colonial countries, the spirit of indulgence is dominant at the core of the bourgeoisie; and this is because the national bourgeoisie identifies itself with the Western bourgeoisie, from whom it has learned its lessons. It follows the Western bourgeoisie along its path of negation and decadence without ever having emulated it in its first stages of exploration and invention, stages which are an acquisition of that Western bourgeoisie whatever the circumstances. In its beginnings, the national bourgeoisie of the colonial countries identifies itself with the decadence of the bourgeoisie of the West. We need not think that it is jumping ahead; it is in fact beginning at the end. It is already senile before it has come to know the petulance, the fearlessness, or the will to succeed of youth.

The national bourgeoisie will be greatly helped on its way towards decadence by the Western bourgeoisies, who come to it as tourists avid for the exotic, for big-game hunting, and for casinos. The national bourgeoisie organises centres of rest and relaxation and pleasure resorts to meet the wishes of the Western bourgeoisie. Such activity is given the name of tourism, and for the occasion will be built up as a national industry. If proof is needed of the eventual transformation of certain elements of the ex-native bourgeoisie into the organisers of parties for their Western opposite numbers, it is worth while having a look at what has happened in Latin America. The casinos of Havana and of Mexico, the beaches of Rio, the little Brazilian and Mexican girls, the half-breed thirteen-year-olds, the ports of Acapulco and Copacabana – all these are the stigma of this depravation of the national middle class. Because it is bereft of ideas, because it lives to itself and cuts itself off from the people, undermined by its hereditary incapacity to think in terms of all the problems of the nation as seen from the point of view of the whole of that nation, the national middle class will have nothing better to do than to take on the role of manager for Western enterprise, and it will in practice set up its country as the brothel of Europe.

Once again we must keep before us the unfortunate example of certain Latin American republics. The banking magnates, the technocrats and the big businessmen of the United States have only to step on to a plane and they are wafted into sub-tropical climes, there for a space of a week or ten days to luxuriate in the delicious depravities which their 'reserves' hold for them.

The behaviour of the national landed proprietors is practically identical with that of the middle classes of the towns. The big farmers have, as soon as independence was proclaimed, demanded the nationalisation of agricultural production. Through manifold scheming practices they manage to make a clean sweep of the farms formerly owned by settlers, thus rein-forcing their hold on the district. But they do not try to introduce new agricultural methods, nor to farm more intensively, nor to integrate their farming systems into a genuinely national economy.

In fact, the landed proprietors will insist that the state should give them a hundred times more facilities and privileges than were enjoyed by the foreign settlers in former times. The exploitation of agricultural workers will be intensified and made legitimate. Using two or three slogans, these new colonists will demand an enormous amount of work from the agricultural labourers, in the name of the national effort of course. There will be no modernisation of agriculture, no planning for development, and no initiative; for initiative throws these people into a panic since it implies a minimum of risk, and completely upsets the hesitant, prudent, landed bourgeoisie, which gradually slips more and more into the lines laid down by colonialism. In the districts where this is the case, the only efforts made to better things are due to the government; it orders them, encourages them and finances them. The landed bourgeoisie refuses to take the slightest risk, and remains opposed to any venture and to any hazard. It has no intention of building upon sand; it demands solid investments and quick returns. The enormous profits which it pockets, enormous if we take into account the national revenue, are never reinvested. The money-in-the-stocking mentality is dominant in the psychology of these landed proprietors. Sometimes, especially in the years immediately following independence, the bourgeoisie does not hesitate to invest in foreign banks the profits that it makes out of its native soil. On the other hand large sums are spent on display: on cars, country houses, and on all those things which have been justly described by economists as characterising an underdeveloped bourgeoisie.

We have said that the native bourgeoisie which comes to power uses its class aggressiveness to corner the positions formerly kept for foreigners. On the morrow of independence, in fact, it violently attacks colonial personalities: barristers, traders, landed proprietors, doctors and higher civil servants. It will fight to the bitter end against these people 'who insult our dignity as a nation'. It waves aloft the notion of the nationalisation and Africanisation of the ruling classes. The fact is that such action will become more and more tinged by racism, until the bourgeoisie bluntly puts the problem to the government by saying 'We must have these posts.' They will not stop their snarling until they have taken over every one.

The working class of the towns, the masses of unemployed, the small artisans and craftsmen for their part line up behind this nationalist attitude; but in all justice let it be said, they only follow in the steps of their bourgeoisie. If the national bourgeoisie goes into competition with the Europeans, the artisans and craftsmen start a fight against non-national Africans. In the Ivory Coast, the anti-Dahoman and anti-Voltaic troubles are in fact racial riots. The

Dahoman and Voltaic peoples, who control the greater part of the petty trade, are, once independence is declared, the object of hostile manifestations on the part of the people of the Ivory Coast. From nationalism we have passed to ultra-nationalism, to chauvinism, and finally to racism. These foreigners are called on to leave; their shops are burned, their street stalls are wrecked, and in fact the government of the Ivory Coast commands them to go, thus giving their nationals satisfaction. In Senegal it is the anti-Sudanese demonstrations which called forth these words from Mr Mamadou Dia:

> The truth is that the Senegalese people have only adopted the Mali mystique through attachment to its leaders. Their adhesion to the Mali has no other significance than that of a fresh act of faith in the political policy of the latter. The Senegalese territory was no less real, in fact it was all the more so in that the presence of the Sudanese in Dakar too obviously manifested for it to be forgotten. It is this fact which explains that, far from being regretted, the break-up of the Federation has been greeted with relief by the mass of the people and nowhere was a hand raised to maintain it.[1]

While certain sections of the Senegalese people jump at the chance which is afforded them by their own leaders to get rid of the Sudanese, who hamper them in commercial matters or in administrative posts, the Congolese, who stood by hardly daring to believe in the mass exodus of the Belgians, decide to bring pressure to bear on the Senegalese who have settled in Leopoldville and Elizabethville and to get them to leave.

As we see it, the mechanism is identical in the two sets of circumstances. If the Europeans get in the way of the intellectuals and business bourgeoisie of the young nation, for the mass of the people in the towns competition is represented principally by Africans of another nation. On the Ivory Coast these competitors are the Dahomans; in Ghana they are the Nigerians; in Senegal, they are the Sudanese.

When the bourgeoisie's demands for a ruling class made up exclusively of Negroes or Arabs do not spring from an authentic movement of nationalisation but merely correspond to an anxiety to place in the bourgeoisie's hands the power held hitherto by the foreigner, the masses on their level present the same demands, confining, however, the notion of Negro or Arab within certain territorial limits. Between resounding assertions of the unity of the continent and this behaviour of the masses which has its inspiration in their leaders, many different attitudes may be traced. We observe a permanent seesaw between African unity, which fades quicker and quicker into the mists of oblivion, and a heartbreaking return to chauvinism in its most bitter and detestable form.

> On the Senegalese side, the leaders who have been the main theoreticians of African unity, and who several times over have sacrificed their local political organisations and their personal positions to this idea, are, though in all good faith, undeniably responsible. Their mistake – our mistake – has been, under pretext of fighting 'Balkanisation', not to have taken into consideration the pre-colonial fact of territorialism. Our mistake has been not to have paid enough attention in our analyses to this phenomenon, which is the fruit of colonialism if you like, but also a sociological fact which no theory of unity, be it ever so laudable or attractive, can abolish. We have allowed ourselves to be seduced by a mirage; that of the structure which is the most pleasing to our minds; and, mistaking our ideal for reality, we have believed it enough to condemn territorialism, and its natural sequel, micro-nationalism, for us to get the better of them, and to assure the success of our chimerical undertaking.[2]

From the chauvinism of the Senegalese to the tribalism of the Yolofs is not a big step. For, in fact, everywhere that the national bourgeoisie has failed to break through to the people as a whole, to enlighten them, and to consider all problems in the first place with regard to them – a failure due to the bourgeoisie's attitude of mistrust and to the haziness of its political tenets – everywhere where that national bourgeoisie has shown itself incapable of extending its vision of the world sufficiently, we observe a falling back towards old tribal attitudes, and, furious and sick at heart, we perceive that race feeling in its most exacerbated form is triumphing. Since the sole motto of the bourgeoisie is 'Replace the foreigner', and because it hastens in every walk of life to secure justice for itself and to take over the posts that the foreigner has vacated, the 'small people' of the nation – taxi drivers, cake sellers and bootblacks – will be equally quick to insist that the Dahomans go home to their own country, or will even go further and demand that the Foulbis and the Peuhls return to their jungle or their mountains.

It is from this viewpoint that we must interpret the fact that in young, independent countries, here and there federalism triumphs. We know that colonial domination has marked certain regions out for privilege. The colony's economy is not integrated into that of the nation as a whole. It is still organised in order to complete the economy of the different mother countries. Colonialism hardly ever exploits the whole of a country. It contents itself with bringing to light the natural resources, which it extracts, and exports to meet the needs of the mother country's industries, thereby allowing certain sectors of the colony to become relatively rich. But the rest of the colony follows its path of underdevelopment and poverty, or at all events sinks into it more deeply.

Immediately after independence, the nationals who live in the more prosperous regions realise their good luck, and show a primary and profound reaction in refusing to feed the other nationals. The districts which are rich in groundnuts, in cocoa and in diamonds come to the forefront, and dominate the empty panorama which the rest of the nation presents. The nationals of these rich regions look upon the others with hatred, and find in them envy and covetousness, and homicidal impulses. Old rivalries which were there before colonialism, old interracial hatreds come to the surface. The Balubas refuse to feed the Luluas; Katanga forms itself into a state, and Albert Kalondji gets himself crowned king of South Kasai.

African unity, that vague formula, yet one to which the men and women of Africa were passionately attached, and whose operative value served to bring immense pressure to bear on colonialism, African unity takes off the mask, and crumbles into regionalism inside the hollow shell of nationality itself. The national bourgeoisie, since it is strung up to defend its immediate interests, and sees no farther than the end of its nose, reveals itself incapable of simply bringing national unity into being, or of building up the nation on a stable and productive basis. The national front which has forced colonialism to withdraw cracks up, and wastes the victory it has gained.

This merciless fight engaged upon by races and tribes, and this aggressive anxiety to occupy the posts left vacant by the departure of the foreigner, will equally give rise to religious rivalries. In the country districts and the bush, minor confraternities, local religions and maraboutic cults will show a new vitality and will once more take up their round of excommunications. In the big towns, on the level of the administrative classes, we will observe the coming to grips of the two great revealed religions, Islam and Catholicism.

Colonialism, which had been shaken to its very foundations by the birth of African unity, recovers its balance and tries now to break that will to unity by using all the movement's weaknesses. Colonialism will set the African peoples moving by revealing to them the existence of 'spiritual' rivalries. In Senegal, it is the newspaper *New Africa* which week by week distils hatred of Islam and of the Arabs. The Lebanese, in whose hands is the greater part of the small trading enterprises on the western seaboard, are marked out for national obloquy. The missionaries find it opportune to remind the masses that long before the advent of European colonialism the great African empires were disrupted by the Arab invasion. There is no hesitation in saying that it was the Arab occupation which paved the way for European colonialism; Arab imperialism is commonly spoken of, and the cultural imperialism of Islam is condemned. Moslems are usually kept out of the more important posts. In other regions the reverse is the case, and it is the native Christians who are considered as conscious, objective enemies of national independence.

Colonialism pulls every string shamelessly, and is only too content to set at loggerheads those Africans who only yesterday were leagued against the settlers. The idea of a Saint Bartholomew takes shape in certain minds, and the advocates of colonialism laugh to themselves derisively when they hear magnificent declarations about African unity. Inside a single nation, religion splits up the people into different spiritual communities, all of them kept up and stiffened by colonialism and its instruments. Totally unexpected events break out here and there. In regions where Catholicism or Protestantism predominates, we see the Moslem minorities flinging themselves with unaccustomed ardour into their devotions. The Islamic feast days are revived, and the Moslem religion defends itself inch by inch against the violent absolutism of the Catholic faith. Ministers of state are heard to say for the benefit of certain individuals that if they are not content they have only to go to Cairo. Sometimes American Protestantism transplants its anti-Catholic prejudices into African soil, and keeps up tribal rivalries through religion.

Taking the continent as a whole, this religious tension may be responsible for the revival of the commonest racial feeling. Africa is divided into Black and White, and the names that are substituted – Africa south of the Sahara, Africa north of the Sahara – do not manage to hide this latent racism. Here, it is affirmed that White Africa has a thousand-year-old tradition of culture; that she is Mediterranean, that she is a Continuation of Europe and that she shares in Graeco-Latin civilisation. Black Africa is looked on as a region that is inert, brutal, uncivilised – in a word, savage. There, all day long you may hear unpleasant remarks about veiled women, polygamy and the supposed disdain the Arabs have for the feminine sex. All such remarks are reminiscent in their aggressiveness of those that are so often heard coming from the settler's lips. The national bourgeoisie of each of these two great religions, which has totally assimilated colonialist thought in its most corrupt form, takes over from the Europeans and establishes in the continent a racial philosophy which is extremely harmful for the future of Africa. By its laziness and will to imitation, it promotes the ingrafting and stiffening of racism which was characteristic of the colonial era. Thus it is by no means astonishing to hear in a country that calls itself African remarks which are neither more nor less than racist, and to observe the existence of paternalist behaviour which gives you the bitter impression that you are in Paris, Brussels, or London.

In certain regions of Africa, drivelling paternalism with regard to the blacks and the loathsome idea derived from Western culture that the black man is impervious to logic and the sciences reign in all their nakedness. Sometimes it may be ascertained that the black minorities are hemmed in by a kind of semi-slavery which renders legitimate that species of wariness, or in other words mistrust, which the countries of Black Africa feel with regard to the countries of White Africa. It is all too common that a citizen of Black Africa hears himself called a 'Negro' by the children when walking in the streets of a big town in White Africa, or finds that civil servants address him in pidgin English.

Yes, unfortunately it is not unknown that students from Black Africa who attend secondary schools north of the Sahara hear their schoolfellows asking if in their country there are houses, if they know what electricity is, or if they practise cannibalism in their families. Yes, unfortunately it is not unknown that in certain regions north of the Sahara Africans coming from countries south of the Sahara meet nationals who implore them to take them 'anywhere at all on condition we meet Negroes'. In parallel fashion, in certain young states of Black Africa members of parliament, or even ministers, maintain without a trace of humour that the danger is not at all of a reoccupation of their country by colonialism but of an eventual invasion by 'those vandals of Arabs coming from the North'.

As we see it, the bankruptcy of the bourgeoisie is not apparent in the economic field only. They have come to power in the name of a narrow nationalism and representing a race; they will prove themselves incapable of triumphantly putting into practice a programme with even a minimum humanist content, in spite of fine-sounding declarations which are devoid of meaning since the speakers bandy about in irresponsible fashion phrases that come straight out of European treatises on morals and political philosophy. When the bourgeoisie is strong, when it can arrange everything and everybody to serve its power, it does not hesitate to affirm positively certain democratic ideas which claim to be universally applicable. There must be very exceptional circumstances if such a bourgeoisie, solidly based economically, is forced into denying its own humanist ideology. The Western bourgeoisie, though fundamentally racist, most often manages to mask this racism by a multiplicity of nuances which allow it to preserve intact its proclamation of mankind's outstanding dignity.

The Western bourgeoisie has prepared enough fences and railings to have no real fear of the competition of those whom it exploits and holds in contempt. Western bourgeois racial prejudice as regards the nigger and the Arab is a racism of contempt; it is a racism which minimises what it hates. Bourgeois ideology, however, which is the proclamation of an essential equality between men, manages to appear logical in its own eyes by inviting the sub-men to become human, and to take as their prototype Western humanity as incarnated in the Western bourgeoisie.

The racial prejudice of the young national bourgeoisie is a racism of defence, based on fear. Essentially it is no different from vulgar tribalism, or the rivalries between septs or confraternities. We may understand why keen-witted international observers have hardly taken seriously the great flights of oratory about African unity, for it is true that there are so many cracks in that unity visible to the naked eye that it is only reasonable to insist that all these contradictions ought to be resolved before the day of unity can come.

The people of Africa have only recently come to know themselves. They have decided, in the name of the whole continent, to weigh in strongly against the colonial regime. Now the nationalist bourgeoisies, who in region after region hasten to make their own fortunes and to set up a national system of exploitation, do their utmost to put obstacles in the path of this 'Utopia'. The national bourgeoisies, who are quite clear as to what their objectives are, have decided to bar the way to that unity, to that coordinated effort on the part of two hundred and fifty million men to triumph over stupidity, hunger and inhumanity at one and the same time. This is why we must understand that African unity can only be achieved through the upward thrust of the people, and under the leadership of the people, that is to say, in defiance of the interests of the bourgeoisie.

As regards internal affairs and in the sphere of institutions, the national bourgeoisie will give equal proof of its incapacity. In a certain number of under-developed countries the parliamentary game is faked from the beginning. Powerless economically, unable to bring about the existence of coherent social relations, and standing on the principle of its domination as a class, the bourgeoisie chooses the solution that seems to it the easiest, that of the single party. It does not yet have the quiet conscience and the calm that economic power and the control of the state machine alone can give. It does not create a state that reassures the ordinary citizen, but rather one that rouses his anxiety.

The state, which by its strength and discretion ought to inspire confidence and disarm and lull everybody to sleep, on the contrary seeks to impose itself in spectacular fashion. It makes a display, it jostles people and bullies them, thus intimating to the citizen that he is in continual danger. The single party is the modern form of the dictatorship of the bourgeoisie, unmasked, unpainted, unscrupulous and cynical.

It is true that such a dictatorship does not go very far. It cannot halt the processes of its own contradictions. Since the bourgeoisie has not the economic means to ensure its domination and to throw a few crumbs to the rest of the country; since, moreover, it is preoccupied with filling its pockets as rapidly as possible but also as prosaically as possible, the country sinks all the more deeply into stagnation. And in order to hide this stagnation and to mask this regression, to reassure itself and to give itself something to boast about, the bourgeoisie can find nothing better to do than to erect grandiose buildings in the capital and to lay out money on what are called prestige expenses.

The national bourgeoisie turns its back more and more on the interior and on the real facts of its undeveloped country, and tends to look towards the former mother country and the foreign capitalists who count on its obliging compliance. As it does not share its profits with the people and in no way allows them to enjoy any of the dues that are paid to it by the big foreign companies, it will discover the need for a popular leader to whom will fall the dual role of stabilising the regime and of perpetuating the domination of the bourgeoisie. The bourgeois dictatorship of underdeveloped countries draws its strength from the existence of a leader. We know that in the well-developed countries the bourgeois dictatorship is the result of the economic power of the bourgeoisie. In the underdeveloped countries on the contrary the leader stands for moral power, in whose shelter the thin and poverty-stricken bourgeoisie of the young nation decides to get rich.

The people who for years on end have seen this leader and heard him speak, who from a distance in a kind of dream have followed his contests with the colonial power, spontaneously put their trust in this patriot. Before independence, the leader generally embodies the aspirations of the people for independence, political liberty and national dignity. But as soon as independence is declared, far from embodying in concrete form the needs of the people in what touches bread, land and the restoration of the country to the sacred hands of the people, the leader will reveal his inner purpose: to become the general president of that company of profiteers impatient for their returns which constitutes the national bourgeoisie.

In spite of his frequently honest conduct and his sincere declarations, the leader as seen objectively is the fierce defender of these interests, today combined, of the national bourgeoisie and the ex-colonial companies. His honesty, which is his soul's true bent, crumbles away little by little. His contact with the masses is so unreal that he comes to believe that his authority is hated and that the services that he has rendered his country are being called in question. The leader judges the ingratitude of the masses harshly, and every day that passes ranges himself a little more resolutely on the side of the exploiters. He therefore knowingly becomes the aider and abettor of the young bourgeoisie which is plunging into the mire of corruption and pleasure.

The economic channels of the young state sink back inevitably into neo-colonialist lines. The national economy, formerly protected, is today literally controlled. The budget is balanced through loans and gifts, while every three or four months the chief ministers themselves or else their governmental delegations come to the erstwhile mother countries or elsewhere, fishing for capital.

The former colonial power increases its demands, accumulates concessions and guarantees and takes fewer and fewer pains to mask the hold it has over the national government. The people stagnate deplorably in unbearable poverty; slowly they awaken to the unutterable treason of their leaders. This awakening is all the more acute in that the bourgeoisie is incapable of learning its lesson. The distribution of wealth that it effects is not spread out between a great many sectors; it is not ranged among different levels, nor does it set up a hierarchy of half-tones. The new caste is an affront all the more disgusting in that the immense majority, nine-tenths of the population, continue to die of starvation. The scandalous enrichment, speedy and pitiless, of this caste is accompanied by a decisive awakening on the part of the people, and a growing awareness that promises stormy days to come. The bourgeois caste, that section of the nation which annexes for its own profit all the wealth of the country, by a kind of unexpected logic will pass disparaging judgements upon the other Negroes and the other Arabs that more often than not are reminiscent of the racist doctrines of the former representatives of the colonial power. At one and the same time the poverty of the people, the immoderate money-making of the bourgeois caste, and its widespread scorn for the rest of the nation will harden thought and action.

But such threats will lead to the re-affirmation of authority and the appearance of dictatorship. The leader, who has behind him a lifetime of political action and devoted patriotism, constitutes a screen between the people and the rapacious bourgeoisie since he stands surety for the ventures of that caste and closes his eyes to their insolence, their mediocrity, and their fundamental immorality. He acts as a braking-power on the awakening consciousness of the people. He comes to the aid of the bourgeois caste and hides his manoeuvres from the people, thus becoming the most eager worker in the task of mystifying and bewildering the masses. Every time he speaks to the people he calls to mind his often heroic life, the struggles he has led in the name of the people and the victories in their name he has achieved, thereby intimating clearly to the masses that they ought to go on putting their confidence in him. There are plenty of examples of African patriots who have introduced into the cautious political advance of their elders a decisive style characterised by its nationalist outlook. These men came from the backwoods, and they proclaimed, to the scandal of the dominating power and the shame of the nationals of the capital, that they came from the backwoods and that they spoke in the name of the Negroes. These men, who have sung the praises of their race, who have taken upon themselves the whole burden of the past, complete with cannibalism and degeneracy, find themselves today, alas, at the head of a team of administrators who turn their back on the jungle and who proclaim that the vocation of their people is to obey, to go on obeying, and to be obedient till the end of time.

The leader pacifies the people. For years on end after independence has been won, we see him, incapable of urging on the people to a concrete task, unable really to open the future to them or of flinging them into the path of national reconstruction, that is to say, of their own reconstruction; we see him reassessing the history of independence and recalling the sacred unity of the struggle for liberation. The leader, because he refuses to break up the national bourgeoisie, asks the people to fall back into the past and to become drunk on the remembrance of the epoch which led up to independence. The leader, seen objectively, brings the people to a halt and persists in either expelling them from history or preventing them from taking root in it. During the struggle for liberation the leader awakened the people and promised them a forward march, heroic and unmitigated. Today, he uses every means to put them to sleep, and three or four times a year asks them to remember the colonial period and to look back on the long way they have come since then.

Now it must be said that the masses show themselves totally incapable of appreciating the long way they have come. The peasant who goes on scratching out a living from the soil, and the unemployed man who never finds employment do not manage, in spite of public holidays and flags, new and brightly-coloured though they may be, to convince themselves that anything has really changed in their lives. The bourgeoisie who are in power vainly increase the number of processions; the masses have no illusions. They are hungry; and the police officers, though they are now Africans, do not serve to reassure them particularly. The masses begin to sulk; they turn away from this nation in which they have been given no place and begin to lose interest in it.

From time to time, however, the leader makes an effort; he speaks on the radio or makes a tour of the country to pacify the people, to calm them and bemuse them. The leader is all the more necessary in that there is no party. During the period of the struggle for independence there was one right enough, a party led by the present leader. But since then this party has sadly disintegrated; nothing is left but the shell of a party, the name, the emblem, and the motto. The living party, which ought to make possible the free exchange of ideas which have been elaborated according to the real needs of the mass of the people, has been transformed into a trade union of individual interests. Since the proclamation of independence the party no longer helps the people to set out its demands, to become more aware of its needs and better able to establish its power. Today, the party's mission is to deliver to the people the instructions which issue from the summit. There no longer exists the fruitful give-and-take from the bottom to the top and from the top to the bottom which creates and guarantees democracy in a party. Quite on the contrary, the party has made itself into a screen between the masses and the leaders. There is no longer any party life, for the branches which were set up during the colonial period are today completely demobilised.

The militant champs on his bit. Now it is that the attitude taken up by certain militants during the struggle for liberation is seen to be justified, for the fact is that in the thick of the fight more than a few militants asked the leaders to formulate a dogma, to set out their objectives and to draw up a programme. But under the pretext of safeguarding national unity, the leaders categorically refused to attempt such a task. The only worthwhile dogma, it was repeatedly stated, is the union of the nation against colonialism. And on they went, armed with an impetuous slogan which stood for principles, while their only ideological activity took the form of a series of variants on the theme of the right of peoples to self-determination, borne on the wind of history which would inevitably sweep away colonialism. When the militants asked whether the wind of history couldn't be a little more clearly analysed, the leaders gave them instead hope and trust, the necessity of decolonialisation and its inevitability, and more to that effect.

After independence, the party sinks into an extraordinary lethargy. The militants are only called upon when so-called popular manifestations are afoot, or international conferences, or independence celebrations. The local party

in Paris or Hamburg. The behaviour of the national bourgeoisie of certain underdeveloped countries is reminiscent of the members of a gang, who after every hold-up hide their share in the loot from the other members who are their accomplices and prudently start thinking about their retirement. Such behaviour shows that more or less consciously the national bourgeoisie is playing to lose if the game goes on too long. They guess that the present situation will not last indefinitely but they intend to make the most of it. Such exploitation and such contempt for the state, however, inevitably gives rise to discontent among the mass of the people. It is in these conditions that the regime becomes harsher. In the absence of a parliament it is the army that becomes the arbiter: but sooner or later it will realise its power and will hold over the government's head the threat of a manifesto.

As we see it, the national bourgeoisie of certain underdeveloped countries has learned nothing from books. If they had looked closer at the Latin American countries they doubtless would have recognised the dangers which threaten them. We may thus conclude that this bourgeoisie in miniature that thrusts itself into the forefront is condemned to mark time, accomplishing nothing. In underdeveloped countries the bourgeois phase is impossibly arid. Certainly, there is a police dictatorship and a profiteering caste, but the construction of an elaborate bourgeois society seems to be condemned to failure. The ranks of decked-out profiteers whose grasping hands scrape up the bank-notes from a poverty-stricken country will sooner or later be men of straw in the hands of the army, cleverly handled by foreign experts. In this way the former mother country practises indirect government, both by the bourgeoisie that it upholds and also by the national army led by its experts, an army that pins the people down, immobilising and terrorising them.

The observations that we have been able to make about the national bourgeoisie bring us to a conclusion which should cause no surprise. In underdeveloped countries, the bourgeoisie should not be allowed to find the conditions necessary for its existence and its growth. In other words, the combined effort of the masses led by a party and of intellectuals who are highly conscious and armed with revolutionary principles ought to bar the way to this useless and harmful middle class.

The theoretical question that for the last fifty years has been raised whenever the history of underdeveloped countries is under discussion –

whether or not the bourgeois phase can be skipped – ought to be answered in the field of revolutionary action, and not by logic. The bourgeois phase in underdeveloped countries can only justify itself in so far as the national bourgeoisie has sufficient economic and technical strength to build up a bourgeois society, to create the conditions necessary for the development of a large-scale proletariat, to mechanise agriculture and finally to make possible the existence of an authentic national culture.

A bourgeoisie similar to that which developed in Europe is able to elaborate an ideology and at the same time strengthen its own power. Such a bourgeoisie, dynamic, educated and secular, has fully succeeded in its undertaking of the accumulation of capital and has given to the nation a minimum of prosperity. In underdeveloped countries, we have seen that no true bourgeoisie exists; there is only a sort of little greedy caste, avid and voracious, with the mind of a huckster, only too glad to accept the dividends that the former colonial power hands out to it. This get-rich-quick middle class shows itself incapable of great ideas or of inventiveness. It remembers what it has read in European textbooks and imperceptibly it becomes not even the replica of Europe, but its caricature.

The struggle against the bourgeoisie of underdeveloped countries is far from being a theoretical one. It is not concerned with making out its condemnation as laid down by the judgement of history. The national bourgeoisie of underdeveloped countries must not be opposed because it threatens to slow down the total, harmonious development of the nation. It must simply be stoutly opposed because, literally, it is good for nothing. This bourgeoisie, expressing its mediocrity in its profits, its achievements and in its thought, tries to hide this mediocrity by buildings which have prestige value at the individual level, by chromium-plating on big American cars, by holidays on the Riviera and weekends in neon-lit nightclubs.

This bourgeoisie which turns its back more and more on the people as a whole does not even succeed in extracting spectacular concessions from the West, such as investments which would be of value for the country's economy or the setting up of certain industries. On the contrary, assembly plants spring up and consecrate the type of neo-colonialist industrialisation in which the country's economy flounders. Thus it must not be said that the national bourgeoisie retards the country's evolution, that it makes it lose time or that it threatens to lead the nation up blind alleys. In fact, the bourgeois phase in the history of underdeveloped countries is a completely useless phase. When this caste has vanished, devoured by its own contradictions, it will be seen that nothing new has happened since independence was proclaimed, and that everything must be started again from scratch. The changeover will not take place at the level of the structures set up by the bourgeoisie during its reign, since that caste has done nothing more than take over unchanged the legacy of the economy, the thought, and the institutions left by the colonialists.

It is all the easier to neutralise this bourgeois class in that, as we have seen, it is numerically, intellectually and economically weak. In the colonised territories, the bourgeois caste draws its strength after independence chiefly from agreements reached with the former colonial power. The national bourgeoisie has all the more opportunity to take over from the oppressor since it has been given time for a leisurely *tête-à-tête* with the ex-colonial power. But deep-rooted contradictions undermine the ranks of that bourgeoisie; it is this that gives the observer an impression of instability. There is not as yet a homogeneity of caste. Many intellectuals, for example, condemn this regime based on the domination of the few. In underdeveloped countries, there are certain members of the elite, intellectuals and civil servants, who are sincere, who feel the necessity for a planned economy, the outlawing of profiteers and the strict prohibition of attempts at mystification. In addition, such men fight in a certain measure for the mass participation of the people in the ordering of public affairs.

In those underdeveloped countries which accede to independence, there almost always exists a small number of honest intellectuals, who have no very precise ideas about politics, but who instinctively distrust the race for positions and pensions which is symptomatic of the early days of independence in colonised countries. The personal situation of these men (breadwinners of large families) or their background (hard struggles and a strictly moral upbringing) explain their manifest contempt for profiteers and schemers. We must know how to use these men in the decisive battle that we mean to engage upon which will lead to a healthier outlook for the nation. Closing the road to the national bourgeoisie is, certainly, the means whereby the vicissitudes of newfound independence may be avoided, and with them the decline of morals, the installing of corruption within the country, economic regression, and the immediate disaster of an anti-democratic regime depending on force and intimidation. But it is also the only means towards progress.

What holds up the taking of a decision by the profoundly democratic elements of the young nation and adds to their timidity is the apparent strength of the bourgeoisie. In newly independent underdeveloped countries, the whole of the ruling class swarms into the towns built by colonialism. The absence of any analysis of the total population induces onlookers to think that there exists a powerful and perfectly organised bourgeoisie. In fact, we know today that the bourgeoisie in underdeveloped countries is non-existent. What creates a bourgeoisie is not the bourgeois spirit, nor its taste or manners, nor even its aspirations. The bourgeoisie is above all the direct product of precise economic conditions.

Now, in the colonies, the economic conditions are conditions of a foreign bourgeoisie. Through its agents, it is the bourgeoisie of the mother country that we find present in the colonial towns. The bourgeoisie in the colonies is, before independence, a Western bourgeoisie, a true branch of the bourgeoisie of the mother country, that derives its legitimacy, its force and its stability from the bourgeoisie of the homeland. During the period of unrest that precedes independence, certain native elements, intellectuals and traders, who live in the midst of that imported bourgeoisie, try to identify themselves with it. A permanent wish for identification with the bourgeois representatives of the mother country is to be found among the native intellectuals and merchants.

This native bourgeoisie, which has adopted unreservedly and with enthusiasm the ways of thinking characteristic of the mother country, which has become wonderfully detached from its own thought and has based its consciousness upon foundations which are typically foreign, will realise, with its mouth watering, that it lacks something essential to a bourgeoisie: money. The bourgeoisie of an underdeveloped country is a bourgeoisie in spirit only. It is not its economic strength, nor the dynamism of its leaders, nor the breadth of its ideas that ensures its peculiar quality of bourgeoisie. Consequently it remains at the beginning and for a long time afterwards a bourgeoisie of the civil service. It is the positions that it holds in the new national administration which will give it strength and serenity. If the government gives it enough time and opportunity, this bourgeoisie will manage to put away enough money to stiffen its domination. But it will always reveal itself as incapable of giving

sure that they really participate in the business of governing the nation, but in order to remind them constantly that the government expects from them obedience and discipline. That famous dictatorship, whose supporters believe that it is called for by the historical process and consider it an indispensable prelude to the dawn of independence, in fact symbolises the decision of the bourgeois caste to govern the underdeveloped country first with the help of the people, but soon against them. The progressive transformation of the party into an information service is the indication that the government holds itself more and more on the defensive. The incoherent mass of the people is seen as a blind force that must be continually held in check either by mystification or by the fear inspired by the police force. The party acts as a barometer and as an information service. The militant is turned into an informer. He is entrusted with punitive expeditions against the villages. The embryo opposition parties are liquidated by beatings and stonings. The opposition candidates see their houses set on fire. The police increase their provocations. In these conditions, you may be sure, the party is unchallenged and 99.99 per cent of the votes are cast for the governmental candidate. We should add that in Africa a certain number of governments actually behave in this way. All the opposition parties, which moreover are usually progressive and would therefore tend to work for the greater influence of the masses in the conduct of public matters, and who desire that the proud, money-making bourgeoisie should be brought to heel, have been by dint of baton charges and prisons condemned first to silence and then to a clandestine existence.

The political party in many parts of Africa which are today independent is puffed up in a most dangerous way. In the presence of a member of the party, the people are silent, behave like a flock of sheep and publish panegyrics in praise of the government or the leader. But in the street when evening comes, away from the village, in the cafés or by the river, the bitter disappointment of the people, their despair but also their unceasing anger makes itself heard. The party, instead of welcoming the expression of popular discontent, instead of taking for its fundamental purpose the free flow of ideas from the people up to the government, forms a screen, and forbids such ideas. The party leaders behave like common sergeant-majors, frequently reminding the people of the need for 'silence in the ranks'. This party which used to call itself the servant of the people, which used to claim that it worked for the full expression of the people's will, as soon as the colonial power puts the country into its control hastens to send the people back to their caves. As far as national unity is concerned the party will also make many mistakes, as for example when the so-called national party behaves as a party based on ethnic differences. It becomes, in fact, the tribe which makes itself into a party. This party which of its own will proclaims that it is a national party, and which claims to speak in the name of the totality of the people, secretly, sometimes even openly, organises an authentic ethnic dictatorship. We no longer see the rise of a bourgeois dictatorship, but a tribal dictatorship. The ministers, the members of the cabinet, the ambassadors and local commissioners are chosen from the same ethnological group as the leader, sometimes directly from his own family. Such regimes of the family sort seem to go back to the old laws of inbreeding, and not anger but shame is felt when we are faced with such stupidity, such an imposture, such intellectual and spiritual poverty. These heads of the government are the true traitors in Africa, for they sell their country to the most terrifying of all its enemies: stupidity. This tribalising of the central authority, it is certain, encourages regionalist ideas and separatism. All the decentralising tendencies spring up again and triumph, and the nation falls to pieces, broken in bits. The leader, who once used to call for 'African unity' and who thought of his own little family, wakes up one day to find himself saddled with five tribes, who also want to have their own ambassadors and ministers; and irresponsible as ever, still unaware and still despicable, he denounces their 'treason'.

We have more than once drawn attention to the baleful influence frequently wielded by the leader. This is due to the fact that the party in certain districts is organised like a gang, with the toughest person in it as its head. The ascendancy of such a leader and his power over others is often mentioned, and people have no hesitation in declaring, in a tone of slightly admiring complicity, that he strikes terror into his nearest collaborators. In order to avoid these many pitfalls an unceasing battle must be waged, a battle to prevent the party ever becoming a willing tool in the hands of a leader. 'Leader': the word comes from the English verb 'to lead', but a frequent French translation is 'to drive'. The driver, the shepherd of the people, no longer exists today. The people are no longer a herd; they do not need to be driven. If the leader drives me on, I want him to realise that at the same time I show him the way; the nation ought not to be something bossed by a Grand Panjandrum. We may understand the panic caused in governmental circles each time one of these leaders falls ill; they are obsessed by the question of who is to succeed him. What will happen to the country if the leader disappears? The ruling classes who have abdicated in favour of the leader, irresponsible, oblivious of everything and essentially preoccupied with the pleasures of their everyday life, their cocktail parties, their journeys paid for by government money, the profits they can make out of various schemes – from time to time these people discover the spiritual wasteland at the heart of the nation.

A country that really wishes to answer the questions that history puts to it, that wants to develop not only its towns but also the brains of its inhabitants, such a country must possess a trustworthy political party. The party is not a tool in the hands of the government. Quite on the contrary, the party is a tool in the hands of the people; it is they who decide on the policy that the government carries out. The party is not, and ought never to be, the only political bureau where all the members of the government and the chief dignitaries of the regime may meet freely together. Only too frequently the political bureau, unfortunately, consists of all the party and its members who reside permanently in the capital. In an underdeveloped country, the leading members of the party ought to avoid the capital as if it had the plague. They ought, with some few exceptions, to live in the country districts. The centralisation of all activity in the city ought to be avoided. No excuse of administrative discipline should be taken as legitimising that excrescence of a capital which is already overpopulated and overdeveloped with regard to nine-tenths of the country. The party should be decentralised in the extreme. It is the only way to bring life to regions which are dead, those regions which are not yet awakened to life.

In practice, there will be at least one member of the political bureau in each area and he will deliberately not be appointed as head of that area. He will have no administrative powers. The regional member of the political bureau is not expected to hold the highest rank in the regional administrative organisation. He ought not automatically to belong to the regional administrative body. For the people, the party is not an authority, but an organism through which they as the people exercise their authority and express their will. The less there is of confusion and duality of powers, the more the party will play its part of guide and the more surely it will constitute for the people a decisive guarantee. If the party is mingled with the government, the fact of being a party militant means that you take the short cut to gain private ends, to hold a post in the government, step up the ladder, get promotion and make a career for yourself.

In an underdeveloped country, the setting up of dynamic district officials stops the progress whereby the towns become top-heavy, and the incoherent rush towards the cities of the mass of country people. The setting up early in the days of independence of regional organisations and officials who have full authority to do everything in their power to awaken such a region, to bring life to it and to hasten the growth of consciousness in it is a necessity from which there is no escape for a country that wishes to progress. Otherwise, the government big-wigs and the party officials group themselves around the leader. The government services swell to huge proportions, not because they are developing and specialising, but because new-found cousins and fresh militants are looking for jobs and hope to edge themselves into the government machine. And the dream of every citizen is to get up to the capital, and to have his share of the cake. The local districts are deserted; the mass of the country people with no one to lead them, uneducated and unsupported, turn their backs on their poorly-laboured fields and flock towards the outer ring of suburbs, thus swelling out of all proportion the ranks of the *lumpen-proletariat*.

The moment for a fresh national crisis is not far off. To avoid it, we think that a quite different policy should be followed: that the interior, the back country, ought to be the most privileged part of the country. Moreover, in the last resort, there is nothing inconvenient in the government choosing its seat elsewhere than in the capital. The capital must be deconsecrated; the outcast masses must be shown that we have decided to work for them. It is with this idea in mind that the government of Brazil tried to found Brazilia. The dead city of Rio de Janeiro was an insult to the Brazilian people. But, unfortunately, Brazilia is just another new capital, as monstrous as the first. The only advantage of this achievement is that, today, there exists a road through the bush to it.

No, there is no serious reason which can be opposed to the choice of another capital, or to the moving of the government as a whole towards one of the most under-populated regions. The capital of underdeveloped countries is a commercial notion inherited from the colonial period. But we who are

controlled. Thus the peasants could no longer go freely to the towns and buy provisions. During this period, the grocers made huge profits. The prices of tea, coffee, sugar, tobacco and salt soared. The black market flourished blatantly. The peasants who could not pay in money mortgaged their crops, in other words their land, or else lopped off field after field of their fathers' farms and during the second phase worked them for the grocer. As soon as the political commissioners realised the danger of the situation they reacted immediately. Thus a rational system of provisioning was instituted: the grocer who went to the town was obliged to buy from nationalist wholesalers who handed him an invoice which clearly showed the prices of the goods. When the retailer got back to the village, before doing anything else he had to go to the political commissioner who checked the invoice, decided on the margin of profit and fixed the price at which the various goods should be sold. However, the retailer soon discovered a new trick, and after three or four days declared that his stocks had run out. In fact, he went on with his business of selling on the black market on the sly. The reaction of the politico-military authorities was thoroughgoing. Heavy penalisations were decided on, and the fines collected were put into the village funds and used for social purposes or to pay for public works in the general interest. Sometimes it was decided to shut down the shop for a while. Then if there was a repetition of black marketeering, the business was at once confiscated and a managing committee elected to carry it on, which paid a monthly allowance to the former owner.

Taking these experiences as a starting point, the functioning of the main laws of economics was explained to the people, with concrete examples. The accumulation of capital ceased to be a theory and became a very real and immediate mode of behaviour. The people understood how that once a man was in trade, he could become rich and increase his turnover. Then and then only did the peasants tell the tale of how the grocer gave them loans at exorbitant interest, and others recalled how he evicted them from their land and how from owners they became labourers. The more the people understand, the more watchful they become, and the more they come to realise that finally everything depends on them and their salvation lies in their own cohesion, in the true understanding of their interests and in knowing who their enemies are. The people come to understand that wealth is not the fruit of labour but the result of organised, protected robbery. Rich people are no longer respectable people; they are nothing more than flesh-eating animals, jackals and vultures which wallow in the people's blood. With another end in view the political commissioners have had to decide that nobody will work for anyone else any longer. The land belongs to those that till it. This is a principle which has through explanation become a fundamental law of the Algerian revolution. The peasants who used to employ agricultural labourers have been obliged to give a share of the land to their former employees.

So it may be seen that production per acre trebled, in spite of the many raids by the French, in spite of bombardments from the air, and the difficulty of getting manures. The *fellahs* who at harvest time were able to judge and weigh the crops thus obtained wanted to know whence came such a phenomenon; and they were quick to understand that the idea of work is not as simple as all that, that slavery is opposed to work, and that work presupposes liberty, responsibility, and consciousness.

In those districts where we have been able to carry out successfully these interesting experiments, where we have watched man being created by revolutionary beginnings, the peasants have very clearly caught hold of the idea that the more intelligence you bring to your work, the more pleasure you will have in it. We have been able to make the masses understand that work is not simply the output of energy, nor the functioning of certain muscles, but that people work more by using their brains and their hearts than with only their muscles and their sweat. In the same way in these liberated districts which are at the same time excluded from the old trade routes we have had to modify production, which formerly looked only towards the towns and towards export. We have organised production to meet consumers' needs for the people and for the units of the national army of liberation. We have quadrupled the production of lentils and organised the manufacture of charcoal. Green vegetables and charcoal have been sent through the mountains from the north to the south, whereas the southern districts send meat to the north. This coordination was decided upon by the FLN and they it was who set up the system of communications. We did not have any technicians or planners coming from big Western universities; but in these liberated regions the daily ration went up to the hitherto unheard-of figure of 3 200 calories. The people were not content with coming triumphant out of this test. They started asking themselves theoretical questions: for example, why did certain districts never see an orange before the war of liberation, while thousands of tons are exported every year abroad? Why were grapes unknown to a great many Algerians whereas the European peoples enjoyed them by the million? Today, the people have a very clear notion of what belongs to them. The Algerian people today know that they are the sole owners of the soil and mineral wealth of their country. And if some individuals do not understand the unrelenting refusal of the FLN to tolerate any encroachment on this right of ownership, and its fierce refusal to allow any compromise on principles, they must one and all remember that the Algerian people is today an adult people, responsible and fully conscious of its responsibilities. In short, the Algerians are men of property.

If we have taken the example of Algeria to illustrate our subject, it is not at all with the intention of glorifying our own people, but simply to show the important part played by the war in leading them towards consciousness of themselves. It is clear that other peoples have come to the same conclusion in different ways. We know for sure today that in Algeria the test of force was inevitable; but other countries through political action and through the work of clarification undertaken by a party have led their people to the same results. In Algeria, we have realised that the masses are equal to the problems which confront them. In an underdeveloped country, experience proves that the important thing is not that three hundred people form a plan and decide upon carrying it out, but that the whole people plan and decide even if it takes them twice or three times as long. The fact is that the time taken up by explaining, the time 'lost' in treating the worker as a human being, will be caught up in the execution of the plan. People must know where they are going, and why. The politician should not ignore the fact that the future remains a closed book so long as the consciousness of the people remains imperfect, elementary, and cloudy. We African politicians must have very clear ideas on the situation of our people. But this clarity of ideas must be profoundly dialectical. The awakening of the whole people will not come about at once; the people's work in the building of the nation will not immediately take on its full dimensions: first because the means of communication and transmission are only beginning to be developed; secondly because the yardstick of time must no longer be that of the moment or up till the next harvest, but must become that of the rest of the world, and lastly because the spirit of discouragement which has been deeply rooted in people's minds by colonial domination is still very near the surface. But we must not overlook the fact that victory over those weaknesses which are the heritage of the material and spiritual domination of the country by another is a necessity from which no government will be able to escape. Let us take the example of work under the colonial regime. The settler never stopped complaining that the native is slow. Today, in certain countries which have become independent, we hear the ruling classes taking up the same cry. The fact is that the settler wanted the native to be enthusiastic. By a sort of process of mystification which constitutes the most sublime type of separation from reality, he wanted to persuade the slave that the land that he worked belonged to him, that the mines where he lost his health were owned by him. The settler was singularly forgetful of the fact that he was growing rich through the death throes of the slave. In fact what the settler was saying to the native was 'Kill yourself that I may become rich.' Today, we must behave in a different fashion. We ought not to say to the people: 'Kill yourselves that the country may become rich.' If we want to increase the national revenue, and decrease the importing of certain products which are useless, or even harmful, if we want to increase agricultural production and overcome illiteracy, we must explain what we are about. The people must understand what is at stake. Public business ought to be the business of the public. So the necessity of creating a large number of well-informed nuclei at the bottom crops up again. Too often, in fact, we are content to establish national organisations at the top and always in the capital: the Women's Union, the Young People's Federation, Trade Unions, etc. But if one takes the trouble to investigate what is behind the office in the capital, if you go into the inner room where the reports ought to be, you will be shocked by the emptiness, the blank spaces, and the bluff. There must be a basis; there must be cells that supply content and life. The masses should be able to meet together, discuss, propose, and receive directions. The citizens should be able to speak, to express themselves and to put forward new ideas. The branch meeting and the committee meeting are liturgical acts. They are privileged occasions given to a human being to listen and to speak. At each meeting, the brain increases its means of participation and the eye discovers a landscape more and more in keeping with human dignity.

The large proportion of young people in the underdeveloped countries raises specific problems for the government, which must be tackled with lucidity. The young people of the towns, idle and often illiterate, are a prey to all sorts of disintegrating influences. It is to the youth of an underdeveloped country that the industrialised countries most often offer their pastimes. Normally, there is a certain homogeneity between the mental and material level of the members of any given society and the pleasures which that society creates for itself. But in underdeveloped countries, young people have at their disposal leisure occupations designed for the youth of capitalist countries: detective novels, penny-in-the slot machines, sexy photographs, pornographic literature, films banned to those under sixteen, and above all alcohol. In the West, the family circle, the effects of education and the relatively high standard of living of the working classes provide a more or less efficient protection against the harmful action of these pastimes. But in an African country, where mental development is uneven, where the violent collision of two worlds has considerably shaken old traditions and thrown the universe of the perceptions out of focus, the impressionability and sensibility of the young African are at the mercy of the various assaults made upon them by the very nature of Western culture. His family very often proves itself incapable of showing stability and homogeneity when faced with such attacks.

In this domain, the government's duty is to act as a filter and a stabiliser. But the youth commissioners in underdeveloped countries often make the mistake of imagining their role to be that of youth commissioners in fully developed countries. They speak of strengthening the soul, of developing the body, and of facilitating the growth of sportsmanlike qualities. It is our opinion that they should beware of these conceptions. The young people of an underdeveloped country are above all idle: occupations must be found for them. For this reason the youth commissioners ought for practical purposes to be attached to the Ministry for Labour. The Ministry for Labour, which is a prime necessity in an underdeveloped country, functions in collaboration with the Ministry for Planning, which is another necessary institution in underdeveloped countries. The youth of Africa ought not to be sent to sports stadiums but into the fields and into the schools. The stadium ought not to be a show place erected in the towns, but a bit of open ground in the midst of the fields that the young people must reclaim, cultivate and give to the nation. The capitalist conception of sport is fundamentally different from that which should exist in an underdeveloped country. The African politician should not be preoccupied with turning out sportsmen, but with turning out fully conscious men, who play games as well. If games are not integrated into the national life, that is to say in the building of the nation, and if you turn out national sportsmen and not fully conscious men, you will very quickly see sport rotted by professionalism and commercialism. Sport should not be a pastime or a distraction for the bourgeoisie of the towns. The greatest task before us is to understand at each moment what is happening in our country. We ought not to cultivate the exceptional or to seek for a hero, who is another form of leader. We ought to uplift the people; we must develop their brains, fill them with ideas, change them and make them into human beings.

We once more come up against that obsession of ours – which we would like to see shared by all African politicians – about the need for effort to be well informed, for work which is enlightened and free from its historic intellectual darkness. To hold a responsible position in an underdeveloped country is to know that in the end everything depends on the education of the masses, on the raising of the level of thought, and on what we are too quick to call 'political teaching'.

In fact, we often believe with criminal superficiality that to educate the masses politically is to deliver a long political harangue from time to time. We think that it is enough that the leader or one of his lieutenants should speak in a pompous tone about the principal events of the day for them to have fulfilled this bounden duty to educate the masses politically. Now, political education means opening their minds, awakening them, and allowing the birth of their intelligence; as Césaire said, it is 'to invent souls.' To educate the masses politically does not mean, cannot mean making a political speech. What it means is to try, relentlessly and passionately, to teach the masses that everything depends on them; that if we stagnate it is their responsibility, and that if we go forward it is due to them too, that there is no such thing as a demiurge, that there is no famous man who will take the responsibility for everything, but that the demiurge is the people themselves and the magic hands are finally only the hands of the people. In order to put all this into practice, in order really to incarnate the people, we repeat that there must be decentralisation in the extreme. The movement from the top to the bottom and from the bottom to the top should be a fixed principle, not through concern for formalism but because simply to respect this principle is the guarantee of salvation. It is from the base that forces mount up which supply the summit with its dynamic, and make it possible dialectically for it to leap ahead. Once again we Algerians have been quick to understand these facts, for no member of the government at the head of any recognised state has had the chance of availing himself of such a mission of salvation. For it is the rank-and-file who are fighting in Algeria, and the rank-and-file know well that without their daily struggle, hard and heroic as it is, the summit would collapse; and in the same way those at the bottom know that without a head and without leadership the base would split apart in incoherence and anarchy. The summit only draws its worth and its strength from the existence of the people at war. Literally, it is the people who freely create a summit for themselves, and not the summit that tolerates the people.

The masses should know that the government and the party are at their service. A deserving people, in other words a people conscious of its dignity, is a people that never forgets these facts. During the colonial occupation the people were told that they must give their lives so that dignity might triumph. But the African peoples quickly came to understand that it was not only the occupying power that threatened their dignity. The African peoples were quick to realise that dignity and sovereignty were exact equivalents, and in fact, a free people living in dignity is a sovereign people. It is no use demonstrating that the African peoples are childish or weak. A government or a party gets the people it deserves and sooner or later a people gets the government it deserves.

Practical experience in certain regions confirms this point of view. It sometimes happens at meetings that militants use sweeping, dogmatic formulas. The preference for this short cut, in which spontaneity and over-simple sinking of differences dangerously combine to defeat intellectual elaboration, frequently triumphs. When we meet this shirking of responsibility in a militant it is not enough to tell him he is wrong. We must make him ready for responsibility, encourage him to follow up his chain of reasoning and make him realise the true nature, often shocking, inhuman and in the long run sterile, of such oversimplification.

Nobody, neither leader nor rank-and-file, can hold back the truth. The search for truth in local attitudes is a collective affair. Some are richer in experience, and elaborate their thought more rapidly, and in the past have been able to establish a greater number of mental links. But they ought to avoid riding roughshod over the people, for the success of the decision which is adopted depends upon the coordinated, conscious effort of the whole of the people. No one can get out of the situation scot free. Everyone will be butchered or tortured; and in the framework of the independent nation everyone will go hungry and everyone will suffer in the slump. The collective struggle presupposes collective responsibility at the base and collegiate responsibility at the top. Yes, everybody will have to be compromised in the fight for the common good. No one has clean hands; there are no innocents and no onlookers. We all have dirty hands; we are all soiling them in the swamps of our country and in the terrifying emptiness of our brains. Every onlooker is either a coward or a traitor.

The duty of those at the head of the movement is to have the masses behind them. Allegiance presupposes awareness and understanding of the mission which has to be fulfilled; in short, an intellectual position, however embryonic. We must not voodoo the people, nor dissolve them in emotion and confusion. Only those underdeveloped countries led by revolutionary elites who have come up from the people can today allow the entry of the masses upon the scene of history. But, we must repeat, it is absolutely necessary to oppose vigorously and definitively the birth of a national bourgeoisie and a privileged caste. To educate the masses politically is to make the totality of the nation a reality to each citizen. It is to make the history of the nation part of the personal experience of each of its citizens. As president Sékou Touré aptly remarked in his message to the second congress of African writers:

> In the realm of thought, man may claim to be the brain of the world;
> but in real life where every action affects spiritual and physical
> existence, the world is always the brain of mankind; for it is at this
> level that you will find the sum total of the powers and units of
> thought, and the dynamic forces of development and improvement;
> and it is there that energies are merged and the sum of man's intell-
> ectual values is finally added together.

Individual experience, because it is national and because it is a link in the chain of national existence, ceases to be individual, limited, and shrunken and is enabled to open out into the truth of the nation and of the world. In the same way that during the period of armed struggle each fighter held the fortune of the nation in his hand, so during the period of national construction each citizen ought to continue in his real, everyday activity to associate himself with the whole of the nation, to incarnate the continuous dialectical truth of the nation and to will the triumph of man in his completeness here and now. If the building of a bridge does not enrich the awareness of those who work on it, then that bridge ought not to be built and the citizens can go on swimming across the river or going by boat. The bridge should not be 'parachuted down' from above; it should not be imposed by a *deus ex machina* upon the social scene; on the contrary it should come from the muscles and the brains of the citizens. Certainly, there may well be need of engineers and architects, sometimes completely foreign engineers and architects; but the local party leaders should be always present, so that the new techniques can make their way into the cerebral desert of the citizen, so that the bridge in whole and in part can be taken up and conceived, and the responsibility for it assumed by the citizen. In this way, and in this way only, everything is possible.

A government which calls itself a national government ought to take responsibility for the totality of the nation; and in an underdeveloped country the young people represent one of the most important sectors. The level of consciousness of young people must be raised; they need enlightenment. If the work of explanation had been carried on among the youth of the nation, and if the Young People's National Union had carried out its task of integrating them into the nation, those mistakes would have been avoided which have threatened or already undermined the future of the Latin American republics. The army is not always a school of war; more often, it is a school of civic and political education. The soldier of an adult nation is not a simple mercenary but a citizen who by means of arms defends the nation. That is why it is of fundamental importance that the soldier should know that he is in the service of his country and not in the service of his commanding officer, however great that officer's prestige may be. We must take advantage of the national military and civil service in order to raise the level of the national consciousness, and to detribalise and unite the nation. In an underdeveloped country every effort is made to mobilise men and women as quickly as possible; it must guard against the danger of perpetuating the feudal tradition which holds sacred the superiority of the masculine element over the feminine. Women will have exactly the same place as men, not in the clauses of the constitution but in the life of every day: in the factory, at school and in the parliament. If in the Western countries men are shut up in barracks, that is not to say that this is always the best procedure. Recruits need not necessarily be militarised. The national service may be civil or military, and in any case it is advisable that every able-bodied citizen can at any moment take his place in a fighting unit for the defence of national and social liberties.

It should be possible to carry out large-scale undertakings in the public interest by using recruited labour. This is a marvellous way of stirring up inert districts and of making known to a greater number of citizens the needs of their country. Care must be taken to avoid turning the army into an autonomous body which sooner or later, finding itself idle and without any definite mission, will 'go into politics' and threaten the government. Drawing-room generals, by dint of haunting the corridors of government departments, come to dream of manifestoes. The only way to avoid this menace is to educate the army politically, in other words to nationalise it. In the same way another urgent task is to increase the militia. In case of war, it is the whole nation which fights and works. It should not include any professional soldiers, and the number of permanent officers should be reduced to a minimum. This is in the first place because officers are very often chosen from the university class, who could be much more useful elsewhere; an engineer is a thousand times more indispensable to his country than an officer; and secondly, because the crystallisation of the caste spirit must be avoided. We have seen in the preceding pages that nationalism, that magnificent song that made the people rise against their oppressors, stops short, falters and dies away on the day that independence is proclaimed. Nationalism is not a political doctrine, nor a programme. If you really wish your country to avoid regression, or at best halts and uncertainties, a rapid step must be taken from national consciousness to political and social consciousness. The nation does not exist in a programme which has been worked out by revolutionary leaders and taken up with full understanding and enthusiasm by the masses. The nation's effort must constantly be adjusted into the general background of underdeveloped countries. The battle line against hunger, against ignorance, against poverty and against unawareness ought to be ever present in the muscles and the intelligences of men and women. The work of the masses and their will to overcome the evils which have for centuries excluded them from the mental

Chapter 6: Conclusion

Come, then, comrades; it would be as well to decide at once to change our ways. We must shake off the heavy darkness in which we were plunged, and leave it behind. The new day which is already at hand must find us firm, prudent, and resolute.

We must leave our dreams and abandon our old beliefs and friendships of the time before life began. Let us waste no time in sterile litanies and nauseating mimicry. Leave this Europe where they are never done talking of Man, yet murder men everywhere they find them, at the corner of every one of their own streets, in all the corners of the globe. For centuries they have stifled almost the whole of humanity in the name of a so-called spiritual experience. Look at them today swaying between atomic and spiritual disintegration.

And yet it may be said that Europe has been successful in as much as everything that she has attempted has succeeded.

Europe undertook the leadership of the world with ardour, cynicism, and violence. Look at how the shadow of her palaces stretches out ever further! Every one of her movements has burst the bounds of space and thought. Europe has declined all humility and all modesty; but she has also set her face against all solicitude and all tenderness.

She has only shown herself parsimonious and niggardly where men are concerned; it is only men that she has killed and devoured.

So, my brothers, how is it that we do not understand that we have better things to do than to follow that same Europe?

That same Europe where they were never done talking of Man, and where they never stopped proclaiming that they were only anxious for the welfare of Man: today we know with what sufferings humanity has paid for every one of their triumphs of the mind.

Come, then, comrades, the European game has finally ended; we must find something different. We today can do everything, so long as we do not imitate Europe, so long as we are not obsessed by the desire to catch up with Europe.

Europe now lives at such a mad, reckless pace that she has shaken off all guidance and all reason, and she is running headlong into the abyss; we would do well to avoid it with all possible speed.

Yet it is very true that we need a model, and that we want blueprints and examples. For many among us the European model is the most inspiring. We have therefore seen in the preceding pages to what mortifying setbacks such an imitation has led us. European achievements, European techniques, and the European style ought no longer to tempt us and to throw us off our balance.

When I search for Man in the technique and the style of Europe, I see only a succession of negations of man, and an avalanche of murders.

The human condition, plans for mankind, and collaboration between men in those tasks which increase the sum total of humanity are new problems, which demand true inventions.

Let us decide not to imitate Europe; let us combine our muscles and our brains in a new direction. Let us try to create the whole man, whom Europe has been incapable of bringing to triumphant birth.

Two centuries ago, a former European colony decided to catch up with Europe. It succeeded so well that the United States of America became a monster, in which the taints, the sickness, and the inhumanity of Europe have grown to appalling dimensions.

Comrades, have we not other work to do than to create a third Europe? The West saw itself as a spiritual adventure. It is in the name of the spirit, in the name of the spirit of Europe, that Europe has made her encroachments, that she has justified her crimes and legitimised the slavery in which she holds four-fifths of humanity.

Yes, the European spirit has strange roots. All European thought has unfolded in places which were increasingly more deserted and more encircled by precipices; and thus it was that the custom grew up in those places of very seldom meeting man.

A permanent dialogue with oneself and an increasingly obscene narcissism never ceased to prepare the way for a half delirious state, where intellectual work became suffering and the reality was not at all that of a living man, working and creating himself, but rather words, different combinations of words, and the tensions springing from the meanings contained in words. Yet some Europeans were found to urge the European workers to shatter this narcissism and to break with this unreality.

But in general, the workers of Europe have not replied to these calls; for the workers believe, too, that they are part of the prodigious adventure of the European spirit.

All the elements of a solution to the great problems of humanity have, at different times, existed in European thought. But the action of European men has not carried out the mission which fell to them, and which consisted of bringing their whole weight violently to bear upon these elements, of modifying their arrangement and their nature, of changing them and finally of bringing the problem of mankind to an infinitely higher plane.

Today, we are present at the stasis of Europe. Comrades, let us flee from this motionless movement where gradually dialectic is changing into the logic of equilibrium. Let us reconsider the question of mankind. Let us reconsider the question of cerebral reality and of the cerebral mass of all humanity, whose connections must be increased, whose channels must be diversified and whose messages must be re-humanised.

Come, brothers, we have far too much work to do for us to play the game of rearguard. Europe has done what she set out to do and on the whole she has done it well; let us stop blaming her, but let us say to her firmly that she should not make such a song and dance about it. We have no more to fear; so let us stop envying her.

The Third World today faces Europe like a colossal mass whose aim should be to try to resolve the problems to which Europe has not been able to find the answers.

But let us be clear: what matters is to stop talking about output, and intensification, and the rhythm of work.

No, there is no question of a return to Nature. It is simply a very concrete question of not dragging men towards mutilation, of not imposing upon the brain rhythms which very quickly obliterate it and wreck it. The pretext of catching up must not be used to push man around, to tear him away from himself or from his privacy, to break and kill him.

No, we do not want to catch up with anyone. What we want to do is to go forward all the time, night and day, in the company of Man, in the company of all men. The caravan should not be stretched out, for in that case each line will hardly see those who precede it; and men who no longer recognise each other meet less and less together, and talk to each other less and less.

It is a question of the Third World starting a new history of Man, a history which will have regard to the sometimes prodigious theses which Europe has put forward, but which will also not forget Europe's crimes, of which the most horrible was committed in the heart of man, and consisted of the pathological tearing apart of his functions and the crumbling away of his unity. And in the framework of the collectivity there were the differentiations, the stratification, and the bloodthirsty tensions fed by classes; and finally, on the immense scale of humanity, there were racial hatreds, slavery, exploitation, and above all the bloodless genocide which consisted in the setting aside of fifteen thousand millions of men.

So, comrades, let us not pay tribute to Europe by creating states, institutions, and societies which draw their inspiration from her.

Humanity is waiting for something from us other than such an imitation, which would be almost an obscene caricature.

If we want to turn Africa into a new Europe, and America into a new Europe, then let us leave the destiny of our countries to Europeans. They will know how to do it better than the most gifted among us.

But if we want humanity to advance a step further, if we want to bring it up to a different level than that which Europe has shown it, then we must invent and we must make discoveries.

If we wish to live up to our peoples' expectations, we must seek the response elsewhere than in Europe.

Moreover, if we wish to reply to the expectations of the people of Europe, it is no good sending them back a reflection, even an ideal reflection, of their society and their thought with which from time to time they feel immeasurably sickened.

For Europe, for ourselves, and for humanity, comrades, we must turn over a new leaf, we must work out new concepts, and try to set afoot a new man.

TOWARD THE AFRICAN REVOLUTION
From Section I: The Problem of the Colonised
The North African syndrome[1]

It is a common saying that man is constantly a challenge to himself, and that were he to claim that he is no longer he would be denying himself. It must be possible, however, to describe an initial, a basic dimension of all human problems. More precisely, it would seem that all the problems which man faces on the subject of man can be reduced to this one question:

'Have I not, because of what I have done or failed to do, contributed to an impoverishment of human reality?'

The question could also be formulated in this way:

'Have I at all times demanded and brought out the man that is in me?'

I want to show in what is to follow that, in the specific case of the North African who has emigrated to France, a theory of inhumanity is in a fair way to finding its laws and its corollaries.

All those men who are hungry, all those men who are cold, all those men who are afraid ...

All those men of whom *we* are afraid, who crush the jealous emerald of our dreams, who twist the fragile curve of our smiles, all those men we face, who ask us no questions, but to whom we put strange ones.

Who are they?

I ask you, I ask myself. Who are they, those creatures starving for humanity who stand buttressed against the impalpable frontiers (though I know them from experience to be terribly distinct) of complete recognition?

Who are they, in truth, those creatures, who hide, who are hidden by social truth beneath the attributes of *bicot, bounioule, arabe, raton, sidi, mon z' ami*?[2]

FIRST THESIS. *That the behaviour of the North African often causes a medical staff to have misgivings as to the reality of his illness.*

Except in urgent cases – an intestinal occlusion, wounds, accidents – the North African arrives enveloped in vagueness. He has an ache in his belly, in his back, he has an ache everywhere. He suffers miserably, his face is eloquent, he is obviously suffering.

'What's wrong my friend?'

'I'm dying, *monsieur le docteur*.'

His voice breaks imperceptibly.

'Where do you have pain?

'Everywhere, *monsieur le docteur*.'

You must not ask for specific symptoms: you would not be given any. For example, in pains of an ulcerous character, it is important to know their frequency. This conformity to the categories of time is something to which the North African seems to be hostile. It is not lack of comprehension, for he often comes accompanied by an interpreter. It is as though it is an effort for him to go back to where he no longer is. The past for him is burning past. What he hopes is that he will never suffer again, never again be face to face with that past. This present pain, which visibly mobilises the muscles of his face, suffices for him. He does not understand that anyone should wish to impose on him, even by way of memory, the pain that is already gone. He does not understand why the doctor asks him so many questions.

'Where does it hurt?'

'In my belly.' (He then points to his thorax and abdomen.)

'When does it hurt?'

'All the time.'

'Even at night?'

'Especially at night.'

'It hurts more at night than in the daytime, does it?'

'No, all the time.'

'But more at night than in the daytime?'

'No all the time.'

'And where does it hurt most?'

'Here.' (He then points to his thorax and abdomen.)

And there you are. Meanwhile patients are waiting outside, and the worst of it is that you have the impression that time would not improve matters. You therefore fall back on a diagnosis of probability and in correlation propose an approximate therapy.

'Take this treatment for a month. If you don't get better, come back and see me.'

There are then two possibilities:

1. The patient is not immediately relieved, and he comes back after three or four days. This sets us against him, because we know that it takes time for the prescribed medicine to have an effect on the lesion. He is made to understand this, or more precisely, he is told. But our patient has not heard what we said. He *is* his pain and he refuses to understand any language, and it is not far from this to the conclusion: it is because I am Arab that they don't treat me like others.

2. The patient is not immediately relieved, but he does not go back to the same doctor, nor to the same dispensary. He goes elsewhere. He proceeds on the assumption that in order to get satisfaction he has to knock at every door, and he knocks. He knocks persistently. Gently. Naïvely. Furiously.

He knocks. The door is opened. The door is always opened. And he tells about *his pain*. Which becomes increasingly his own. He now talks about it volubly. He takes hold of it in space and puts it before the doctor's nose. He takes it, touches it with his ten fingers, develops it, exposes it. It grows as one watches it. He gathers it over the whole surface of his body and after fifteen minutes of gestured explanations the interpreter (appropriately baffling) translates for us: he says he has a belly ache.

All those forays into space, all those facial spasms, all those wild stares were only meant to express a vague discomfort. We experience a kind of frustration in the field of explanation. The comedy, or the drama, begins all over again: approximate diagnosis and therapy.

There is no reason for the wheel to stop going round. Some day an X-ray will be taken of him which will show an ulcer or gastritis. Or which in most cases will show nothing at all. His ailment will be described as 'functional'.

This concept is of some importance and is worth looking into. A thing is said to be vague when it is lacking in consistency, in objective reality. The North African's pain, for which we can find no lesional basis, is judged to have no consistency, no reality. Now the North African is a-man-who-doesn't-like-work. So that whatever he does will be interpreted *a priori* on the basis of this.

A North African is hospitalised because he suffers from lassitude, asthenia, weakness. He is given active treatment on the basis of restoratives. After twenty days it is decided to discharge him. He then discovers that he has another disease.

'My heart seems to flutter inside here.'

'My head is bursting.'

In the face of this fear of leaving hospital one begins to wonder if the debility for which he was treated was not due to some giddiness. One begins to wonder if one has not been the plaything of this patient whom one has never too well understood. Suspicion rears its head. Henceforth one will mistrust all the alleged symptoms.

The thing is perfectly clear in the winter; so much so that certain wards are literally submerged by North Africans during the severe cold spells. It's so comfortable within the hospital walls. In one ward, the doctor was scolding a European suffering from sciatica who spent the day visiting in the different rooms. The doctor explained to him that with his particular ailment, rest constituted one half of the therapy. With the North Africans, he added, for our benefit, the problem is different: there is no need to prescribe rest; they're always in bed.

In the face of this pain without lesion, this illness distributed in and over the whole body, this continuous suffering, the easiest attitude, to which one comes more or less rapidly, is the negation of any morbidity. When you come down to it, the North African is a simulator, a liar, a malingerer, a sluggard, a thief.[3]

SECOND THESIS. *That the attitude of medical personnel is very often an a priori attitude. The North African does not come with a substratum common to his race, but on a foundation built by the European. In other words, the North African, spontaneously, by the very fact of appearing on the scene, enters into a pre-existing framework.*

For several years medicine has shown a trend which, in a very summary way, we can call neo-Hippocratism. In accordance with this trend, doctors when faced with a patient, are concerned less with making a diagnosis of an organ than with a diagnosis of a function. But this orientation has not yet found favour in the medical schools where pathology is taught. There is a flaw in the practitioner's thinking. An extremely dangerous flaw.

We shall see how it manifests itself in practice.

I am called in to visit a patient on an emergency. It is two o'clock in the morning. The room is dirty, the patient is dirty. His parents are dirty. Everybody weeps. Everybody screams. One had the impression that death is hovering nearby. The young doctor does not let himself be perturbed. He 'objectively' examines the belly that has every appearance of requiring surgery.

He touches, he feels, he taps, he questions, but he gets only groans by way of response. He feels again, taps a second time, and the belly contracts, resists. ... He 'sees nothing'. But what if an operation is really called for? What if he is overlooking something? His examination is negative, but he doesn't dare to leave. After considerable hesitation, he will send his patient to a centre with a diagnosis of an abdomen requiring surgery. Three days later he sees the patient with the 'abdomen requiring surgery' turn up smilingly in his office, completely cured. And what the patient is unaware of is that there is an exacting medical philosophy, and he has flouted this philosophy.

Medical thinking proceeds from the symptom to the lesion. In the illustrious assemblies, in the international medical congresses, agreement has been reached as to the importance of the neuro-vegetative systems, the diencephalon, the endocrine glands, the psychosomatic links, the sympathalgias, but doctors continue to be taught that every symptom requires its lesion. The patient who complains of headaches, ringing in the ears, and dizziness, will also have high blood pressure. But should it happen that along with these symptoms there is no sign of high blood pressure, nor brain tumour, in any case nothing positive, the doctor would have to conclude that medical thinking was at fault; and as any thinking is necessarily thinking about something, he will find the *patient* at fault – an indocile, undisciplined patient, who doesn't know the rules of the game. Especially the rule, known to be inflexible, which says: any symptom presupposes a lesion.

What I am to do with this patient? From a specialist to whom I have sent him for a probable operation, he comes back to me with a diagnosis of 'North African syndrome'. And it is true that the newly arrived medico will run into situations reminiscent of Molière through the North Africans he is called upon to treat. A man who fancies himself to be ill! If Molière (what I am about to say is utterly stupid, but all these lines only explicate, only make more flagrant, something vastly more stupid), if Molière had the privilege of living in the twentieth century, he would certainly have written *Le Malade Imaginaire*, for there can be no doubt that Argan is ill, is actively ill:

'*Comment, coquine! Si je suis malade! Si je suis malade, impudente!*'[4]

206

The North African Syndrome. The North African today who goes to see a doctor bears the dead weight of all compatriots. Of all those who had only symptoms, of all those about whom the doctors said, 'Nothing you can put your teeth into'. (Meaning: no lesion). But the patient who is here in front of me, this body which I am forced to assume to be swept by a consciousness, this body which is no longer altogether a body or rather which is doubly a body since it is beside itself with terror – this body which asks me to listen to it without, however, paying too much heed to it – fills me with exasperation.

'Where do you hurt?'

'In my stomach.' (He points to his liver.)

I lose my patience. I tell him that the stomach is to the left, that what he is pointing to is the location of the liver. He is not put out, he passes the palm of his hand over that mysterious belly.

'It all hurts.'

I happen to know that this 'it all' contains three organs; more exactly five or six. That each organ has *its* pathology. The pathology invented by the Arab does not interest us. It is a pseudo-pathology. The Arab is a pseudo-invalid.

Every Arab is a man who suffers from an imaginary ailment. The young doctor or the young student who has never seen a sick Arab *knows* (the old medical tradition testifies to it) that 'those fellows are humbugs'. There is one thing that might give food for thought. Speaking to an Arab, the student or the doctor is inclined to use the second person singular. It's a nice thing to do, we are told ... to put them to ease ... they're used to it ... I am sorry but I find myself incapable of analysing this phenomenon without departing from the objective attitude to which I have constrained myself.

'I can't help it,' an intern once told me, 'I can't talk to them the same way I talk to other patients.'

Yes, to be sure: 'I can't help it.' If only you knew the things in my life that I can't help. If you only knew the things in my life that plague me during the hours when others are benumbing their brains. If you only knew ... but you will never know.

The medical staff discovers the existence of a North African syndrome. Not experimentally, but on the basis of oral tradition. The North African takes his place in this asymptomatic syndrome and is automatically put down as undisciplined (cf. medical discipline), inconsequential (with reference to the

'THE GRANTING OF FRENCH CITIZENSHIP, CONFERRING EQUALITY OF RIGHTS, SEEMS TO HAVE BEEN TOO HASTY AND BASED ON POLITICAL REASONS, RATHER THAN ON THE FACT OF THE SOCIAL AND INTELLECTUAL EVOLUTION OF A RACE HAVING CIVILISATION THAT IS AT TIMES REFINED BUT STILL PRIMITIVE IN ITS SOCIAL, FAMILY AND SANITARY BEHAVIOUR.' (p. 45)

Need anything be added? Should we take up these absurd sentences one after the other? Should we remind Dr Mugniery that if the North Africans in France content themselves with prostitutes, it is because they find prostitutes here in the first place, and also because they do not find any Arab women (who might invade the nation)?

4. *His inner tension.* Utterly unrealistic! You might as well speak of the inner tension of a stone. Inner tension indeed! What a joke!

5. *His sense of security or of insecurity.* The first term has to be struck out. The North African is in a perpetual state of insecurity. A multi-segmented insecurity.

I sometimes wonder if it would not be well to reveal to the average Frenchman that it is a misfortune to be a North African. The North African is never sure. He has rights, you will tell me, but he doesn't know what they are. Ah! Ah! It's up to him to know them. Yes, sure, we are back on our feet! Rights, Duties, Citizenship, Equality, what fine things! The North African on the threshold of the French Nation – which is, we are told, his as well – experiences in the political realm, on the plane of citizenship, an imbroglio which no one is willing to face. What connexion does this have with the North African in a hospital setting? It so happens that there *is* a connexion.

6. *The dangers that threaten him.* Threatened in his affectivity, threatened in his social activity, threatened in his membership in the community – the North African combines all conditions that make a man sick.

Without a family, without love, without human relations, without communion with the group, the first encounter with himself will occur in a neurotic mode, in a pathological mode; he will feel himself emptied, without life, in a bodily struggle with death, a death on this side of death, a death in life – and what is more pathetic than this man with robust muscles who tells us in his truly broken voice, 'Doctor, I'm going to die'?

7. *His evolution and the story of his life.* It would be better to say the history of his death. A daily death.

A death in the tram,
a death in the doctor's office,
a death with the prostitutes,
a death on the job site,
a death at the movies,
a multiple death in the newspapers,
a death in the fear of all decent folk of going out after midnight.
A death,
yes a DEATH.

All this is very fine, we shall be told, but what solutions do you propose?

As you know, they are vague, amorphous ...

'You constantly have to be on their backs.'

'You've got to push them out of the hospital.'

'If you were to listen to them you would prolong their convalescence indefinitely.'

'They can't express themselves.'

And are they liars
and also are they thieves
and also and also and also
the Arab is a thief
all Arabs are thieves
It's a do-nothing race
dirty
disgusting
Nothing you can do about them
nothing you can get out of them
sure, it's hard for them being the way they are
being that way
but anyway, you can't say it's our fault.

– But that's just it, it *is* our fault.

It so happens that the fault is YOUR fault.

Men come and go along the corridor you have built for them, where you have provided no bench on which they can rest, where you have crystallised a lot of scarecrows that viciously smack them in the face, and hurt their cheeks, their chests, their hearts.

Where they find no room

where you leave them no room

where there is absolutely no room for them

and you dare tell me it doesn't concern you!

that it's no fault of yours!

This man whom you thingify by calling him systematically Mohammed, whom you reconstruct, or rather whom you dissolve, on the basis of an idea, an idea you know to be repulsive (you know perfectly well you rob him of something, that something for which not so long ago you were ready to give up everything, even your life) well, don't you have the impression that you are emptying him of his substance?

Why don't they stay where they belong?

Sure! That's easy enough to say: why don't they stay where they belong? The trouble is, they have been told they were French. They learned it in school. In the street. In the barracks. (Where they were given shoes to wear on their feet.) On the battlefields. They have had France squeezed into them wherever, in their bodies and in their souls, there was room for something apparently great.

Now they are told in no uncertain terms that they are in 'our' country. That if they don't like it, all they have to do is go back to their Casbah. For here too there is a problem.

Whatever vicissitudes he may come up against in France, so some people claim, the North African will be happier at home …

It has been found in England that children who were magnificently fed, each having two nurses entirely at his service, but living away from the family circle, showed a morbidity twice as pronounced as children who were less fed but who lived with their parents. Without going so far, think of all those who lead a life without a future in their own country and who refuse fine positions abroad. What is the good of a fine position if it does not culminate in a family, in something that can be called home?

Psychoanalytical science considers expatriation to be a morbid phenomenon. In which it is perfectly right.

These considerations allow us to conclude:

1. The North African will never be happier in Europe than at home, for he is asked to live without the very substance of his affectivity. Cut off from his origins and cut off from his ends, he is a thing tossed into the great sound and fury, bowed beneath the law of inertia.

2. There is something manifestly and abjectly disingenuous in the above statement. If the standard of living made available to the North African in France is higher than the one he was accustomed to at home, this means that there is still a good deal to be done in his country, in that 'other part of France'.

That there are houses to be built, schools to be opened, roads to be laid out, slums to be torn down, cities to be made to spring from the earth, men and women and children to be adorned with smiles.

This means that there is work to be done over here, human work, that is, work which is a meaning of a home. Not that of a room or a barrack building. It means that over the whole territory of the French nation (the metropolis and the French Union), there are tears to be wiped away, inhuman attitudes to be fought, condescending ways of speech to be ruled out, men to be humanised.

Your solution, sir?

Don't push me too far. Don't force me to tell you what you ought to know, sir. If YOU do not reclaim the man who is before you, how can I assume that you reclaim the man that is in you?

If YOU do not want the man who is before you, how can I believe the man that is perhaps in you?

If YOU do not demand the man, if YOU do not sacrifice the man that is in you so that the man who is on this earth shall be more than a body, more than a Mohammed, by what conjurer's trick will I have to acquire the certainty that you, too, are worthy of my love?

NOTES

1 First published in *L'Esprit*, February 1952.

2 Terms of contempt applied in France to Arabs in general and to Algerians in particular. (Translator's note)

3 *Social Security? It's we who pay for it!*

4 'What, you hussy! You doubt if I'm sick! You doubt if I'm sick, you impudent wench!'

5 Dr E. *Stern*. '*Médicine psychosomatique*', *Psyché* (January–February 1949), p. 128. Emphasis added.

6 Emphasis added.

7 Emphasis added.

From Section III: For Algeria

Letter to the resident minister (1956)

Monsieur le Docteur Frantz Fanon
Médecin des Hôpitaux Psychiatriques
Médecin-Chef de Service à
l'Hôpital Psychiatriques de
BLIDA-JOINVILLE

à Monsieur le Ministre Résident,
Gouverneur Général de l'Algérie
ALGER

Monsieur le Ministre,

At my request and by decree under date of 22 October 1953, the Minister of Public Health and Population was good enough to put me at the disposal of the Governor-General of Algeria to be assigned to a Psychiatric Hospital in Algeria.

Having been given a post at the Psychiatric Hospital of Blida-Joinville on 23 November 1953, I have since that date performed the duties of medical director here.

Although the objective conditions under which psychiatry is practised in Algeria constituted a challenge to common sense, it appeared to me that an effort should be made to attenuate the viciousness of a system in which the doctrinal foundations are a daily defiance of an authentically human outlook.

For nearly three years I have placed myself wholly at the service of this country and of the men who inhabit it. I have spared neither my effort nor my enthusiasm. There is not a parcel of my activity that has not had as its objective the unanimously hoped-for emergence of a better world.

But what can a man's enthusiasm and devotion achieve if everyday reality is a tissue of lies, of cowardice, of contempt for man?

What good are intentions if their realisation is made impossible by the indigence of the heart, the sterility of the mind, the hatred of the natives of this country?

215

Madness is one of the means man has of losing his freedom. And I can say, on the basis of what I have been able to observe from this point of vantage, that the degree of alienation of the inhabitants of this country appears to me frightening.

If psychiatry is the medical technique that aims to enable man no longer to be a stranger to his environment, I owe it to myself to affirm that the Arab, permanently an alien in his own country, lives in a state of absolute depersonalisation.

What is the status of Algeria? A systematised de-humanisation.

It was an absurd gamble to undertake, at whatever cost, to bring into existence a certain number of values, when the lawlessness, the inequality, the multi-daily murder of man were raised to the status of legislative principles.

The social structure existing in Algeria was hostile to any attempt to put the individual back where he belonged. Monsieur le Ministre, there comes a moment where tenacity becomes morbid perseverance. Hope is then no longer an open door to the future but the illogical maintenance of a subjective attitude in organised contradiction with reality.

Monsieur le Ministre, the present-day events that are steeping Algeria in blood do not constitute a scandal for the observer. What is happening is the result neither of an accident nor of a breakdown in the mechanism.

The events in Algeria are the logical consequence of an abortive attempt to decerebralise a people.

One did not have to be a psychologist to divine, beneath the apparent good nature of the Algerian, behind his stripped humility, a fundamental aspiration to dignity. And nothing is to be gained, with respect to non-simplifiable manifestations, by appealing to some form of civic conscience.

The function of a social structure is to set up institutions to serve man's needs. A society that drives its members to desperate solutions is a non-viable society, a society to be replaced.

It is the duty of the citizen to say this. No professional morality, no class solidarity, no desire to wash family linen in private, can have a prior claim. No pseudo-national mystification can prevail against the requirement of reason.

Monsieur le Ministre, the decision to punish the workers who went out on strike on 5 July 1956, is a measure which, literally, strikes me as irrational.

Either the strikers have been terrorised in their flesh and that of their families, in which case there was an obligation to understand their attitude, to regard it as normal, in view of the atmosphere.

Or else their abstention expressed a unanimous current of opinion, an unshakeable conviction, in which case any punitive attitude was superfluous, gratuitous, inoperative.

I owe it to the truth to say that fear has not struck me as being the dominant mood of the strikers. Rather, there was the inevitable determination to bring about, in calm and silence, a new era of peace and dignity.

The worker in the commonwealth must cooperate in the social scheme of things. But he must be convinced of the excellence of the society in which he lives. There comes a time when silence becomes dishonesty.

The ruling intentions of personal existence are not in accord with the permanent assaults on the most commonplace values.

For many months my conscience has been the seat of unpardonable debates. And their conclusion is the determination not to despair of man, in other words, of myself.

The decision I have reached is that I cannot continue to bear a responsibility at no matter what cost, on the false pretext that there is nothing else to be done.

For all these reasons I have the honour, Monsieur le Ministre, to ask you to be good enough to accept my resignation and to put an end to my mission in Algeria.

Yours sincerely

From Section IV: Toward the Liberation of Africa

French intellectuals and democrats and the Algerian Revolution[1]

1

One of the first duties of intellectuals and democratic elements in colonialist countries is unreservedly to support the national aspiration of colonised peoples. This attitude is based on very important theoretical considerations: the defence of an idea of man challenged in the Western countries, the refusal to participate institutionally in the degradation and negation of certain values, the community of interests between the working classes of the conquering country and the combined population of the conquered and dominated country, and finally the feeling that the government must be made to respect the right of peoples to self-determination.

This support and this solidarity find their expression, before the period of armed struggle, in the holding of a few meetings and in the adoption of motions. Sometimes, when a suddenly very fierce repression occurs, which is an obvious forerunner of a more thoroughgoing, more extensive repression (in the case of Algeria, M. Naegelen's election and the 1950–51 plot), a press campaign, statements, warnings, appeals are prepared.

It must be pointed out that not a single attempt at an explanation is undertaken on the level of the population of the colonialist country. Because it has no hold on the people, the democratic Left, shut in upon itself, convinces itself in endless articles and studies that Bandung has sounded the death-knell of colonialism. But it is the real people, the peasants and the workers, who must be informed. Incapable of reaching the millions of workers and peasants of the colonialists' people and of explaining and commenting on the realities of the drama that is beginning, the Left finds itself being reduced to the role of a Cassandra. It announces cataclysms, but because public opinion has not been adequately prepared, these prophecies, inexplicable in the pre-insurrectional period, will, at the time of explosion, be regarded as proof of complicity.

A PAINFUL INEFFECTIVENESS

Thus, in the special case of Algeria, after the acute pre-insurrectional phase (1952–3), when the period of the armed phase began (sabotaging, raids), the Left was paradoxically caught off its guard and proved helpless.

The French democratic elements and intellectuals are familiar with the problem. Having seeing it at close range and having studied it for a long time, they know its complexity, its depth, and its tension. But all this knowledge proves futile because it is utterly disproportionate to the simple ideas current among the people.

Encumbered by this unusable knowledge, the Left enjoys the status of a prophet. For a long time it has repeated to those who govern: 'You were forewarned; all this is happening through no fault but your own.'

In this effervescent phase of alignment of forces and of organisation of the armed struggle of the colonised people, we witness a partial communication between the people in revolt and the democratic elements. This is because very often the intellectuals and the democrats have personally known the present leaders of the armed struggle. There thus develops between them a kind of apparent complicity. But this active pseudo-solidarity is very quickly swept away by events. In the course of the second period, characterised by engagements, ambushes, and assaults, the guilt so generously projected on the official heads tends in fact to be displaced. The repression goes deeper, becomes organised, diversified. Torture chambers appear. Over the whole Algerian national territory tens and hundreds of patriots are murdered.

The real people, the men and women, the children and the old people in the colonised country, take it for granted that existing, in the biological sense of the word, and existing as a sovereign people are synonymous. The only possible issue, the sole way of salvation for this people is to react as energetically as it can to the genocide campaign being conducted against it. The reaction is becoming progressively more absolute.

NATIONALISM AND 'BARBARISM'

Here we encounter a double phenomenon. First of all an ultra-chauvinistic, nationalistic, patriotic propaganda, mobilising the implicit racist elements of the collective consciousness of the colonialist people, introduces a new element. It immediately becomes obvious that it is no longer possible to back the colonised without at the same time opposing the national solution. The fight against colonialism becomes a fight against the nation. The war of conquest is assumed by the colonialist country as a whole, and anti-colonialist arguments lose their efficacy, become abstract theories and finally disappear from democratic literature.

In the case of Algeria, it was after March 1955, with the calling out of the contingent, that the French nation took over the war of colonial reconquest. The demonstrations of the draftees were at that point the last symptoms of a war whose doctrinal motivations had no popular support.

From 1956 onwards the Algerian war was accepted by the nation. France wants the war, as M. Guy Mollet and M. Bourgès-Maunoury have explicitly stated; and the people of Paris, on 14 July 1957, conveyed to Massu's parachutist torturers the country's deep gratitude. The liberals abandoned the struggle at this stage. The accusation of treason to which the adversaries of the Algerian war exposed themselves became a formidable weapon in the hands of the French Government. Thus in early 1957 many democrats ceased their protests or were overwhelmed by the clamour for vengeance, and a clumsily structured elementary patriotism manifested itself, steeped in racism – violent, totalitarian, in short, fascist.

The French Government was to find its second argument in what is called terrorism. Bombs in Algiers have been exploited by the propaganda service. Innocent children who got hurt, who did not answer to the name of Borgeaud or who did not fit the classic definition of the 'ferocious colonialist', created unexpected problems for French democrats. The Left was staggered; Sakamody accentuated this reaction. Ten French civilians, in this case, were killed in an ambush and the entire French Left, in a unanimous outburst, cried out: we can no longer follow you! The propaganda became orchestrated, wormed its way into people's minds and dismantled convictions that were already crumbling. The concept of barbarism appeared and it was decided that France in Algeria was fighting barbarism.

A large portion of the intellectuals, almost the entire democratic Left, collapsed and laid down its conditions before the Algerian people: condemn Sakamody and the bombs and we shall continue to give you our friendly support.

On the dawn of the fourth year of the war of national liberation, in the face of the French nation and in the face of the bombs that had been exploded on the rue Michelet, the French Left was more and more conspicuous by its absence.

Some took refuge in silence; others chose certain themes, which reappear periodically. The Algerian war must end for it is too costly (the Algerian war is again becoming unpopular, simply because it costs 1,200 billion francs), it isolates France or makes possible her replacement by the Anglo-Saxons or by the Russians or by Nasser, etc...

In France it becomes less and less clear why the Algerian war must end. People forget more and more that France, in Algeria, is trampling popular sovereignty underfoot, flouting the right of peoples to self-determination, murdering thousands of men and women.

In France, among the Left, the Algerian war is tending to become a disease of the French system, like ministerial instability, and colonial wars a nervous tic with which France is afflicted, a part of the national panorama, a familiar detail.

2

Since 1956, France intellectuals and democrats have periodically addressed themselves to the FLN. Most of the time they have proffered either political advice or criticisms concerning this or that aspect of the war of liberation. This attitude of the French intelligentsia must not be interpreted as the consequence of an inner solidarity with the Algerian people. This advice and these criticisms are to be explained by the ill-repressed desire to guide, to direct the very liberation movement of the oppressed.

Thus can be understood the constant oscillation of the French democrats between a manifest or latent hostility and the wholly unreal aspiration to militate 'actively to the end'. Such a confusion indicates a lack of preparation for the facing of concrete problems and a failure on the part of French democrats to immerse themselves in the political life of their own country.

Along this oscillating line the French democrats – outside the struggle or intent upon observing it from within, and even participating in it in the capacity of censors, of advisers, unable or refusing to choose a precise ground on which to fight within the French system – issue threats and practise blackmail.

The pseudo-justification for this attitude is that in order to have an influence on French public opinion, certain facts must be condemned, the unexpected excrescences must be rejected, the 'excesses' must be disavowed. In these moments of crisis, of face-to-face opposition, the FLN is being asked to direct its violence, and to make it selective.

THE MYTH OF FRENCH ALGERIA

At this level, reflection enables us to discover an important peculiarity of colonial reality in Algeria. Within a nation it is usual and commonplace to identify two antagonistic forces: the working class and bourgeois capitalism. In a colonial country this distinction proves totally inadequate. What defines the colonial situation is rather the undifferentiated character that foreign domination presents. The colonial situation is first of all a military conquest continued and reinforced by a civil and police administration. In Algeria, as in every colony, the foreign oppressor looks upon the native as marking a limit to his dignity and defines himself as constituting an irreducible negation of the colonised country's national existence.

The status of the foreigner, of the conqueror, of the Frenchman in Algeria, is the status of an oppressor. The Frenchman in Algeria cannot be neutral or innocent. Every Frenchman in Algeria oppresses, despises, dominates. The French Left, which cannot remain indifferent and impervious to its own phantasms, adopted paradoxical positions in Algeria, during the period preceding the war of liberation.

WHAT IS COLONIALISM?

French democrats, in deciding to give the name of 'colonialism' to what has never ceased to be military conquest and occupation, have deliberately simplified facts. The term of colonialism created by the oppressor is too affective, too emotional. It is placing a national problem on a psychological level. This is why, as conceived by these democrats, the contrary of colonialism is not the recognition of the right of peoples to self-determination, but the necessity, on an individual level, for less racist, more open, more liberal types of behaviour.

Colonialism is not a type of individual relation but the conquest of a national territory and the oppression of a people: that is all. It is not a certain type of human behaviour or a pattern of relations between individuals. Every Frenchman in Algeria is at the present time an enemy soldier. So long as Algeria is not independent, this logical consequence must be accepted. M. Lacoste shows that he has understood it, by his 'surface mobilisation' of the Frenchmen and Frenchwomen residing in Algeria.

At the end of this analysis we perceive that, far from reproaching the National Liberation Front for some of its urban actions, we should on the contrary appreciate the efforts that it imposes on the people.

It is because they have failed to understand that colonialism is only military domination that the French democrats have reached a paradoxical extreme.

Victims of the myth of French Algeria, the parties of the Left create Algerian sections of the French political parties on Algerian territory. The slogans, the programmes, the methods of struggle are identical to those of the 'metropolis'. A doctrinal position, unchallenged until just recently, has justified this attitude. In a colonial country, it used to be said, there is a community of interests between the colonised people and the working class of the colonialist country. The history of the wars of liberation waged by the colonised peoples is the history of the non-verification of this thesis.

COLONIALISM IS NOT M. BORGEAUD

The Algerian people has proved refractory to the over-simple imagery according to which a colonialist is a special type of man who can be readily recognised. Thus it has been claimed that all Frenchmen in Algeria are not colonialists, and that there are different degrees of colonialism. Now, neither M. Borgeaud nor M. de Sérigny wholly characterise French colonialism in Algeria. French colonialism, French oppression in Algeria, form a coherent whole which does not necessarily require the existence of M. Borgeaud. French domination is the totality of the forces that are opposed to the existence of the Algerian nation, and for the Algerian, concretely, M. Blachette is no more 'colonialist' than a police officer, a rural policeman, or a school teacher.

The Algerian experiences French colonialism as an undifferentiated whole, not out of simplemindedness or xenophobia but because in reality every Frenchman in Algeria maintains, with reference to the Algerian, relations that are based on force. The evocation of special cases of Frenchmen who are abnormally nice to Algerians does not modify the nature of the relations between a foreign group that has seized the attributes of national sovereignty and the people which finds itself deprived of the exercise of power. No personal relation can contradict this fundamental datum: that the French nation through its citizens opposes the existence of the Algerian nation.

In colonies that are held solely by occupying forces, the colonial people is represented by the soldiers, the police, and the technicians. Under those conditions the colonialist people can take refuge in ignorance of the facts and claim to be innocent of the colonisation. In settlement colonies, on the other hand, this running away from oneself becomes impossible. Because, in accordance with famous formula of a French chief of state, 'there is not a single Frenchman who does not have a cousin in Algeria', the whole French nation finds itself involved in the crime against a people and is today an accomplice in the murders and the tortures that characterise the Algerian war.

The authentic French democrat cannot just be *against* M. Borgeaud or M. Blachette; he must avoid choosing arbitrarily a few scapegoats who cannot express the 130 years of colonialist oppression. The French democrat must judge and condemn colonisation as a whole in its category of military and police oppression. He must convince himself that every Frenchman in Algeria reacts as M. Borgeaud does. Because there is not a Frenchman in Algeria who is not justified in his very existence by this domination.

Unable to adopt this attitude, through lack of courage or failure of analysis, the French democrat is constantly resorting to abstractions as points of reference: colonialism in general is dying, colonialism is inhuman, France must remain faithful to its history, thus pointedly forgetting that colonialism constitutes an important part of French history.

Colonialism is the organisation of the domination of a nation after military conquest. The war of liberation is not a seeking for reforms but the grandiose effort of a people, which had been mummified, to rediscover its own genius, to reassume its history and assert its sovereignty.

Frenchmen, within the framework of NATO, refuse to serve under the orders of German General Speidel, but are willing to fight against the Algerian people. But, strictly speaking, fidelity to the spirit of the French resistance should impel Frenchmen who find it distasteful to serve under Speidel to refuse, in terms of their own logic, to fight under Massu or Salan.

3

The men who govern France are obviously right when they claim that the Algerian problem is shaking the very foundation of the Republic. For some years the myth of French Algeria has been put to severe tests, and a dose of uncertainty has crept into the French consciousness as to the truth of this thesis.

On the international level, repercussions of this destruction have been noted. Such progress, however, has not totally solved the problem of the mystification engendered by dozens of years of wrong teaching and of systematised historic falsification.

THE PRICE OF MYSTIFICATION

When one closely examines the colonial relations that have existed between Algeria and France one notes that the Algerian territory, by the very characteristics of the conditions of its conquest, has always represented for France a more or less real prolongation. At no time has France indicated in identical terms its property rights over Africa south of the Sahara, or over any other fragment of 'French Empire'. Africa south of the Sahara may have been decreed French territory, but never was it decided that Africa south of Sahara was France.

France's right in Africa was based rather on a right of property, whereas in Algeria, from the beginning, relations of identity were affirmed. We have seen that French democrats, with rare exceptions, have adapted their attitude to this view. French political parties have not concealed the necessity they felt to mark obedience to this mystification. M. Laurent Cassanova, in a speech to the communist students delivered on 17 March 1957 in Paris, in response to criticisms levelled at him by the Communist youth on the attitude of the French Communist Party in respect to the Algerian problem, justified himself by asking them to take into account 'the spontaneous attitude of the French popular masses on the question'.

Because for 130 years the French national consciousness has been conditioned by one simple basic principle – Algeria *is* France – we today find ourselves up against instinctive, passionate, anti-historic reactions, at a moment when a large proportion of the French people rationally realises that its interest can best be served by putting an end to the war and recognising an independent Algerian State.

Never was the principle according to which no one can enslave another so wholly true. After having domesticated the Algerian people for more than a century, France finds herself a prisoner of her conquest and incapable of detaching herself from it, of defining new relations, of making a fresh start.

It would be a great mistake, however, to believe the problem to be exhausted by these psychological considerations. The encounters with the representatives of the French Left bring out much more complex concerns. Thus, on the precise point of the future of independent Algeria, we face two contradictory demands which, incidentally, match at a higher level the Manichean conception of good and evil that for some years now has divided the world.

The non-Communist Left assures us of its support, promises to act in our behalf, but asks us to give our guarantee that Algeria will never fall into the Communist bloc or into the so-called neutralist bloc. The anti-colonialism of these democrats is therefore not unreserved and unconditional, but assumes a precise political choice. They do not lack arguments, to be sure. Exchanging French colonialism for a red or Nasserian 'colonialism' appears to them to be a negative operation, for, they claim, at the present historic hour of great combinations, an alignment is compulsory and there is nothing veiled about their advice: one must choose the Western bloc.

This non-Communist Left is generally reticent when we explain to them that, for the moment, the Algerian people must first of all liberate itself from the French colonialist yoke. Refusing to confine itself to the strict ground of decolonisation and national liberation, the French non-Communist Left implores us to combine the two efforts: rejection of French colonialism and of Soviet-neutralist communism.

The same problem, in obedience to an opposite dynamism, arises with the French Communist Left. The French Communist Party, it says, can support only certain national liberation movements, for what would be the advantage, for us French Communists, of having American imperialism take over Algeria? Here again guarantees are demanded of us. Pressure is put upon us to give promises, assurances.

It will be understood that such difficulties stand in the way of the anti-colonialist action of the French Left. This is because the not yet independent Algeria has already become a bone of contention on an international scale. For whom, indeed, is Algeria going to be liberated? For three years the Algerian people has not ceased repeating that it proposes to liberate itself for its own sake, that what is important for it is first of all to reconquer its sovereignty, to establish its authority, to achieve its humanisation, its economic and political freedom; but these obvious objectives do not seem to find acceptance.

The Algerian people is undergoing its birth to independence in the midst of terrifying suffering and already the slightest bit of support is being haggled over with unaccustomed aggressiveness. Thus it is not rare to hear certain democratic Frenchmen tell us: help us to help you. Which clearly means: give us some idea of which direction you expect to take afterwards.

This summons, which is always proffered on an individual level between Frenchmen and Algerians, certainly represents one of the most painful aspects of the struggle for independence. Certain French democrats are at times shocked by the sincerity of the Algerian fighter. This is because the total character of the war that we wage has a repercussion on the no less radical manner in which we conduct individual exchanges. And we must confess that it is unendurably painful for us to see certain Frenchmen whom we had considered our friends behave with us like tradesmen and practise this kind of hateful blackmail whereby solidarity is hedged about with all sorts of fundamental restrictions as to our objectives.

A FUNDAMENTAL DISAGREEMENT

If we examine the attitude of the French Left with respect to the objectives of our struggle, we perceive that no faction admits the possibility of a real national liberation.

The non-Communist Left concedes that the colonial status must disappear. But, between the liquidation of the colonial system – reduced under the circumstances to a preferential system, with a struggle of castes within a whole – and the recognition of an Algerian nation, independent of France, this Left has interposed a multitude of stages, of sun-stages, of original solutions, of compromises.

It is clear that for this part of the Left the end of the Algerian war must bring about a kind of international federalism and renovated French Union. Our disagreement with this French opinion is thus neither of a psychological order nor of a tactical order, as some pretend. The Left-wing radicals, the minority socialists, and the Left Wing of the MRP[2] have not accepted the idea of an Algerian independence. There is therefore something radically false about positions that begin with the formula: 'We agree in substance but not as to the methods …'

The Communist Left, for its part, while proclaiming the necessity for colonial countries to evolve towards independence, requires the maintenance of special links with France. Such positions clearly manifest that even the so-called extremist parties consider that France has rights in Algeria and that the lightening of domination does not necessarily imply the disappearance of every link. This mental attitude assumes the guise of a technocratic paternalism, of a disingenuous warning against the danger of regression.

After breaking all links with France, it is argued, what will you do?

You need technicians, currency, machines …

Not even the catastrophic prospect of an Algeria consumed by the desert, infested by marshes, and ravaged by disease, is spared us in the campaign to give us pause.

The colonialists tell the French people in their propaganda: France cannot live without Algeria.

The French anti-colonialists say to the Algerians: Algeria cannot live without France.

The French democrats do not always perceive the colonialist, or – to use a new concept – the neo-colonialist character of their attitude.

The demand for special links with France is a response to the desire to maintain colonial structures intact. What is involved here is a kind of terrorism of necessity on the basis of which it is decided that nothing valid can be conceived or achieved in Algeria independently of France. In fact, the demand for special links with France comes down to a determination to maintain Algeria eternally in a stage of a minor and protected State. But also to a determination to guarantee certain forms of exploitation of the Algerian people. It is unquestionably proof of a grave failure to understand the revolutionary implications of the national struggle.

IS IT TOO LATE?

The French democrats must rise above the contradictions that sterilise their positions if they wish to achieve an authentic democratisation with the colonialists. It is to the extent to which French democratic opinion is without reticences that its action can be effective and decisive.

Because the Left unconsciously obeys the myth of French Algeria, its action does not go beyond aspiring to an Algeria in which more justice and freedom would prevail or, at most, an Algeria less directly governed by France. The passion-charged chauvinism of French public opinion on the Algerian question exerts pressure on this Left, inclines it to excessive caution, shakes is principles, and places it in a paradoxical and increasingly sterile situation.

The Algerian people considers that the French Left has not done everything it should within the framework of the Algerian war. It is not up to us to accuse the French democrats, but we feel duty bound to draw their attention to certain attitudes that appear to us to be contrary to the principles of anti-colonialism.

It is perhaps worth recalling the attitude of the Socialist International on this question. No one has forgotten that in 1956 the French delegation led by M. Pineau was condemned by the International and that Mr Bevan in 1957, at the Socialist Congress in Toulouse, publicly expressed his disappointment and his anger at the racism and the colonialism manifested by SFIO.[3]

Since 1954 the Algerian people has been fighting for national independence. What is involved is a territory conquered more than a century ago which express its will to set itself up as a sovereign nation. The French Left should unreservedly support this effort. Neither the presence of a European minority, nor Sakamody, can or should affect the determination of an authentic Left. We have seen that M. Lacoste's propaganda keeps affirming that France, in Algeria, is fighting barbarism. The Left must prove itself immune to this campaign and demand the end of the war and the recognition of Algeria's independence.

It has happened, as we have seen, that certain democrats resort to the following reasoning: if you wish our aid to continue, condemn such and such acts. Thus the struggle of a people for its independence must be diaphanous if it would enjoy the support of democrats.

Here, paradoxically, may be recognised the attitude of M. Guy Mollet who, in order to continue his war, appoints a safeguard commission assigned to call attention to 'excesses', thus spectacularly isolating the bad soldiers from the good and true and fertile French army.

THE TASKS OF THE FRENCH LEFT

The FLN addresses itself to the entire French Left and asks of it, in this fourth year, to become concretely involved in the fight for peace in Algeria.

There can be no question, at any moment, of French democrats joining our ranks or betraying their country. Without renouncing their nation, the

French Left must fight to make the government of their country respect the values which we call the right of peoples to self-determination, recognition of the national will, liquidation of colonialism, mutual and enriching relations among free peoples.

The FLN addresses itself to the French Left, to French democrats, and asks them to encourage every strike undertaken by the French people against the rise in the cost of living, new taxes, the restriction of democratic freedoms in France, all of which are direct consequences of the Algerian war.

The FLN asks the French Left to strengthen its action in spreading information and to continue to explain to the French masses the characteristics of the struggle of the Algerian people, the principles that animate it, the objectives of the Revolution.

The FLN salutes the French who have had the courage to refuse to take up arms against the Algerian people and who are now in prison.

These examples must be multiplied in order that it may become clear to everyone and first of all to the French Government that the French people refuses this war which is being waged in its name against the right of peoples, for the maintenance of oppression, against the reign of freedom.

NOTES

1 The series of three articles appeared in El *Moudjahid* (1, 15 and 30 December 1957).

2 Popular Republican Movement, the French Catholic party. (Translator's note)

3 SFIO – *Section Française de L'Internationale Ouvrière*, the French Socialist Party. (Translator's note)

From Section V: African Unity

THIS AFRICA TO COME

[At the end of 1958 the *wilaya* colonels of the ALN held a meeting in the Nord-Constantinois. On this occasion they took note of the danger of a progressive strangling of the armed struggle in the interior as a result of the disposition of the enemy forces (forbidden areas, regrouping camps tending to cut off the ALN from the population).

It was decided to send Colonel Amirouche (colonel of *wilaya* III) to Tunis to explain the situation to the GPRA (Provisional Government of the Algerian Republic) and define the means whereby the interior could be supplied with arms, munitions, and finances.

Colonel Amirouche never reached Tunis, for he was killed by the enemy during this voyage in the region of Bou-Saâda in March 1959.

It was in order to meet this situation that the CNRA (National Committee of the Algerian Revolution) decided at its meeting in the fall of 1959 to create the General Staff.

The French army having reinforced its army at the frontiers (the Challe line) it was becoming difficult to supply the interior via Morocco and Tunisia.

In March 1960 Fanon was appointed to Accra. During his stay in West Africa he found that there was a possibly of strengthening the situation within by way of the southern frontier, namely the Mali frontier. He made contact with the Mali authorities and communicated his suggestions to the Algerian leaders who decided to set up a third base south of the Sahara for the shipment of arms to *wilayas* I and V. The notes that follow were written by Fanon in the course of the mission for the reconnaissance and setting up of this base during the summer of 1960.

To this logbook are added a number of technical problems in the form of hasty and unfinished notes in which Fanon examines the various solutions that might be adopted on the strictly operational level.]

To put Africa in motion, to cooperate in its organisation, in its regrouping, behind revolutionary principles, to participate in the ordered movement of a continent – this was really the work I had chosen. The first point of departure, the first base was represented by Guinea. Then Mali, ready for anything,

231

fervent and brutal, coherent and singularly keen, extended the bridgehead and opened valuable prospects. To the East, Lumumba was marking time. The Congo which constituted the second landing beach for revolutionary ideas was caught in an inextricable network of sterile contradictions. The colonialist citadels of Angola, Mozambique, Kenya, the Union of South Africa were not ripe to be effectively blockaded.

Yet everything was set. And here the colonialist system of defence, while discordant, was reviving old particularisms and breaking up the liberating lava. For the moment it was therefore necessary to hang on in the Congo and advance in the West. For us Algerians the situation was clear. But the terrain remained difficult, very difficult. Taking the West as a starting point, we had to prove, by concrete demonstrations, that this continent was one. That behind the general choices of the leaders, it was possible to determine the precise points at which the peoples, the men and the women, could meet, help one another, build in common. The spectre of the West, the European tinges, was everywhere present and active. The French, English, Spanish, Portuguese areas remained living. Oxford was opposed to the Sorbonne, Lisbon to Brussels, the English bosses to the Portuguese bosses, the pound to the franc, the Catholic Church to Protestantism or to Islam. And above all this, the United States had plunged in everywhere, dollars in the vanguard, with Armstrong as herald and American Negro diplomats, scholarships, the emissaries of the Voice of America ... And one must not forget hard-working Germany, Israel reclaiming the desert ...

A difficult task. Fortunately, in every corner arms make signs to us, voices answer us, hands grasp ours. Things are on the move.

The rapid and reassuring sound of the liberated cities that break their moorings and move forward, grandiloquent but by no means grandiose, these former militants now having definitely passed their examinations who sit down and remember.

... But the sun is still very high in the heaven and if one listens with one ear glued to the red earth one very distinctly hears the sound of rusty chains, groans of distress, and the bruised flesh is so constantly present in this stifling noonday that one's shoulders droop with the weight of it. The Africa of everyday, oh not the poets' Africa, the one that puts to sleep, but the one that prevents sleep, for the people is impatient to do, to play, to say. The people that says: I want to build myself as a people, I want to build, to love, to respect, to create. This people that weeps when you say: I come from a country where the women have no children and the children have no mothers and that sings: Algeria, brother country, country that calls, country that hopes.

That is real Africa, the Africa that we had to let loose in the continental furrow, in the continental direction. The Africa that we had to guide, mobilise, launch on the offensive. This Africa to come.

The West. Conakry, Bamako. Two cities dead on the surface, but underneath, the temperature is unendurable for those who calculate, who manoeuvre, who settle. In Conakry and in Bamako men and women strike Africa, forge it with love and enthusiasm.

Moumié. On 30 September we met on the Accra airfield. He was going to Geneva for some very important meetings. In three months he told us, we would witness a mass ebbing of colonialism in Cameroon.

In Tripoli, a fog prevented any landing and for three hours the plane circles above the airfield. The pilot wanted to land at any cost. The control tower refused the requested authorisation but the courageous and heedless pilot had decided to land his tens of thousands of tons. 'Those fellows gamble with people's lives,' Félix said to me.

It was true. But we are not gambling with ours? What was this pilot's intrepidity compared to our lives perpetually in suspense? Today Félix is dead. In Rome, two weeks later, we were to have met again. He was absent. His father standing at the arrival in Accra saw me coming, alone, and great sadness settled on his face.

Two days later a message told us that Félix was hospitalised. Then that poisoning was suspected. Kingue, the vice-president of the UPC[1] and Marthe Moumié decide to go to Geneva. A few days later the news reached us: Félix was dead.

We hardly felt this death. A murder, but a bloodless one. There were neither volleys nor machines guns nor bombs. Thallium poisoning. It made no sense. Thallium! How was one to grasp such a cause? An abstract death striking the most concrete, the most alive, the most impetuous man. Félix's tone was constantly high. Aggressive, violent, full of anger, in love with his country, hating cowards and manoeuvrers. Austere, hard, incorruptible. A bundle of revolutionary spirit packed into sixty kilos of muscle and bone.

In the evening we went to comfort the Cameroon comrades. The father, his face seamed, impassive, inexpressive, listened to me speak of his son. And progressively the father yielded place to the militant. Yes, he said, the programme is clear. We must stick to the programme. Moumié's father, at the moment, reminded me of those parents in Algeria who listen in a kind of stupor to the story of the death of their children. Who from time to time ask a question, require a detail, then relapse into that inertia of communion that seems to draw them towards where they think their sons have gone.

Action, however, will not be forgotten. Tomorrow, presently, the war must be carried to the enemy, who must be given no rest, pursued, knocked out.

We are off. Our mission: to open the southern front. To transport arms and munitions from Bamako. Stir up the Saharan population, infiltrate to the Algerian high plateaus. After carrying Algeria to the four corners of Africa, move up with all Africa towards African Algeria, towards the North, towards Algiers, the continental city. What I should like: great lines, great navigation channels through the desert. Subdue the desert, deny it, assemble Africa, create the continent. That Malians, Senegalese, Guineans, Ghanaians should descend from Mali on to our territory. And those of the Ivory Coast, of Nigeria, of Togoland. That they should all climb the slopes of the desert and pour over the colonialist bastion. To turn the absurd and the impossible inside out and hurl a continent against the last ramparts of colonial power.

There are eight of us: a commando, the army, transmission, political commissars, the sanitary corps. Each of the pairs is to prospect the working possibilities in respect of his own field. We must work fast. Time presses. The enemy is still stubborn. In reality he does not believe in military defeat. But I have never felt it so possible, so within reach. We need only march, and charge. It is not even a question of strategy. We have mobilised furious cohorts, loving our combat, eager to work. We have Africa with us. A continent is getting into motion and Europe is languorously asleep. Fifteen years ago it was Asia that was stirring. Today 650 million Chinese, calm possessors of an immense secret, are building a world by themselves alone. The giving birth of a world.

Chawki. A funny chap. A major in the ALN, born in the Souf. Small, lean, with the implacable eyes of an old *maquis* fighter. Those eyes tell their own story. They say openly that they have witnessed hard things: repressions, tortures, cannon fire, hunts, liquidations ... One notes in those eyes a kind of haughtiness, of almost murderous hardness. Of non-intimidation too. One quickly forms the habit of paying attention to such men. One can say anything to them but they need to feel and to touch the Revolution in the words uttered. They are very difficult to deceive, to get around.

For the time being Chawki and I share the same bed. Our discussions last rather late into the night and I constantly marvel at the intelligence and the clarity of his ideas. Having received a degree at the Islam University of Zitouna in Tunisia, he wanted to make contact with Western civilisation. He settled in Algiers to learn French, to see, judge, discriminate. But the atmosphere of Algiers with the contemptuous settlers, his total ignorance of the French language, the closed nature of the European circles made him decide to go to France. For two years he lived in Paris, mixed in European circles, haunted the libraries and devoured hundreds of books.

He finally returned to Algeria and planned to develop his father's land. 1954. He took down his hunting rifle from its hook and joined the brothers. He knows the Sahara like the palm of his hand. When he speaks of that inhuman desert immensity it assumes an infinity of details. Hospitable corners, dangerous roads, mortal regions, points of penetration, the Sahara is a world in which Chawki moves with the boldness and the perspicacity of a great strategist. The French do not suspect the tricks this man is ready to play on them.

Our mission nearly ended in the third-degree rooms of Algeria. From Accra the Ghana Airways clerk Mensah, who requires some tens of thousands of francs for each reservation, had confirmed our Monrovia-to-Conakry flight. But at the Liberian airport we were told that the plane was full and that we would have to wait till the next day to fly to Conakry by an Air France plane. The employees were abnormally attentive to us and offered to have the company pay all our stop-over expenses. This exemplary solicitude, the French nationality of several employees, and the bar-maid allure of a voluble and excruciatingly boring French lady led us to change our route. We decided to leave Monrovia by road and enter Guinea at night via N'Zérékoré.

Until the last moment the employees were convinced that we were taking the plane which was two hours late that day.

The French Intelligence had indeed taken the matter in hand. Instead of heading for Freetown on leaving Robertsfield, the plane turned back and landed at Abidjan, where it was searched by French forces.

It is clear that the Ivory Coast Government has a prime responsibility in this affair. Such an operation could not have taken place without its connivance or at least its benediction. Houphouët-Boigny, whom certain people try to exonerate, continues to play a leading role in the French colonial system, and the African peoples would have a great deal to gain by isolating him and hastening his downfall. Houphouët-Boigny is objectively the most conscious curb on the evolution and the liberation of Africa. In the end the Intelligence Office had to rue it. Such an operation is a paying proposition only if it succeeds. A public failure under such conditions reveals bandit methods which may cause even those who have been willing to shut their eyes to harden their attitude.

I hope in any case, that the French authorities have lost track of us.

Here we are in Bamako, the Mali capital. Modibo Keita, ever militant, quickly understands. No need for great speeches. Our working sessions move fast. Without any loss of time the brothers of the Transmission Services discuss with him the problem with which they are concerned and reach the decision to set up a listening post in Kayes. I believe it should be in operation by 5 December. For the time being we are lodged at the rest centre of the Bamako barracks. Great agitation these last days. Nkrumah is arriving on the 21st on an official visit.

In Bamako the French element of the population is still considerable. Bookshops, pharmacies, business houses belong in the majority to French settlers. Here and there one comes across a major, a sergeant or two … Yesterday, which was Sunday, the 20th, a French adjutant serving in the Mali Army coming from Ségou with a company arrived at the rest centre. He introduced himself very politely and shook hands with us. He wanted to know if we could not put a bed at his disposal. One has to have a certain sense of humour about these things. In any case we were able to obtain an armed sentinel who went on duty at eight in the evening. From time to time cars driven by Europeans would cruise round the villa. Not a very safe district. Fortunately things moved fast. On Tuesday the 22nd at five in the morning we left for Gao. The Bamako-Timbuktu road was not passable.

From Bamako we reached Ségou where Jouanelle welcomed us. We refuelled and reached San. Then Mopti. At Mopti we hit a snag. As we left town we ran into a police barrier and the sentinels demanded our passports. There ensued a painful discussion, for in spite of the document issued by the

Minister of the Interior the *gendarmes* wanted to check our identities. Finally the chief of the post arrived, and I had of necessity to present myself. But he was not a man to be put off. He wanted to know the nature of our mission and the qualifications of those who accompanied me.

Then I got angry and asked him to hold me and put me under arrest for refusal to present our papers. Faced with this ultimatum he realised that he had blundered and let us go, at the same time promising absolute secrecy.

The road from Mopti to Douentza is a joke. In the middle of a forest one follows by guess-work the tracks of a car that must have passed there six months before. Such feeling one's way in the middle of the night is very painful and more than once we lost our way. At last, at two in the morning, we arrived. There was no one in the village. The commandant was absent and his wife sent us to the encampment which was closed. We somehow managed, with some in the car, others outside, to get a little rest. At seven we set off for Gao via Hombori. At nine at night we knocked at the commandant's. Ten minutes later we were hard at work. Everything seemed favourable and the Malians were quite determined to help us in creating this third front. People used to speak admiringly of the Odyssey of General Leclerc's march across the Sahara. The one that we are preparing, if the French Government does not realise it in time, we will make the Leclerc episode look, by comparison, like a Sunday-school picnic. In Gao we found a complete documentation left by the French secret service on the Algerian Moroccan border country. All the names of the Algerians living there were mentioned. In the margin were also mentioned their greater or lesser good-will in respect to nationalist ideas. With no trouble at all we found the negative of the skeleton of a working and transit cell. Thanks to Commandant Cardaire.

After two days in Gao we headed for Aguerhoc. The Gao commandant made us take off our peuhl garments and offered each a good Arab scout outfit with a Mas 36 gun and 20 cartridges. We were to have occasion, in fact, to kill a bustard and several does.

In Aguerhoc, at about 11 at night, we met chief of the Kidal subdivision who was accompanied by the post commander of Tessalit. Introductions all around. Thirty minutes later we were discussing strategy, terrain, passage ...

It is thrilling to experience these moments. These two officers had only to know who we were to make a whole immense collusion, latent until then, come out into the open. What we want, they give us. Did we want to see at close range the frontier, Tessalit, Bouressa across from Tir Zaouaten where the French, caught short, are building an airfield … ? O.K.

And off we are, across one hundred kilometres of dirt road. This part of the Sahara is not monotonous. Even the sky up there is constantly changing. Some days ago we saw a sunset that turned the robe of heaven a bright violet. Today it is a very hard red that the eye encounters. Aguerhoc, Tessalit, Bouressa. At Tessalit we cross the French military camp. A French soldier, bared to the waist, gives us a friendly wave. His arms would drop off him if he could guess whom these Arab outfits conceal.

At Bouressa we made contact with a Malian nomad group. We are learning more and more details about the French forces. Bordj le Prieur, Tir Zaouaten, Bidon V.

And, beyond, Tamanrasset where, by piecing things together, we managed to get a fairly exact idea of the French forces. The guides that we found in Bouressa seem reliable and determined. We shall have to give them priority when we need guides later.

In Kidal I plunge into some books on the history of the Sudan. I relive, with the intensity that circumstances and the place confer upon them, the old empires of Ghana, of Mali, of Gao, and the impressive Odyssey of the Moroccan troops with the famous Djouder. Things are not simple. Here Algeria at war comes to solicit aid from Mali. And during this time Morocco is demanding Mauritania and a part of Mali … Also a part of Algeria.

This Saharan region worked over by so many influences and where French officers are constantly creating nests of dissidence we are now preparing to stir to its depths round a battlefield which will require a great deal of rigour and cool thinking. A few observations picked up here and there, with always a special emphasis when Islam and the race is mentioned, require extra caution.

Colonialism and its derivatives do not, as a matter of fact, constitute the present enemies of Africa. In a short time this continent will be liberated. For my part, the deeper I enter into the cultures and the political circles the surer I am that the great danger that threatens Africa is the absence of ideology. Old Europe had toiled for centuries before completing the national unity of the States. And even when a final period could be put to it, how many wars still! With the triumph of socialism in Eastern Europe we witness a spectacular disappearance of old rivalries, of the traditional territorial claims. That nucleus of wars and political assassinations that Bulgaria, Hungary, Estonia, Slovakia, Albania represented, has made way for a coherent world whose objective is the building of a socialist society.

In Africa, on the other hand, the countries that come to independence are as unstable as their new middle classes or their renovated princes. After a few hesitant steps in the international arena the national middle classes, no longer feeling the threat of the traditional colonial power, suddenly develop great appetites. And as they do not yet have any political experience they think they can conduct political affairs like their business. Perquisites, threats, even despoiling of the victims. All of which is of course regrettable, for the small states have no other choice but to beg the former metropolis to remain just a little longer. In these imperialist pseudo-states, likewise, an extreme militarist policy leads to a reduction of public investments in countries which in certain respects are still medieval. The discontented workers undergo a repression as pitiless as that of the colonial periods. Trade unions and opposition political parties are confined to a quasi-clandestine state. The people, the people who had given everything in the difficult moments of the struggle for national liberation wonder, with their empty hands and bellies, as to the reality of their victory.

For nearly three years I have been trying to bring the misty idea of African Unity out of the subjectivist bogs of the majority of its supporters. African Unity is a principle on the basis of which it is proposed to achieve the United States of Africa without passing through the middle-class chauvinistic national phase with its procession of wars and death tolls.

To initiate this unity all combinations are possible.

Some, like Guinea, Ghana, Mali and tomorrow perhaps Algeria, put political action to the forefront. Others like Liberia and Nigeria insist on economic cooperation. The UAR on its side puts more emphasis on the cultural aspect. Everything is possible and the different states should avoid discrediting or denouncing those that see this unity, this coming-together of African states, in a way that differs from theirs. What must be avoided is the Ghana–Senegal tension, the Somali–Ethiopia, the Morocco–Mauritania, the Congo–Congo tensions ... In reality the colonised states that have reached independence by the political path seem to have no other concern than to find themselves a real battlefield with wounds and destruction. It is clear, however, that this psychological explanation, which appeals to a hypothetical need for release of pent-up aggressiveness, does not satisfy us. We must once again come back to the Marxist formula. The triumphant middle classes are the most impetuous, the most enterprising, the most annexationist in the world (not for nothing did the French bourgeoisie of 1789 put Europe to fire and sword).

TECHNICAL PROBLEMS

1. Passages by truck: difficult to achieve in the immediate. The thing has to be prepared. Contact the driver. Then study the process. Study the filling stations. Will require, if one is to provide minimum of safeguards and ensure a maximum of success, at least three months of preparation from the time the project is really begun.

2. The whole problem is to know whether what is wanted is:

(a) either to supply the forces already in existence in the Sahara;

(b) or supply *wilayas* I, V and the remains of VI;

(c) or literally create a series of lines of attack perpendicular to the Tellien Atlas which could possibly meet up with and work with the already existing *wilayas*. Of course it can be said that these choices are not mutually exclusive and that these three possibilities can be included in a single programme. In any case one of these three possibilities must be given priority even if the Sahara operation as a whole were to contain all three.

Personally I incline to point to c.

How is it to be carried out?

Before anything else, bring the maximum of equipment up to the frontier. In the two months to come: 10 000 rifles, 4 000 P.M., 1 500 F.M., 600 machine-guns, three to four rocket-throwers.

The mines and grenades that cannot be directly used in the Sahara should be reserved to supply the *wilayas* of the North. But what is to be done with these weapons, in other words, how is the action to be carried out?

I see the thing in terms of two different directions; one vertical, the other horizontal.

Some forty individuals having a good knowledge of the Sahara and being first-rate militants could be appointed commando chiefs.

These commandos would operate in sections of ten. Each commando could be composed at the outset of twenty to twenty-five members, it being up to the chiefs to bring the number rapidly up to one hundred, even one hundred and fifty. Recruitment would be done locally at the outset. Either Algerians living in Mali or Malian Touaregs themselves. This can be done in a month and a half. Between now and 15 January it is possible to arm and introduce into Algeria 500 to 800 armed men.

The first wave should be one of politicalisation, mobilisation. It should avoid encounters and let opportunities to strike the enemy slip by, even if success seems assured. Its role is to rouse the populations, to reassure them as to the future, to show the armament of the ALN, to detach them psychologically and mentally from enemy ascendancy.

In every sizable tribe met up with, the commando must recruit three to four new members and leave three or four of its original members. The reason:

(a) the new recruits know the terrain beyond, and at the beginning serve as a contact, as political interpreters, with the Northern tribes;

(b) the members of the commando left on the spot prepare the various liaison channels that will receive the following waves.

One would then have the following pattern:

       ↑ ❐ 80 to
       ↓ ❐ 100 km.

11th base ❐ A ❐ B ❐ C ❐ D ❐ E ❐ F ❐ G ❐ H ❐ I ❐ J

       ↑ ❐ 100 to
       ↓ ❐ 150 km.

10th base ❐ A ❐ B ❐ C ❐ D ❐ E ❐ F ❐ G ❐ H ❐ I ❐ J

9th base →

8th base →

7th base → (There would thus be a frontal position and a perpendicular
         direction.)

6th base →

5th base →

4th base →

3rd base →

2nd base →

1st base →

0   base →

At the same time supply columns would be moving up to base 1.

Base 2 would send supply columns to base 1.

Base 3 to base 2 ... and so forth. It is only when the advanced bases have received 3 or 4 shipments of supplies that the question of beginning operations can be considered.

At that time, moreover, contacts with the drivers and perhaps a better situation in the Fezzan will enable us to supply the ALN groups regularly.

Every group of twenty-five should have the following weaponry:

2 rocket-throwers and 20 shells;

2 machine-guns, 1 of which should be anti-aircraft;

3 F.M.

The groups would leave at two-day intervals. One radio sending station should be provided at the outset for base 0 located at D,

for the 4th base located at J,

for the 9th base located at A,

and 2 or 3 stations along the frontier.

These frontier stations would have listening-times in conjunction with the North General Staff and each of the stations of bases 0, 4, and 9.

NOTE

1   UPC – Union of the Populations of the Cameroons. (Translator's note)

Reflections on Fanon and his legacy

Fanon with Roberto Holden (founder and leader of the National Liberation Front of Angola, on the left), Abdelaziz Bouteflika (2nd from right) and others. Bouteflika is the current president of Algeria and was secretary to Fanon during the last year of his life.

INTERVIEWS: PIERRE CHAULET, NIGEL GIBSON AND DAVID MACEY

Knowing Fanon: Pierre Chaulet

Leo Zeilig interviewed Pierre and Claudine Chaulet in September and October 2011 in Algiers as part of his research into the Algerian national struggle. Pierre and Claudine Chaulet joined the struggle in Algeria in the early 1950s, marrying later in the decade. They were part of a small group of Algerians of European origin who were committed to the revolution. Both were close friends of Fanon and introduced him to militants in the FLN. After Pierre was released from prison in 1957, the couple joined Fanon in exile in Tunisia, where they worked together on *El Moudjahid*, the FLN paper.

What follows are some of Pierre Chaulet's memories of Fanon as a friend, and brother, involved in the Algerian struggle. Sadly, Pierre died on 5 October 2012.

Leo Zeilig (LZ): Could you please give me a description of what Fanon was like, his personality and character?

Pierre Chaulet (PC): He was a brilliant talker, a charmer who adored using words from the medical and psychiatric lexicon to express a core meaning. He seemed to have read everything. Sometimes he was in a spin of words, taking lyrical flight, pushing reason to the point of paradox to provoke discussion. Yet at the same time he was a disciplined militant, modest and accepting criticism of certain improper expressions or exaggerations.

LZ: You were with Fanon as he was writing his final, greatest book in 1961. Could you describe what it was like, the atmosphere at that time?

PC: *The Wretched of the Earth* should be read like an urgent message, delivered in a raw state and uncorrected. He was sick, and aware that he was condemned. But he desired with all his force to say what he had to say... Fanon's vivid style – of a psychiatrist, philosopher and poet, more than a political thinker – gives a particular power to his flashes of prophetic brilliance and even to his errors ...

LZ: How would you describe the crucial role Algeria played in Fanon's life?

PC: He participated in the liberation struggle of a settler colony, with the aim of abolishing a colonial system that rested on exploitation and racism. This was the realisation of his dream as a young Caribbean man confronted with a similar system as a child.

LZ: How was it collaborating with Fanon on the newspaper El Moudjahid, *which you both worked on in Tunisia from 1957?*

PC: The freedom of discussion was total within the editorial committee. Each one of us would speak in turn on a certain theme. But we shared the same analysis and we had the same objectives within the editorial committee. Fanon was one of us and what we wrote was a reflection of the collective. Neither more nor less.

LZ: You also knew Fanon in Algeria, when he worked as a radical psychiatrist in the hospital at Blida. Can you tell me what Fanon achieved in the hospital with his reforms?

PC: Fanon not only removed the chains of certain patients, but he also abolished the use of straitjackets. He organised social and leisure activities, including a café, a football pitch, concerts with Algerian musicians, religious events for Muslim patients and a printing press for a hospital newspaper.

Studying Fanon: Nigel Gibson

Nigel Gibson is one of the world's leading scholars on Frantz Fanon's revolutionary thought. He has written one of the most important studies of Fanon's ideas, and his political and philosophical writing, *Fanon: The Postcolonial Imagination*. Leo Zeilig interviewed Gibson on 3 November 2010.

Leo Zeilig (LZ): How satisfactory is the label 'Third Worldist' to describe Fanon's thinking and life?

Nigel Gibson (NG): Yes and no. All the labels are problematic. Depends who the other Third Worldists are. Certainly, Fanon argues that Europe is a creation of the Third World. That is (like Walter Rodney), slavery and colonialism are essential to capitalist development. But he is not an economic theorist.

LZ: What are the major ways that we misunderstand Fanon?

NG: That Fanon is a prophet of violence or theorist of violence.

LZ: Is there any misunderstanding of Fanon derived from Sartre's preface to The Wretched of the Earth?

NG: Sure, once again on violence especially. But a lot of people read the book through the preface (not Sartre's fault).

LZ: What was the nature of the intellectual relationship between Sartre and Fanon?

NG: For both it was important. Sartre's preface may be the most radical thing he wrote; Fanon's critique of Jean-Paul Sartre in *Black Skin, White Masks* is essential to understanding Fanon's notion of the dialectic (his footnote to Sartre on ontology is important too). Fanon is indebted to Sartre's anti-Semitism and the Jew, and continues to engage Sartre in his last book (*Critique of Dialectical Reason*). So, for Fanon, Sartre was the most important intellectual interlocutor, especially since Sartre was against French colonialism. That Fanon wanted to see him in Rome in 1961 and stay up into the early hours (at a time I think when Fanon knew he was sick with leukaemia) says a lot about Fanon ... that quote from De Beauvoir about this is always telling.

LZ: How would you interpret the role of Algeria in Fanon's life? I get the sense that Fanon made great professional and political leaps the moment he arrived in Algeria.

NG: I am not sure about professional leaps. Tosquelles might be more important. But don't forget that Fanon was in Algiers when the Battle of Algiers developed. He made contact with the FLN underground (I think through Chaulet) and began seeing the tortured and the torturers in the context of the radical changes in social relations that a revolutionary situation creates. *Studies in a Dying Colonialism* really speaks of this experience of revolution. It is interesting that many criticised Fanon as a 'romantic' or 'utopian', but I was just re-reading Bourdieu's book on the Algerians and he says the same thing. The revolution, as revolutions do, turned things upside down, upset the old social relations. That these changes did not remain, that they were turned back (re-revolved?) does not mean that they didn't happen. I think Fanon also understood the fragility of new social relations, not only from outside but also from inside the revolution, and that is a reason why he remains relevant today.

LZ: What was Fanon's relationship with François Tosquelles? We know, for example, that Tosquelles was an important psychiatrist who carried out innovative work at the hospital in Saint-Alban in France. But Tosquelles was also a revolutionary from Spain who was from an anti-Stalinist Marxist background. How influenced was Fanon in a range of areas by his friendship with Tosquelles?

NG: Cherki says that Fanon admired Tosquelles politically. On the Trotskyists, difficult to say. He went to some meetings in Lyon (in the late 1940s) and I think Cherki talks about some individual relationships in Paris like Pierre Broué, the French historian and Trotskyist (another through-the-night talk before he gave the racism and culture speech) after he left Algiers and before going to Tunis. The year 1956 is an important one in European communism but Fanon isn't attracted to a group like socialism or barbarism which, ideologically, would make some sense. His focus is Algeria and the anti-colonial revolutions and the Trotskyists are in the main Eurocentric.

LZ: What do you see as the relationship between Black Skin, White Masks *and* The Wretched of the Earth?

NG: Big question. The topics are different but in a sense not. In other words, there are ways that *Black Skin, White Masks* talks of a postcolonial situation and the postcolonial middle class is the subject. The conclusion speaks of Fanon's vision but it remains a little abstract. Things change with the Algeria experiences. In other words, lived experience – revolutionary lived experience – is important; he doesn't 'concretise' in *Black Skin, White Masks*, but in *The Wretched of the Earth* his work, especially the critique of the postcolonial parties/intellectuals/middle class is connected.

LZ: In The Wretched of the Earth *I am struck by Fanon's sharp analysis of the class of nationalist leaders who become a sort of sub-bourgeoisie after independence and are happy to make deals with the parting colonial powers. Originally I saw these insights as a product of Fanon's extensive scholarship and as an intellectual and militant from Latin America, an area that had already witnessed so-called 'independence'. However, I wonder now whether it was equally part of his own direct experiences in Ghana witnessing early independence (the Congo crisis, etc.) and the political degeneration of figures he had previously admired … including Césaire and Senghor. Is this an accurate picture of his development and experiences?*

NG: You mean from Africa? He is interested in stuff going on in Latin America but I don't think particularly directly informed. Yes, I think it is absolutely about his insights from Algeria, from the Congo (especially Lumumba) and Ghana. He meets a lot of these leaders at conferences in 1959 and 1960.

LZ: What, according to Fanon, was to stop Algeria becoming the independent state he saw elsewhere and describes in The Wretched of the Earth? *Are these tensions in his work?*

NG: Sure. I think *The Wretched* is also about Algeria. A great tension. He keeps quiet about Abane, he knows about the militarists. Look at the difference between the hope of *A Dying Colonialism* and the 'pessimism' or 'realism' of *The Wretched of the Earth*; this stuff is taking place as he writes; and he is so inside and also critically engaged that he can write it.

LZ: Fanon saw the nation as the 'dynamic creation of the action of the

famous project for an African legion which marches as a body across the Sahara, failed as a military act and, as far as I can work out, Fanon never had any approval or any discussion in the FLN military.

LZ: What remains to be written or studied on Fanon's life and work?

DM: I think we need to look much more at his background in Martinique … what does it mean in the 1940s, 1950s to grow up in Martinique believing you're French and then being told in no uncertain terms that you aren't? And, sadly, this is still very relevant to the experience of people brought up in France today … 'I'm French' – 'No you're not, you're from Martinique.' It's alarmingly widespread. So I think there are whole kinds of problems to it. Is Fanon French? Is he Martiniquan? Is he Algerian by adoption? Is he simply black? Is he simply not-white? And there isn't a simple answer for any of those questions and we need to make his identity more complex. With Algeria, I think you have to begin with what the Algerian Revolution was actually about and how Fanon distorted things. But there's no notion in Fanon, or indeed Sartre, or much of the French Left, that the FLN defined *themselves* as an Arab-Islamic state. And the Islamic bit gets forgotten about. And I'm not saying it's the equivalent of what we'd now call Islamism or Fundamentalism but there is a cultural-religious dimension to it – it's not just secular nationalism. And I think the entire French-Left failed to see that. So Fanon talks hopefully about a role for the European minority, which was just never going to be possible. And by 1961/1962 it was obvious that that they certainly couldn't stop the mass exodus of the white population.

So somehow you've got to reconcile what actually happened with either Fanon's generosity or naivety, I don't know which. I suppose ultimately you have to ask why did Algeria have to become an Arab-Islamic state? There were other possibilities, you know, the possibility of some kind of Franco-Algerian alliance.

LZ: You get in The Wretched of the Earth *this brilliant sense of what happened after independence, you know, the vengeance as it's called, and the degeneration of the class of independence leaders after national freedom. Fanon was asking, what was this Algeria becoming? Was* The Wretched *written partly as a warning to Algeria?*

DM: I think it's interesting that, according to Algeria ... there's not much interest in Fanon ... Well actually, I think if there's an answer, it's in Sartre's *Critique of Dialectical Reason* that you cannot sustain the dynamism of the revolution beyond a certain point. It would collapse back into practical inertia or the practice of dense structures. And I think that probably, if there is a theoretical underpinning behind it, that must be it.

You can seize power but then if that's your only goal, then everything falls apart. And there does seem to be on Fanon's part a very healthy mistrust of colonels in particular – the FLN had a lot of colonels. So, yeah, there's a danger of militarisation ... And I think the reality is that after 1961 and 1962, the sudden exodus of French powers, French expertise, French everything – there was a vacuum, so you had a brief interlude of what was called, somewhat politically, self-management. Which, actually, as far as I can see, was taking over anything you could.

LZ: Is Fanon posing an alternative Algeria in the self-activity of Algerians in the making of the revolution?

DM: Yes, I think he is. There's no real structure however ... what's striking about Fanon is that for a Third Worldist revolutionary of the period there is no theory of a party, or avant-garde, it's not theorised in any real sense. Instead he falls back on the need for continuity and that was actually unsustainable by any standard. So he's let down by his own voluntarism or nationalism in the real struggle ...

LZ: How does Fanon develop such a powerful critique of independence? Is it his disillusionment with people like Senghor and Césaire, or do you think it's probably a combination of all those things, including his time working in Ghana?

DM: I think it's probably a combination of all those things, certainly his experience of so-called diplomatic mission in West Africa and his first-hand observations of what went on in Ghana, the Gambia, Congo must have been terribly disillusioning, well they still are in retrospect ... African independence kind of imploded into this bureaucratic military

253

hell, which is true. There was an awful lot of Western interference in this process – the collapses of the Congo were not just internal – there was awful Belgian interference, etc. And the French colonies got so involved and also France was intent on maintaining some kind of colonial/neo-colonial presence, and has done so ever since. The irony of Senegal is that it is actually quite a peaceful place! Not terribly prosperous but it's actually quite a stable society.

In terms of Césaire, he did become, I suppose, a very compromised figure. But was there an alternative? And Césaire through all this is much loved, very popular and in many ways very successful. But, OK, a form of neo-colonialism does exist in Martinique.

LZ: How confusing was Sartre's preface to understanding Fanon's The Wretched of the Earth? *Do you think that some misunderstanding of* The Wretched of the Earth *for example, stems from that preface? And that the preface is sometimes where people stop?*

DM: Yes. I think Sartre does out-Fanon Fanon. Sartre talks about killing two birds with one stone – that's actually Sartre not Fanon ['To shoot down a European is to kill two birds with one stone, to destroy an oppressor and the man he oppresses at the same time: there remains a dead man and a free man.'] But in the same context and in its own terms I think it's perfectly justifiable. Well, understandable, in that virtually no one on the French Left was an out-and-out supporter of Algeria. The Communist Party and communist powers were ambiguous and often supported these colonial troops. The socialist party was compromised – so there's only a kind of handful of people on the far left who were independent ... So I think Sartre's extreme position is actually quite understandable. Sartre does tend to take a very extreme position for his own reasons.

LZ: Fanon was enthusiastic about the preface.

DM: Partly, yes, he was desperate to be prefaced by Sartre. I think it's very difficult to reconstruct what Fanon read but it's clear that, going back to *Black Skin, White Masks,* Sartre was a very important influence on Fanon. A lot of analysis of anti-black racism comes from Sartre on anti-

Semitism … The reflections on the Jewish questions are very important. You'd have to go into it in much more detail than I've done but I suspect the relationship between the *Wretched of the Earth* and the *Critique of Dialectical Reason* is actually very close. For example, the embryonic party can sustain itself on its own energy to a point and probably not beyond. And also the idea that the party is bound together by fraternity and at the same time fear that some one in it is a traitor. It's the fear of treachery that's *very dangerous* … so there may well be a kind of interplay between the two texts. Certainly at the time if you wanted to be prefaced by anyone in France who else could it be?

LZ: I got a strong sense of the role of Algeria in Fanon's life from your book, and there's this sense of a very significant break or shift from someone who wasn't particularly political (not with a big 'p') to political engagement and revolution. And it reminded me of Orwell's 'Why I write'… a sense of this significant crossroads, Spain for Orwell and Algeria for Fanon. Is that an accurate summary?

DM: I think if there's a crunch point in Fanon and it comes very early, in the Second World War … There are probably similarities in that for a lot of Algerians too – volunteering for the French army and it's hard to imagine how you'd get through the confusion – black volunteers integrated into colonial French troops and you invade the south of France and by the time you arrive it's snowing, but the French military command pull back the black Senegalese troops while the black West Indian troops were somehow reclassified as white. So that, on the one hand you're not a black *person* you're French, yet you're not French, you're a black colonial. You're not a black infantry, you're a white infantry now fighting in snow you've never seen before at the age of 18, 19. Can you imagine anything to be more bloody confusing?! And then of course you find that you've been decorated as a military hero. It's very hard to imagine a more confusing experience … So it's not surprising the confusion about who you are, what you are and what on earth France is … So it must have been quite a common experience of the so-called colonial troops … I think it must have been a very widespread disillusionment and the breaking point for a lot of people who'd had an education in France, which is certainly the case with Fanon. Studying medicine in France when he was very young and certainly encountering what it was like to be Algerian in metropolitan France, and the severe destitution of Algerian men in Lyon.

LZ: I get a sense of – and you talk about them having professional arguments - of the important connection between Fanon and Tosquelles. Tosquelles is this figure of the radical left, who fights in a position of some authority during the Spanish Civil War, gets out, becomes this brilliant avant-garde psychiatrist. So I'm curious in terms of an exposure for Fanon to a non-dogmatic, anti-Stalinist left.

DM: Possibly – we don't know enough about their relationship. Tosquelles isn't the most coherent writer. But, as far as I know, there's no serious book on him. So he seems to have been forgotten. In terms of psychiatry, it's clear that Tosquelles is a hugely important figure – even if a somewhat forgotten one. And it's part of this shift away from the hospital as a place of incarceration to a place of psychotherapy where it does become a community that's partly self-remedying. So that's the beginning of a huge shift in psychiatric care, which was happening in England too. It's a shift towards the humanisations of experience, which is what Fanon tried to recreate and develop in Blida. With, I think, a kind of huge amount of good will and voluntarism but again a certain amount of naivety, in that he doesn't mention the fact that when he's talking to patients he didn't actually speak Arabic, and for the life of me I don't see how you can be a useful psychiatrist without language, only interpreters.

LZ: Fanon was very critical of psychoanalysis.

DM: Fanon was quite happy prescribing heavy drugs. That's what psychiatry's all about! So it's interesting that because of the dominance of psychoanalysis we forgot all this, that it's not about endless analysis. But certainly there's an interest in psychology ... And you get a sense of the endless curiosity of the guy ...

LZ: Hungry intellect.

DM: Yeah, it's extraordinary.

LZ: You mentioned in passing this romantic notion of Fanon taking over in Algeria and unchaining patients. And you're critical of that image …

DM: It is hard to get to the bottom of that. Unchaining patients is this founding myth in psychiatry in France … and restraints would have certainly been used at the time. I think Fanon's critique of psychiatry in Algiers was well founded. But psychiatry was probably more advanced in Algeria than in France; publications suggest there may have been more progressive forces than Fanon makes allowances for. Whether he was unaware of it or not I don't know.

LZ: Can I ask you about Black Skin, White Masks? *Gibson writes about the continuity between Fanon's earliest work and his last book. What do you feel are the connections?*

DM: The interesting thing about *Black Skin, White Masks* is that we don't know very much about how he worked on it, or his working method, except that it wasn't written – it was dictated. So we're actually dealing with oral text, and we don't know to what extent he was able to read it. I suspect he wasn't … which would explain why some of the strange Creole expressions survived, because they don't mean anything to the French. But I think if there is a continuity, it's not so much a theory of even conscious thought, it's the central idea that comes up in both books – the idea of the slave revolt. Aimé Césaire's poem about the slave revolt in the West Indies ['And the Dogs were Silent', 'It was me, it was indeed me, I told him, the good faithful slave, the slave, and suddenly my eyes were two roaches frightened on a rainy day … I struck, the blood spurted: it is the only baptism that today I remember.'] I don't want to over interpret but for someone who knew he was dying, it's actually an extraordinarily powerful image. Yes, the rebel's going to die but we'll still take the house. It takes you a world away from any kind of critical theory. This is a very personal vision and it's just this cry of revolt and this is just some of the ideas that Fanon did identify with …

LZ: If we can identify in the late 1960s that Fanon radicalises movements in the West, for all sorts of reasons – his work on racism, his work on Third World liberation what are the continued interests in Fanon, how can we explain the continued interests in Fanon now and who's he speaking to?

DM: Good question. There seems to be almost no reference to Fanon in Martinique in the West Indies; he's almost forgotten about in France … I suppose mid- to late-70s any form of Third-World liberation is seen as totalitarian and potentially oppressive. Now Fanon has become a celebrity of postcolonial studies. Which, for better or worse, I think they use Fanon to an alarming degree because for the simple reason that postcolonialism is an English discipline – coming out of the English and literature departments. It's a monolingual phenomenon – they don't read French, they don't read Spanish, they certainly don't read Arabic, and I think that's been limiting.

Although if you pushed in that direction, Fanon is still a very good guide to the structures of racism, especially in France – I think it's a very French-specific analysis and I'm not sure it applies so much to England, for instance. But if you go back to reading *Black Skin, White Masks*, it's still relevant to the kind of experience of people travelling to France from Martinique as French citizens and being treated as other than French citizens – that still goes on and it's a very common experience being treated as foreigners.

Fanon's certainly been extremely popular for quite a few years now. It's sad in a sense that he is forgotten in France. North Africans might not be the wretched of the earth in his sense but they're certainly almost dispossessed. I mean surely if the Third World is here, as well as the Caribbean and Algeria then … we have to come to terms with that. And we won't do that by discussing Fanon in seminars at Yale University, which is certainly a valid activity but it's got to go beyond that. And I think that's the problem with postcolonial studies, as far as I can see – it doesn't actually link up with what virtually anybody who lives in a city, is poor, marginalised, in the Third World, goes through daily …

LZ: Just a last word on Fanon's relationship with Negritude and Senghor. It was very mixed wasn't it? On the one hand, it was early black pride and then later on it becomes solidified in early state systems; it becomes problematic, even reactionary.

DM: Yeah, I think Negritude was a very double-edged thing. It's probably more complex than is allowed for. It seems there's a split between African, mainly Senegalese, versions of it and the West Indian versions.

In Senegal, with Senghor's poetry, it very rapidly becomes a hymn to a mythical Africa, possibly pre-colonial Africa which is almost idyllic and it changes the African soul. Which is very appealing in a lot of ways but more static and confining. So you get a very idyllic static portrait of Africa in which nothing changes.

Whereas the West Indian, in Césaire, it is much more to do with revolt and of course the lasting memory of the slave culture – everyone does their best to forget about it but it's still there.

But, for Fanon, the real problem with Negritude is, well in my own view, that Negritude was a very necessary expression as a reaction against white racism and white supremacy. And I think maybe throughout all of Fanon's books there's a refusal to be defined as black, West Indian, and the black man has to be briefly freed from the blackness that's imposed upon him; the white man has to be freed from the whiteness that he imposes upon himself and the black man. There has to be at some point in Fanon's vision a freedom that doesn't recognise any determination between race, class … but is this vision totally utopian? Human freedom that is precisely that, escaping all determination – he says, 'I will be my own foundation' – maybe totally utopian, maybe unreliable.

That said, at its best I think Negritude is still fantastically exciting.

LZ: Senghor was a brilliant poet and I return often to his writing.

DM: Yes, he's a great poet. But there's something uncomfortable about the first leader of a black independent state in Africa writing poems for the first war dead in France on French war memorials. One of the most bizarre memories I have of my couple of weeks in Martinique was a war memorial to those who died in the Second World War who were almost exclusively black and yet the statue was white. So, if that can still go on in the 1990s you still need someone to say that it's fine and beautiful to be black.

LZ: And Negritude does that.

DM: Yes. In the same way that whatever was wrong with it there is a certain validity in Malcolm X and Stokely Carmichael … they haven't become invalid and wouldn't – it's still inspiring whether you're black or not.

LZ: And these figures were inspired by their reading of Fanon.

DM: To some extent. Stokely Carmichael's claim that 'every brother on a roof top can quote Fanon' was probably true at the time. So some forms of Negritude are still evidently valid and still true – even if it's just the American soul singer James Brown!

LZ: (laughs) Exactly, exactly. I suppose that's part of the tension in Fanon because here's someone who saw himself as writing very much for Third World revolution, and in many respects there is a rejection of Europe, but there's an occasional sense of the global dimension to Fanon's project when he writes, '…when the European working class stops playing their games … then maybe we can talk about an alliance.'

DM: It is the case that from the late 1920s/early 1930s the Communist Party in Europe and Socialist Party did lose interest in any form of Third World, colonial liberation – it wasn't prioritised. The French Communist Party certainly did – the liberation of French colonies would come *after* revolution in France and would be dependent upon it, and Algeria wasn't recognised as an even potential relation by the French Left. And it's one of the, probably for reasons which are explicable, failings of the entire *Marxist* tradition in Europe – it did not break this paradigm. In some sense, the rest of the world has to go through European-style capitalist development before this can happen, and there isn't room for alternative experiments – it's a very uni-centric tradition. I'm not even sure that Chinese communism escapes from that entirely.

UNPICKING FANON'S LEGACY: LESSONS AND POSSIBILITIES
Leo Zeilig

Among the most effective oppositional organisations in contemporary Pakistan is the Baloch Student Federation (BSO). It is, however, not strictly a student organisation, but more akin to a secular nationalist organisation. Its membership is found among rural youth who have fled to Pakistan's growing cities looking for work. The BSO's manifesto is the Urdu translation of *The Wretched of the Earth*. One outgrowth of the BSO is the organisation's armed wing, the Baloch Liberation Army. The BSO's ideological orientation is characterised by a degree of confusion, as the Pakistani socialist, Sartaj Khan, has explained:

> The BSO was inspired by the guerrilla struggle of Che Guevara, and in the past was influenced by both Maoism and Stalinism. Many of its leaders, like Dr Allah Nazar Baloch, claim to be Marxists. But, like others, the Baluchi nationalist movement suffered serious political disorientation in the wake of the collapse of the Berlin Wall.[2]

It would be unfair to leave Fanon's legacy with the Baloch Student Federation. His influence was far greater, and more difficult to chart. But the confusing combination of Marxism, Maoism and guerrilla war does point to an uncomfortable reality. Fanon was the brilliant and angry champion of national liberation and revolution, but his refusal to see how a movement could be centred on the power of the organised working class and independent working-class politics limited the positive reach of his ideas. Instead, Fanon's orientation to the countryside and the lumpenproletariat won him many supporters in the 1960s and 1970s but helped to tie up his own alternatives into a delimiting prison.[3] The real history of working-class action in the Third World has often been concealed. Fanon's role in helping to conceal this reality makes his legacy decidedly ambiguous for those of us who seek to develop (and recover) such a politics today.[4]

However, the removal of the working class from Fanon's paradigm can be contextualised. The setback of the urban movement after the Battle of Algiers – largely a campaign of urban terror and limited strike action – led to a withdrawal of the FLN and the political struggle from towns. Increasingly, union members and urban FLN sympathisers and members were encouraged to leave the cities and workplaces and move to the countryside to work in *wilayas* (FLN-organised countryside districts). The war had shifted back to the countryside, the military campaign and the exiled leadership. What became known as Fanonist revolutionary strategy after 1961 spoke, in large part, of the failures and divisions of the Algerian war and the political choices made by the FLN.[5]

Fanon also tended to fetishise the armed struggle as the real struggle.[6] He was right to confront the hypocrisy of the European left, who frequently refused to support and defend Algeria's right to violent resistance against the French. But his championing of the Algerian method of insurrection was deeply problematic. At times Fanon uniformly presented this model to countries that were ill-suited to such a tactic, condemning Angola's nationalists for refusing to launch their own insurrection regardless of timing or local circumstances.[7]

Yet Fanon's writing and life offers us so much to celebrate and study. Fanon belongs to the radical tradition of decolonisation. Modestly, he helped to promote and influence the FLN, but *Studies in a Dying Colonialism* and, especially, *The Wretched of the Earth* – with its capacity to capture the anger of the world – had an important impact on national liberation movements across the African continent and the world. He was perhaps the most important figure in the ideological struggle against colonialism in the 20th century.

In the West, Fanon's writings were taken up in the mid-1960s by a new Black Power movement, principally in the United States. Fanon's analysis of racism, the necessity of organising the wretched of the earth (the unemployed and disenfranchised lumpenproletariat) and his insistence on the complex therapy of violence and self-defence against oppression were interpreted as tools that could be used in the liberation of the colonised black communities in the United States. Bobby Seale, co-founder of the Black Panther Party for Self-Defence, credited Fanon as a key influence on their ideas.

Fanon's literary output was relatively limited; indeed it could be argued that we approach his work as oral texts. He was a reluctant writer. He dictated his books and articles. He needed to pace around the room when he was dictating, his arms flying, his mind searching for another metaphor or expression that would encapsulate the passion and anger he felt, or synthesise the philosophy of praxis that the revolution needed.

Fanon's activism, the need to practically do something, lived in him deeply. In 1955 he was so insistent that he wanted actively to fight – take up arms – that the organisation was forced to tell him in no uncertain terms that they had enough volunteers. In the late 1950s he tried to argue and lobby for an African legion – an all-African military force – to counter Western imperialism. In 1960 he tried to establish a southern front in the Algerian war, leading an expeditionary force on a clandestine 2000-mile[8] mission through West Africa, to assess possible supply routes for an eventual rearguard force that could liberate Algeria by penetrating the country from sub-Saharan Africa. For Fanon, this would be a demonstration of real and practical pan-Africanism.[9]

Fanon only dictated his books when there was a force beyond his control that made him unable to travel. Examples include after his accident in Morocco in 1959 and when he was dying of leukaemia in 1961 and writing *The Wretched of the Earth*, desperate to prevent the revolution from possible degeneration and decay. In his final months of life, knowing he was probably not going to see the year out, Fanon rushed to the Algerian/Tunisian border to tell those fighting for independence about the dangers of national liberation. Although we can only guess from the book Fanon published later in the year what he said, it must surely have been something like: '... care must be taken to avoid turning the army into an autonomous body which sooner or later ... will "go into politics"... the only way to avoid this menace is to educate the army politically.'[10] Fanon was a bristling and ferocious revolutionary in constant motion.

In his commitment to the FLN, as a propagandist and a disciplined militant, Fanon was the champion of the Algerian Revolution and of African liberation. He also provided us with a warning about the dangers of postcolonial power, even if he could not adequately pose an alternative to the limitations threatening the very freedom to which he had devoted himself. Writing in 1960, he says, 'Colonialism and its derivations do not, as a matter of fact, constitute the present enemies of Africa. In a short time this continent will be liberated. For my part, the deeper I enter into the cultures and the political circles, the surer I am that the great danger that threatens Africa is the absence of ideology.'[11] This inability to chart a clear alternative is the tantalising failure in Fanon's work. Though unique among his contemporaries, he examined the dangers of postcolonial independence. So he wrote how after independence the aspirations of real independence are jettisoned. For much of Africa, the seemingly radical structures of the nationalist revolution hardened into the quasi-Stalinist mould of the one-party state.[12] Fanon diagnosed the snare of national liberation, but his conception of a nation as the dynamic creation of popular action did not provide a solution to the prison of independence that he described. Still, his monumental contribution was posing questions and explaining the curse which national liberation would become for the new decolonised nations. It was for other movements and leaders, influenced by Fanon's work, to propose alternatives to the failures and imprisonment of independence.

In Fanon's adopted Algeria, which won independence from France on 5 July 1962, after a gruelling eight-year war that left a million Algerians dead, he has received an uneasy recognition, with his work translated and his old hospital in Blida named after him, but his warnings about the failures of national liberation grimly fulfilled. Independence for Algeria followed negotiations, known as the Évian Accords, between the FLN leadership and the French government led by General Charles de Gaulle. The Algerian Revolution had defeated the French in the most violent war of decolonisation in Africa. No other national liberation movement had come to power, with international hope so high. Yet Algeria's own postcolonial history provides a tragic confirmation of Fanon's 1961 thesis.

Algerian independence for the rest of Fanon's Third World seemed to represent the real struggle, with huge potential to become a model for the radical projects of national liberation around the world. Algiers became the safe haven for revolutionaries who sought to understand the Algerian experience first hand or simply seek exile from their own governments' repression. Eldridge Cleaver, the prominent Black Panther, fled to Algeria in the late 1960s, and learnt about the armed struggle, which he sought to export to the United States.[13]

In North Africa and the Middle East, the new independent governments aligned themselves with the Egyptian president Gamal Abdel Nasser, riding a radical wave of national liberation that had ejected the British invasion of Suez and the French from Algeria, and had brought new governments to power across North Africa and the Middle East. The post-independent revolutionary regime in Libya, led by Colonel Gaddafi, seemed to seal the fate of the region's petrol states.[14] In Algeria, the government committed itself to a programme of industrialisation and nationalisation, culminating in February 1971 with the nationalisation of the oil industry. For ordinary Algerians, however, these initiatives, state-led industrialisation and nationalisation, did not flow from their own endeavours, the popular participation and involvement in society that Fanon had envisaged. Instead, the dividends of independence trickled down unevenly into Algerian society.

Popular ownership was largely absent in a statist project that was led from above. The nationalist leadership of the new state assumed a dictatorial character, concentrating power in a few hands around the political leadership. Houari Boumediene ruled ruthlessly as Algeria's *Président du Conseil de la Révolution et du Conseil des Ministres* (President of the Revolutionary Council and the Council of Ministers) after his 1965 coup against Ahmed Ben Bella. Political expression, organisations and basic freedoms were severely curtailed - what the FLN had been to its opponents in the war against the French, it was now in government.[15]

Since the 1980s, the Algerian regime – led since 1999 by Abdelaziz Bouteflika (who had worked in the last year of his life as Fanon's secretary) – has followed pro-market economic reforms, pursuing aggressive privatisation and liberalisation that has impoverished Algeria. The UK-based Algerian writer, Hamza Hamouchene, has described a 'bazaar economy based on import-import ... when the economy relies essentially on oil revenues and when the Algeria of today imports even the food it eats.'[16]

Fanon wanted much more for Algeria and the world. He was an internationalist and understood that transforming the world, and creating a new and socialist humanity, would ultimately necessitate unity between the North and South; but that this could only happen once the European working class stopped playing the game of 'sleeping beauty'. Today, in the context of the struggles taking place across North Africa and elsewhere in the world – and with the distinct possibility of these spreading – we need to revisit Fanon for his extraordinary insights into revolutionary processes and his warnings of the pitfalls of national consciousness and the national bourgeoisie.

FANON'S REVOLUTIONARY CULTURE AND NATIONALISM
Hamza Hamouchene

Fanon died a few months before Algeria's independence in July 1962. He did not live to see his adopted country become free from French colonial domination, something he believed had become inevitable. This radical intellectual and revolutionary devoted himself, mind, body and soul, to the Algerian National liberation. He was a prism, through which many revolutionaries abroad understood Algeria and one of the reasons the country became synonymous with Third World revolution.

With the weight of its long war of independence, as well as its history, Algeria served as a model for several liberation fronts across the globe, and given its assertive diplomacy and audacious foreign policy in the 1960s and 70s, the Algerian capital became a Mecca for many revolutionaries. As Amilcar Cabral announced at a press conference at the margins of the first Pan-African Festival held in Algiers in 1969: 'Pick a pen and take note: the Muslims make the pilgrimage to Mecca, the Christians to the Vatican and the national liberation movements to Algiers!'[17] Fanon would surely have been proud of that moment of Algeria and Africa's history. The festival was impregnated with a revolutionary fervour and with his ideas around a combative culture that is fuelled by people's daily struggles. The radical atmosphere of these few days in July was captured in an important and powerful film by William Klein, *The Pan-African Festival of Algiers, 1969*, which attests that this Pan-African gathering was not merely an exercise in flag waving or a momentary utopia, but a genuine meeting of African cultures united in their denunciation of colonialism and in their fight for freedom.

This historic festival and the film were also an offensive against Senghor's vision of Negritude and a critique of the World Festival of Negro Arts he had organised in Dakar in 1966. France's high-profile involvement in its organisation and its running, as well as particularly the presence of André Malraux, who was the French minister for culture at the time, were strongly denounced by critics. This condemnation of Senghor and his festival focused on criticism of its dependence on Europe and the conservatism of the president's writings that were influenced by colonial anthropology. The philosopher Adotevi, following in the footsteps of Fanon, points out the limits of the Negritude espoused by Senghor: 'The enforced search for traditions, we repeat Fanon's view, is a banal search for exoticism. Negritude, hollow, vague, is ineffectual as an ideology. There is no longer room, in Africa for literature that is outside the revolutionary struggle.'[18] The critique of Negritude culminates in the film with the affirmation: African culture will be revolutionary or will not be!

Political leaders like António Agostinho Neto and Cabral saw culture at the heart of their concerns because they associated it with liberation that they theorised as a form of political action. They strongly echo Fanon's words in *The Wretched of the Earth*:

A national culture is not a folklore, nor an abstract populism that
believes it can discover the people's true nature. It is not made up of
the inert dregs of gratuitous actions, that is to say actions which are
less and less attached to the ever-present reality of the people ... It
is around the people's struggles that African-Negro culture takes on
substance and not around songs, poems or folklore.[19]

It is worth bearing this in mind when we think about the role and the conception of culture today. Is it simply a culture that entertains people and diverts them from the real issues? Or is it a culture that speaks to the people and advances their resistance and struggles? Is it an independent and free culture that fosters dissent and criticism, or is it a folkloric one that comes under the suffocating patronage of some authoritarian elites?

Fanon's high hopes for, and profound belief in, revolutionary Algeria, as well as his understanding that liberation does not come as a gift, are attested to in *L'An Cinq de la Révolution Algérienne* (*Studies in a Dying Colonialism*). It is seized by the masses with their own hands, and by seizing it they themselves are transformed. He strongly argued that for the masses, the most elevated form of culture, that is to say, of progress, is to resist imperialist domination and penetration. For Fanon, revolution is a transformative process that will create 'new souls'.[20] For this reason, Fanon concludes his 1959 book, *Studies in a Dying Colonialism*, with the words: 'The revolution in depth, the true one, precisely because it changes man and renews society, has reached an advanced stage. This oxygen which creates and shapes a new humanity – this, too, is the Algerian revolution.'[21]

Fanon's concern with what the masses do and say and think, and his belief that it is the masses, and not leaders or systems, who make and determine history, is at the centre stage in his books. It is crucial to analyse Fanon's arguments because they illustrate how, in the midst of the worst disasters, the masses find the means of reorganising themselves and continuing their existence when they have a common objective. In that respect, Fanon's descriptions of the conduct of the masses are of great importance, as they show how the masses go on living and how they go forward.[22]

This focus and vivid attachment to the masses, the wretched of the earth, their lives and their struggle, is put in opposition to an instinctive aversion to a national bourgeoisie that will betray the masses, halt liberation and set up a national system of tyranny and exploitation, reminiscent of its colonial counterpart. Fanon rightly observed how nationalist consciousness can very easily lead to 'frozen rigidity', merely replacing the departed white masters with dark-skinned equivalents.

Understanding Africa: Fanon today

More than five decades after his death, the question seems to be why is Fanon relevant now? rather than is he relevant at all? It would be instructive to explore how this revolutionary would think and act in the face of contemporary issues in Africa and the world.

Fanon's work, written in the 1950s and early 60s, still bears a prophetic power as an accurate description of what happened in Algeria after independence and beyond. Reading Fanon's words – especially 'The Pitfalls of National Consciousness', his famous chapter in *The Wretched of the Earth* (based on his reflections on his West African experiences, as well as his concerns about the Algerian revolution)[23] – one cannot help being absorbed and shaken by their truth and foresight on the bankruptcy and sterility of national bourgeoisies in Africa and the Middle East today. These are bourgeoisies that tended to replace the colonial force with a new class-based system, replicating the old colonial structures of exploitation and oppression. Today, we can see states across the formerly colonised world that have 'bred pathologies of power' as Eqbal Ahmad has called them – giving rise to national-security states, dictatorships, oligarchies and one-party systems.[24]

What has become of Algeria today, with oil money playing an enormously important role in pacifying the population and paying for a bloated and ubiquitous security force, corresponds to what Fanon had feared. His vision and politics were not, and still are not, to the taste of the ruling class, which is the reason he is marginalised today and reduced to just another anti-colonial figure, stripped of his incandescent attack on the stupidity of the national bourgeoisies and their intellectual and spiritual poverty.

As Edward Said, the cultural theorist and activist, argued, the true prophetic genius of *The Wretched of the Earth* is when Fanon senses the divide between the nationalist bourgeoisie in Algeria and the FLN's liberationist tendencies. Fanon was the first major theorist of anti-imperialism to realise that orthodox nationalism followed the same track hewn out by imperialism, which, while it appeared to concede authority to the nationalist bourgeoisie, was really extending its hegemony.[25] Fanon put it to us bluntly: 'History teaches clearly that the battle against colonialism does not run straight away along the lines of nationalism.'[26] He then warns us that we must take a rapid step from national consciousness to political and social consciousness if we really wish our countries to avoid regression and uncertainties.

In this state of affairs, the national bourgeoisie dispenses with popular legitimacy and increasingly turns its back on the interior and the realities of uneven development, with its only interest in exporting the enormous profits it derives from the exploitation of people to foreign countries. Current events confirm this assertion as we see the scandalous and endemic corruption and 'legalised' robbery in Algeria, Nigeria, Egypt, Ben Ali's Tunisia and South Africa, to mention only a few.

In Algeria for example, an anti-national, sterile and unproductive bourgeoisie is getting the upper hand in running state affairs and in directing its economic choices. This comprador elite is the biggest threat to the sovereignty of the nation as it is selling off the economy to foreign capital and multinationals. This same elite is cooperating with imperialism in its 'war on terror', which is merely a pretext for imperialists to expand their domination and scramble for resources.[27] It is a bourgeoisie that renounced the autonomous development project initiated in the 1960s and 70s, and, as Fanon eloquently put it, is 'incapable of great ideas and inventiveness and does not even succeed in extracting spectacular concessions from the West, such as investments which would be of value for the country's economy.'[28] On the contrary, it now offers one concession after another – such as the exploitation of shale gas, for example – for blind privatisation and projects that will undermine the country's sovereignty and will endanger its population and environment.[29] Today, Algeria – as well as Tunisia, Egypt, Nigeria and South Africa, among others – follow the dictates of the new instruments of imperialism, such as the International Monetary Fund, the World Bank and the World Trade Organization. Some African countries still use the CFA franc, including Senegal, the Ivory Coast and Burkina Faso, a currency inherited from French colonialism and still under the control of the French Treasury. Fanon would have been revolted at this *bêtise* (stupidity) and sheer mindlessness. How can we go on being submissive to imperialism, bowing to every folly to satisfy foreign capital?

Fanon had predicted this ominous situation and the shocking behaviour of the national bourgeoisie when he noted that its mission has nothing to do with transforming the nation but rather consists of 'being the transmission line between the nation and capitalism, rampant though camouflaged, which today puts on the masque of neo-colonialism.'[30] This is where we can appreciate the lasting value of employing Fanon's critical insights when he describes for us the contemporary postcolonial reality, a reality shaped by a national bourgeoisie 'unabashedly ... anti-national,' opting, he adds, for an abhorrent path of a conventional bourgeoisie, 'a bourgeoisie which is stupidly, contemptibly and cynically bourgeois'.[31]

That is exactly what happened in Algeria and other countries in Africa. These regimes are content with their role as the business agents of Western capital, and are only preoccupied with filling their pockets as rapidly as possible, ignoring the deplorable stagnation into which their countries further and deeper sink. Fanon would have been shocked by the ongoing international division of labour where Africans 'still export raw materials' and continue 'being Europe's small farmers who specialise in unfinished products.'[32]

Fanon's critique of tourism, which he regarded as a quintessential post-colonial industry, must be revisited and pondered on. He condemns the fact that nationalist elites have become 'the organisers of parties' for their Western counterparts in the midst of the overwhelming poverty of their populations. Bereft of ideas and cut off from the people, these elites, he argues, will in practice set up their countries as 'the brothel of Europe'.[33] This is not just a Caribbean experience; it has become the experience of many countries in Africa, such as post-apartheid South Africa, and Tunisia, Egypt and Morocco.

> In these poor, underdeveloped countries, where the rule is that the greatest wealth is surrounded by the greatest poverty, the army and the police constitute the pillars of the regime; an army and a police force (another rule which must not be forgotten) which are advised by foreign experts. The strength of the police and the power of the army are proportionate to the stagnation in which the rest of the nation is sunk. By dint of yearly loans, concessions are snatched up by foreigners; scandals are numerous, ministers grow rich, their wives doll themselves up, the members of parliament feather their nests and there is not a soul down to the simple policeman or the customs officer who does not join in the great procession of corruption.[34]

This raging passage from *The Wretched of the Earth* is a fairly accurate portrayal of the situation in many African countries where repression and suppression of freedoms are the rule – helped, of course, by foreign expertise – and where greedy elites institutionalise corruption and serve foreign interests.

Fanon was one of only a few radical intellectuals to point out the dangers of the influence of a 'carefully nurtured' nativism, to borrow Edward Said's words, on a sociopolitical movement like decolonisation.[35] From nationalism, we pass to ultra-nationalism, then to chauvinism, and finally to racism and tribalism. This is seen in several exclusionary and dogmatic ideologies like Arabism, Negritude and the appeals to pure or authentic Islam, all of which have had disastrous consequences on national populations. Algeria suffices as a good example, where cultural diversity was ignored for a narrower culturalist conception of Algerian identity, when the Berber dimension of the Algerian cultural heritage was marginalised and reduced to folkloric manifestations, and when the elite engaged in a sclerotic Arabisation policy in which it developed a conservative interpretation of religion and a reactionary vision of the role of women in society by adopting Islamist-appeasing social measures, such as the notorious and retrograde Family Code of 1984.

Edward Said notes that more effort seemed to be spent in bolstering the idea that to be Syrian, Iraqi, Egyptian or Saudi is a sufficient end, rather than in thinking critically, even audaciously, about the national programme itself.[36] Identity politics assumes the primary place, and 'African unity takes off the mask and crumbles into regionalism inside the hollow shell of nationalism itself'.[37] In his work Fanon argues for the converse – for going beyond the first steps of nativist assertive identity towards true liberation that involves a transformation of social consciousness beyond national consciousness.[38]

Fanon's vision of the future Algeria, which he shared with his mentor, Abane Ramdane, the architect of the revolution, was a secular democratic society with the primacy of citizenship over identities (Arab, Amazigh, Muslim, Jewish, Christian, European, white, black, etc): '... in the new society that is being built,' Fanon wrote in *Studies in a Dying Colonialism*, 'there are only Algerians. From the outset, therefore, every individual living in Algeria is an Algerian ... We want an Algeria open to all, in which every kind of genius can grow.'[39] He did not forget the role of women in the new society when he said that every effort has to be made to mobilise men and women as quickly as possible and admonished against 'the danger of perpetuating the feudal tradition which holds sacred the superiority of the masculine element over the feminine'.[40] Fanon demonstrated in an essay he wrote in his 1959 book, entitled 'Algeria Unveiled', how women were essential elements in the Algerian Revolution and how the necessities of combat gave rise to new attitudes and new modes of behaviour: '... the virtually taboo character assumed by the veil in the colonial situation disappeared almost entirely in the course of the liberating struggle.'[41]

Alternatives: A second Fanonian moment?

Alas, such a generous vision of a pluralist society is yet to be achieved and this moment of flowering humanity is the second Fanonian moment of decolonisation, a moment that breaks away with the hierarchies, divisions and regionalisms constituted by imperialism, by embracing a universal humanism and by building regional and international solidarities.

The sad contemporary reality that Fanon described and warned against more than five decades ago leaves little doubt that were he alive today, he would have been hugely disappointed at the result of his efforts and those of other revolutionaries. He turned out to be right about the rapacity and divisiveness of national bourgeoisies, and the limits of conventional nationalism, but he did not offer us a prescription for making the transition after decolonisation to a new liberating political order. Perhaps, there is no such thing as a detailed plan or solution. Perhaps he viewed it as a protracted process that would be informed by praxis and, above all, by confidence in the masses and their revolutionary potential in figuring out the liberating alternative.

Fanon does, however, alert us to the fact that the scandalous enrichment of this profiteering caste will be accompanied by 'a decisive awakening on the part of the people and a growing awareness that promised stormy days to come'.[42] So we can see Fanon's rationale for revolt and rebellion, suddenly made absolutely clear by the Arab uprisings in 2011. What started in Tunisia and then Egypt's Tahrir Square has become a new global revolt, spreading to Spain and the Indignados movement, to Athens against the vicious austerity measures, to the urban revolt in the UK, to the massive student mobilisation to end education for profit in Chile, to the Occupy Movement against the 1 per cent, to the revolts in Turkey and Brazil, and so on. The rebellion of the popular masses in all these countries has been against the violence of the contemporary world that offers them only growing pauperisation and marginalisation, while the few are enriched at the expense and damnation of the majority.

Countries like Egypt and Tunisia were long praised for the 'wonderful' achievements of their economies with high economic growths, but which do not at all reflect the abject poverty and the deep inequalities entrenched in those countries. The masses, however, erupted onto the political scene, discovered their political will and power, and began again to make history. As the Egyptians said of 25 January, the start of their revolution, 'When we stopped being afraid, we knew we would win. We will not again allow ourselves to be scared of a government. This is the revolution in our country, the revolution in our minds.'[43] Egyptians and Tunisians did not only revolt to demand democracy and freedom, they also rebelled for bread and dignity, against the oppressive socio-economic conditions under which they lived for decades. They rose up to challenge the Manichean geographies of oppressor and oppressed (so well described by Fanon in *The Wretched*), geographies imposed on them by the globalised capitalist-imperialist system.

What can Fanon tell us about what has happened in Egypt since 2011, with the July 2013 military coup and the undergoing counter-revolution? While we cannot be certain what Fanon would say, there is little doubt that his words would be along these lines:

The bourgeoisie should not be allowed to find the conditions necessary for its existence and its growth. In other words, the combined effort of the masses led by a party and of intellectuals who are highly conscious and armed with revolutionary principles ought to bar the way to this useless and harmful middle class.[44]

Liberals, Islamists or military generals, what's the difference? All of them belong to a sterile bourgeoisie aligned with the demand of global neo-liberal capitalism.

Fanon would also probably repeat to us an important observation he made on some African revolutions (including the Algerian one), which is their unifying character that sidelines any thinking of a sociopolitical ideology on how radically to transform society. This is a great weakness that we witnessed with the Egyptian Revolution. 'Nationalism is not a political doctrine, nor a programme,' says Fanon.[45] He insists on the necessity of a revolutionary political party that can take the demands of the masses forward, a political party that will educate the people politically, that will be 'a tool in the hands of the people' and that will be the energetic spokesperson and the 'incorruptible defender of the masses'. For Fanon, reaching such a conception of a party, first and foremost necessitates ridding ourselves of the bourgeois notion of elitism and 'the contemptuous attitude that the masses are incapable of governing themselves'.[46]

For Fanon, the 'we' was always a creative 'we', a 'we' of political action and praxis, thinking and reasoning.[47] For him, the nation does not exist except in a sociopolitical and economic programme 'worked out by revolutionary leaders and taken up with full understanding and enthusiasm by the masses'.[48] Unfortunately, what we see today is the antithesis of what Fanon strongly argued for. We see the stupidity of the anti-democratic bourgeoisies embodied in their tribal and family dictatorships, banning their people, often with crude force, from participating in their country's development and fostering a climate of immense hostility between rulers and ruled. Fanon, in his conclusion of *The Wretched*, argues that we have to work out new concepts of liberation and philosophical thought through an ongoing political education that gets enriched through mass struggle. Political education for him is not merely about political speeches; instead, it is about 'opening the minds' of the people, 'awakening them, and allowing the birth of their intelligence'.[49]

This is perhaps one of the greatest legacies of Fanon. His radical and generous vision is so refreshing and rooted in the people's daily struggles that it opens up spaces for new ideas and imaginings. For him, everything depends on the masses, which underpins his idea of radical intellectuals engaged in and with people's movements that are capable of coming up with new concepts in a non-technical and non-professional language. For Fanon, culture has to become a fighting culture, education has to become about total liberation too. He says, 'If nationalism is not made explicit, if it is not enriched and deepened by a very rapid transformation into a consciousness of social and political needs, in other words into humanism, it leads up a blind alley.'[50] And that is what we need to bear in mind when we talk about education in schools and universities. Decolonising education in the Fanonian sense is an education that helps create a social consciousness and a social individual.

For Fanon, the militant or the intellectual must not take short cuts in the name of getting things done, as this approach is inhuman and sterile. Instead, getting things done is all about coming and thinking together, which is the foundation of the liberated society. Fanon's notions in this respect are not mere abstractions, as he gives us concrete examples from the Algerian revolution, writing of how the creation of production/consumption committees among the peasants and FLN gave rise to theoretical questions about the accumulation of capital:

> In those regions where we have been able to carry out successfully these interesting experiments, where we have watched man being created by revolutionary beginnings, because people began to realise that one works more with one's brain and one's heart than with one's muscles and sweat.[51]

In *Studies in a Dying Colonialism*, in an essay on the radio, 'The voice of Algeria', he also tells us about another experience.[52] He describes a meeting in a room where people are listening to the radio with the militant (teacher) in their midst. This form of the classroom he wrote about is a democratic space where the teacher is an informed discussant, not a director, and where the purpose of political education is self-empowerment.

Fanon argued that an intellectual or a militant cannot be truly productive in their mission of serving the people without being committed to radical change, without giving up the position of privilege (careerism) and without challenging the divisions that prevail under capitalism: leader vs. the masses, mental vs. manual labour, urban vs. rural, centre vs. periphery and so on. For Fanon, the centre (capital city, official culture, appointed leader) must be deconsecrated and demystified. He argues for a new system of mobile relationships that must replace the hierarchies inherited from imperialism.[53] In order to achieve liberation, the consciousness of self, a never-ending process of discovery, empathy, encouragement and communication with the other, must be unleashed. That is one of the fundamental lessons that we must heed when we build grassroots social movements that are diverse, non-hierarchical and intersectional.

Fanon was not a Marxist, but he strongly believed that capitalism, with imperialism and its divisions, enslaves people. Moreover, his precocious diagnosis of the incapability of the nationalist elites in fulfilling their historical mission demonstrates the continuing relevance of Fanon's thought today. In spite of his own failure – his early death at the age of 36 might be to blame here – to put forward a detailed ideology of how to go beyond imperialism and orthodox nationalism in order to achieve liberation and universalism, he surely managed in his illuminating conception of education to provide us with crucial tools to work it out for ourselves: education must always be influenced by practice; it must also be transformative, striving to liberate all of humanity from imperialism. This is the living legacy of a revolutionary and a great thinker.

NOTES

1   This interview was conducted in 2010.

2   S. Khan, 'Crisis and Conflict in Pakistan', *International Socialism*, 126 (2010.)

3   Chaulet highlights another weakness, which he argues comes from Fanon's celebrated strengths: 'Fanon's vivid style – of a psychiatrist, philosopher and poet, more than a political thinker – gives a particular power to his flashes of prophetic brilliance and even to his errors ...' (Interview). Fanon's general and unspecific statements give them an enormous power, but also a tendency to broad and problematic interpretation.

4   This point, however, is controversial. So Hamza Hamouchene has argued, 'I would argue that this claim is based on a unilinear and exclusively-based conception of Marxism. In Algeria and other parts of the colonial world at the time, the working class was not developed. Even, 50 years later, the working class is still the minority with informal work dominating the scene.' (Personal communication, 10 June 2014.)

5 It should be clear that Fanon was not trying to develop such a 'strategy' whatever subsequent writers and activists have said. His last book was a work in progress. It is also important not to present a Manichean version of the Algerian revolution – divided neatly between city and countryside phases.

6 For a discussion on Fanon as a 'voluntarist', see P. Hallward, '*Fanon et la Volonté Politique*', *Contretemps* 2:10 (2011).

7 B. Davidson, 'On Revolutionary Nationalism: the Legacy of Cabral', *Race and Class* 27:21 (1986).

9 3 200 kilometres.

9 See L. Turner, 'Fanon and the FLN: Dialectics of Organisation and the Algerian Revolution' in N. Gibson (ed), *Rethinking Fanon*.

10 Fanon, *Les Damnés*, p. 163.

11 F. Fanon, *Towards the African Revolution: Political Essays* (New York: Grove, 1967), p. 186.

12 J. Molyneux, *What is the Real Marxist Tradition?* (London: Bookmarks, 1983).

13 K. Cleaver and G. Katsiaficas, *Liberation, Imagination, and the Black Panther Party* (New York: Routledge, 2001).

14 R. First, *Libya: The Ellusive Revolution* (London: Peguin, 1974).

15 M. Evans and J. Phillips, *Algeria: anger of the dispossessed* (New Haven: Yale University Press, 2007).

16 See Hamza Hamouchene, 'Algeria, 50 Years of Independence: Hopes and Lost Illusions', http://www.algeriasolidaritycampaign.com/algerias-independence50achievements/ (accessed August 2013).

17 Hadouchi, *Third Text*, pp. 117–128.

18 O. Hadouchi, 'African culture will be revolutionary or will not be: William Klein's Film of the First Pan-African Festival of Algiers (1969)', *Third Text* 25:1, pp. 117–128.

19 F. Fanon, *The Wretched of The Earth* (Penguin, 1967), pp. 188–189.

20 The phrase 'new souls' was borrowed from Aimé Césaire.

21 F. Fanon, *A Dying Colonialism* (Grove Press, 1967), p. 181.

22 A deeper analysis is provided in *A Dying Colonialism*.

23 F. Fanon, 'The Pitfalls of National Consciousness' in *The Wretched of the Earth*, pp. 119–165.

24 E. Ahmad, 'The Neo-Fascist State: Notes on the Pathology of Power in the Third World, *Arab Studies Quarterly* 3:2 (spring 1981), pp. 170–180.

25 E. Said, *Culture and Imperialism* (Vintage, 1994), p. 328.

26 Fanon, *The Wretched of The Earth*, p. 119.

27 H. Hamouchene, 'Is Algeria an Anti-Imperialist State?', *Jadaliyya* (October 2013).

28 Fanon, *The Wretched of The Earth*, p. 141.

29 H. Hamouchene, 'Algeria, an Immense Bazaar: The Politics and Economic Consequences of Infitah', *Jadaliyya* (January 2013).

30 Fanon, *The Wretched of The Earth*, p. 122.

31 Fanon, *The Wretched of The Earth*, p. 121.

32 Fanon, *The Wretched of The Earth*, p. 122.

33 Fanon, *The Wretched of The Earth*, p. 123.

34 Fanon, *The Wretched of The Earth*, p. 138.

35 Said, *Culture and Imperialism*, p. 371.

36 Said, *Culture and Imperialism*, pp. 361–362.

37 Fanon, *The Wretched of The Earth*, p. 128.

38 Fanon, *The Wretched of The Earth*, p. 165.

39 Fanon, *A Dying Colonialism*, pp. 32, 152.

40 Fanon, *The Wretched of The Earth*, p. 163.

41 Fanon, *A Dying Colonialism*, p. 61.

42 Fanon, *The Wretched of The Earth*, p. 134.

43 A quote by Ahmad Mahmoud in C. McGreal, 'Mubarak is still here, but there's been a revolution in our minds, say protesters', *The Guardian*, 5 February 2011.

44 Fanon, *The Wretched of The Earth*, p. 140.

45 Fanon, *The Wretched of The Earth*, p. 163.

46 Fanon, *The Wretched of The Earth*, p. 151.

47 N. C. Gibson, '50 Years Later: Frantz Fanon's Legacy to the Caribbean and the Bahamas', keynote address at the Caribbean Symposium Series, December 2011.

48 Fanon, *The Wretched of The Earth*, p. 164.

49 Fanon, *The Wretched of The Earth*, p. 159.

50 Fanon, *The Wretched of The Earth*, p. 165.

51 Fanon, *The Wretched of The Earth*, p. 154.

52 Fanon, *A Dying Colonialism*, pp. 69–97.

53 Said, *Culture and Imperialism*, p. 330.

SELECT BIBLIOGRAPHY

Books by Frantz Fanon

Black Skin, White Masks (London: Pluto Press, 1986).

L'an V de la révolution algérienne (Paris, François Maspero, 1959).

Les Damnés de la Terre (Paris, François Maspero, 1961).

Pour la Révolution Africaine (Paris: François Maspero, 1964).

Peau noire, masques blancs (Paris: Editions du seuil, 1952)

Studies in a Dying Colonialism (Monthly Review Press, 1965; London: Earthscan, 1989).

The Wretched of the Earth (New York: Grove Press 1963, 2004).

Toward the African Revolution (Monthly Review Press, 1967; London: Penguin, 1970).

Resources on Frantz Fanon and his context

Ahmad E. 'The Neo-Fascist State: Notes on the Pathology of Power in the Third World, *Arab Studies Quarterly* 3:2 (spring 1981), pp. 170–180.

Alessandrini A. C. (ed) *Frantz Fanon: Critical Perspectives* (New York: Routledge, 1999).

Bernasconi R. 'Fanon's *The Wretched of the Earth* as the Fulfilment of Sartre's Critique of Dialectical Reason', *Sartre Studies International* 16(2) (2010).

Birchall I. (ed) 'European Revolutionaries and Algerian Independence 1954–1962' (special issue), *Revolutionary History* 16:4 (2012).

Birchall I. 'Socialism or Identity Politics: A Reply to Linda A Bell' *Sartre Studies International* 4(2) (1998).

Bond P. (ed) *Fanon's Warning: A Civil Society Reader on the New Partnership for Africa's Development* (Trenton, NJ: Africa World, 2002).

Bulhan H. *Frantz Fanon and the Psychology of Oppression* (London: Plenum Press, 1985).

Caute D. *Frantz Fanon* (New York: The Viking Press, 1970).

Césaire A. *Cahier d'un Retour au Pays Natal* (Paris: Présence Africaine, 1983).

Cherki A. *Frantz Fanon: Portrait* (Paris: Seuil, 2000).

Cleaver K. and G. Katsiaficas *Liberation, Imagination, and the Black Panther Party* (New York: Routledge, 2001).

Davidson B. 'On Revolutionary Nationalism: The Legacy of Cabral, *Race and Class* 27(21) (1986).

Ehlen P. *Frantz Fanon: A Spiritual Biography* (New York: Crossroad, 2001).

Elsenhans H. '*Les manifestations de Décembre 1960 et la Reconnaisance de la révolution algérienne*' in *11 Décembre 1960. Le Diên Biên Phu Politique de la Guerre d'Algérie* (Petite collection – Histoire), 2010.

Evans M. and J. Phillips *Algeria: Anger of the Dispossessed* (New Haven: Yale University Press, 2007).

First, R. Libya: *The Elusive Revolution* (London: Penguin, 1974).

Geismar P. *Fanon* (New York: Grove Press, 1971).

Gendzier I. *Frantz Fanon* (Paris: Editions du Seuil, 1976).

Gibson N. *Fanon: The Postcolonial Imagination* (London: Polity Press, 2003).

Gibson N. *Fanonian Practices in South Africa* (London: Palgrave Macmillan, 2011).

Gibson N. (ed) *Rethinking Fanon: the continuing dialogue* (New York: Humanity Books, 1999).

Gordon L. *Fanon and the Crisis of European Man: An Essay on Philosophy and the human sciences* (New York: Routledge, 1995)

Hadouchi O. 'African culture will be revolutionary or will not be: William Klein's Film of the First Pan-African Festival of Algiers (1969)', *Third Text* 25:1, pp. 117–128.

Hallward P. *'Fanon et la Volonté Politique'*, *Contretemps* (2)10 (2011).

Hamouchere H. See Hamza Hamouchene, 'Algeria, 50 Years of Independence: Hopes and Lost Illusions', accessed August 2013.

Hamouchere H. 'Algeria, an Immense Bazaar: The Politics and Economic Consequences of Infitah', *Jadaliyya* (January 2013).

Hansen E. *Frantz Fanon: Social and Political Thought* (Columbus: Ohio State University Press, 1977).

Harbi M. and B. Stora *La Guerre d'Algérie* (Paris: Robert Laffont, 2004).

Høgsbjerg C. 'CLR James and the Black Jacobins', *International Socialism*, www.isj.org.uk/index.php4?id=639&issue=126.

James C. L. R. *The Black Jacobins: Toussaint L'Ouverture and the San Domingo Revolution* (London: Vintage, 1989).

Jeanson F. *La Révolution Algérienne* (Paris: Feltrinelli, 1962).

Jinadu A. *Fanon: In Search of the African Revolution* (Enugu, Nigeria: Fourth Dimension, 1980)

Khan S. 'Crisis and Conflict in Pakistan', *International Socialism* www.isj.org.uk/index.php4?id=636&issue=126.

Lazarus N. *The Postcolonial Unconscious* (Cambridge: Cambridge University Press, 2011).

Macey D. *Frantz Fanon: A Life* (London: Granta, 2000).

Macey D. '"I am my own foundation": Frantz Fanon as a Source of Continued Political Embarrassment', *Theory, Culture and Society* 27(7–8) (2011).

Macey D. *Frantz Fanon: A Biography* (New York: Picodor, 2001).

Molyneux J. *What is the Real Marxist Tradition?* (London: Bookmarks, 1983).

Murray R. and T. Wengraf 'The Algerian Revolution – 1', *New Left Review* 1:22 (1963).

Onwuanibe R. *Critique of Revolutionary Humanism: Frantz Fanon* (Saint Louis: Warren H. Green, 1983).

Pattieu S. *Les Camarades des Frères: Trotskistes et Libertaires dans la Guerre d'Algérie* (Paris: Editions Syllepse, 2002).

Planche J.L. *Sétif 1945: Histoire d'un Massacre Annoncé* (Paris: Perrin, 2006).

Read A. *The Fact of Blackness: Frantz Fanon and Visual Representation* (London: Institute of Contemporary Arts, 1996).

Said E. *Culture and Imperialism* (Vintage, 1994), p. 328.

Sekyi-Out A. *Fanon's Dialectic of Experience* (Harvard: Harvard University Press, 1996).

Sharpley-Whiting T. D. *Frantz Fanon: Conflicts and Feminisms* (New York City: Rowman & Littlefield, 1997).

Silverman M. (ed) *Frantz Fanon's Black Skin, White Masks: New Interdisciplinary Essays* (Manchester: Manchester University Press, 2005).

Singh N. P. 'The Black Panthers and the "Undeveloped Countries" of the Left', Charles E. Jones (ed), *Black Panther Party Reconsidered* (Baltimore: Black Classic Press, 1998).

Turner L. 'Fanon and the FLN: Dialectics of Organisation and the Algerian Revolution' in N. Gibson (ed) *Rethinking Fanon* (New York: Humanity Books, 1999).

Turshen M. 'Algerian Women in the Liberation Struggle and the Civil War: From Active Participants to Passive Victims?', *Social Research* 69:3 (2002).

Zeilig L. 'Frantz Fanon, Une Vie Révolutionnaire', *Contretemps* 2:10 (2011).

Zeilig L. (ed), *Class Struggle and Resistance in Africa* (Chicago: Haymarket, 2009).

Zeilig L. *Voices of Liberation: Patrice Lumumba* (Cape Town: HSRC Press, 2013).

Films, novels and plays about Frantz Fanon and his context

Churchill, Caryl 'The Hospital at the Time of the Revolution' in *Caryl Churchill: Shorts* (London: Nick Hern Books, 2008).

Concerning Violence (2014). Documentary. Directed by Göran Hugo Olsson.

Days of Glory (2006). Drama. Directed by Rachid Bouchareb.

Frantz Fanon: Black Skin, White Marks (1996). Documentary. Directed by Isaac Julien (San Francisco: California Newsreel).

Outside the Law (2010). Drama. Directed by Rachid Bouchareb.

Rare recording of Fanon speaking in 1956 at the Congrès des Écrivains et Artistes Noirs in Paris, http://www.ina.fr/audio/PH909013001/conference-de-frantz-fanon-au-congres-international-des-ecrivains-et-artistes-noirs-audio.html.

The Battle of Algiers (1966). Drama/documentary. Directed by Gillo Pontecorvo (Rizzoli, Rialto Pictures).

Wideman J. E. *Fanon* (a novel) (New York: Houghton Mifflin, 2008).

Websites

http://frantzfanonfoundation-fondationfrantzfanon.com

http://algeriasolidarity.org/

http://www.marxists.org/subject/africa/fanon/

Interviews

Telephone interview with Pierre Chaulet, 14 November 2010, in Paris, by Leo Zeilig.

Interview with Pierre and Claudine Chaulet, 29 September 2011, in Algiers, by Leo Zeilig.

Interview with David Macey, 14 October 2010, in Leeds, by Leo Zeilig.

Interview with Nigel Gibson, 3 November 2010, in London, by Leo Zeilig.

Interview with Moutif Mohamed, 4 October 2011, in Algiers, by Leo Zeilig.

INDEX

ABOUT HAYMARKET BOOKS

Haymarket Books is a nonprofit, progressive book distributor and publisher, a project of the Center for Economic Research and Social Change. We believe that activists need to take ideas, history, and politics into the many struggles for social justice today. Learning the lessons of past victories, as well as defeats, can arm a new generation of fighters for a better world. As Karl Marx said, "The philosophers have merely interpreted the world; the point, however, is to change it."

We take inspiration and courage from our namesakes, the Haymarket Martyrs, who gave their lives fighting for a better world. Their 1886 struggle for the eight-hour day reminds workers around the world that ordinary people can organize and struggle for their own liberation.

For more information and to shop our complete catalog of titles, visit us online at www.haymarketbooks.org.

ALSO AVAILABLE FROM HAYMARKET BOOKS

African Struggles Today: Social Movements Since Independence
Peter Dwyer and Leo Zeilif

Apartheid Israel: The Politics of an Analogy
Edited by Jon Soske and Sean Jacobs, Foreword by Achille Mbembe

BRICS: An Anti-Capitalist Critique
Edited by Ana Garcia and Patrick Bond

Clsss Struggle and Resistance in Africa
Edited by Leo Zeilig

*Concerning Violence: Fanon, Film, and Liberation in Africa,
Selected Takes 1965–1987*
Edited by Sophie Vukovic and Göran Olsson,
foreword by Gayatri Chakravorty Spivak

Reading Revolution: Shakespear on Robben Island
Ashwin Desai

Urban Revolt: State Power and the Rise of People's Movements in the Global South
Trevor Ngwane, Emmanuel Ness, and Luke Sinwell

Printed in the USA
CPSIA information can be obtained
at www.ICGtesting.com
JSHW022210140824
68134JS00018B/968